The Historicity of
*Romantic
Discourse*

The Historicity of
Romantic
Discourse

Clifford Siskin

New York   Oxford
OXFORD UNIVERSITY PRESS
1988

Oxford University Press

Oxford New York Toronto
Delhi Bombay Calcutta Madras Karachi
Petaling Jaya Singapore Hong Kong Tokyo
Nairobi Dar es Salaam Cape Town
Melbourne Auckland

and associated companies in
Beirut Berlin Ibadan Nicosia

Copyright © 1988 by Oxford University Press, Inc.

Published by Oxford University Press, Inc.,
200 Madison Avenue, New York, New York 10016

Oxford is a registered trademark of Oxford University Press.

Library of Congress Cataloging-in-Publication Data
Siskin, Clifford.
The historicity of romantic discourse.
Bibliography: p.
Includes index.
1. English literature—19th century—History and
criticism. 2. Romanticism—England. 3. Literature and
history—Great Britain. 4. English literature—18th Century—
History and criticism I. Title.
PR468.H57S57   1988   820'.9'145   87-18421
ISBN 0-19-504470-3

Part of chapter 3 appeared in earlier form as "A Preface to Creative Criticism," published in *The Kenyon Review*—New Series, Spring 1983, Vol. 5,
No. 2. Copyright © by Kenyon College. Reprinted with permission of the
author and *The Kenyon Review*. Part of chapter 4 appeared in earlier form as
"Personification and Community: Literary Change in the Mid and Late Eighteenth Century," published in *Eighteenth-Century Studies,* 15, No. 4 (Summer 1982), 371–401. Parts of chapter 5 appeared in earlier forms as "Revision
Romanticized: A Study in Literary Change," published in *Romanticism Past
and Present,* 7, No. 2 (Summer 1983), 1–16, and as "Romantic Genre: Lyric
Form and Revisionary Behavior in Wordsworth," published in *Genre,* XVI
(Summer 1983), 137–55. The former is reprinted by permission of Northeast-
ern University. The latter is copyright © 1983 by The University of Okla-
homa, all rights of reproduction in any form reserved. Part of chapter 6
appeared in earlier form as "A Formal Development: Austen, the Novel, and
Romanticism," published in *The Centennial Review,* XXVIII, No. 4 (Fall
1984)—XXIX, No. 1 (Winter 1985), 1–28. I wish to thank the editors of these
journals for permission to use and revise this material.

1 3 5 7 9 8 6 4 2

Printed in the United States of America
on acid-free paper

To Roy and Dorothy Siskin

Acknowledgments

Manys act of kindness facilitated the writing of this book. For questions that have demanded a different kind of literary history, I thank Ralph Cohen. To Robert Langbaum I owe a sense of the power of the poetry of experience. For their insights into the politics both of literature and of our profession, as well as their toughness and patience as readers of my work, I thank my colleagues Nancy Armstrong and Leonard Tennenhouse. Patricia Spacks, Stuart Curran (whose recent work on Romantic forms appeared too late to be discussed here), and Mary Poovey have provided timely advice and support. Anne Mellor has proven, over the years, to be exceptionally generous with her critical expertise and knowledgeable enthusiasm. So, too, has Herbert Lindenberger, whose work has helped occasion our discipline's turn toward history and genre. Among the other scholars whose written comments and conversation have contributed to what is best in this book are Todd Bender, Peter Manning, Arthur Marotti, Stuart Peterfreund, Jeffry Plank, Christopher Ricks, Gene Ruoff, Ron Schleifer, Michael Scrivener, Ronald Sharp, and James Thompson.

John Rowlett's knowledge of matters of kind in literature is matched only by his willingness to exercise kindness toward others. I hope that, having enjoyed the latter, I have written a book that clarifies the value of this knowledge and adds to it. Such a contribution would have been far more difficult to attempt without Leslie Siskin's intellectual kinship and editorial expertise.

My special thanks to William P. Sisler, Executive Editor at Oxford University Press, for his efficient, courteous, and knowledgeable handling of this project from the initial inquiry to final production. Oxford's Linda D. Robbins and Woody Gilmartin facilitated that process, and Henry Krawitz proved to be an exceptionally able and articulate editor. I am indebted also to the careful work of my copy editor, Clifford Browder.

Help of an ongoing and often timely sort came from those Wayne State University students who, over the past five years, participated in my graduate seminars on the eighteenth century and on Romanticism, as well as those who joined me in surveying English literature from 1700 to 1900. Thanks are also due Wayne State for the sabbatical leave and summer fellowships that eased the temporal and financial hardships of scholarly writing. Support of another kind came from my children—Corin, Nathaniel, and Johanna—who provided me with their patience and the pleasures of their company.

Contents

I
Present and Past: The Lyric Turn

1

Introduction:
A New Literary History

It is strange to realize how many things that are taken for granted
as natural and eternal were invented at a specific time and place.
OTTO FRIEDRICH IN A NATIONAL NEWSMAGAZINE[1]

This book historicizes the discursive power of English Romanticism
in both its time and ours. So pervasive has that power been for over
150 years that mine is among the initial inquiries into Romanticism
that treat as artifacts not only its disciplinary boundaries (literary
versus nonliterary), hierarchical differences (creative versus critical),
aesthetic values (spontaneity and intensity), and natural truths (development and the unconscious), but also the distinction between the
organic and the ironic/deconstructive that informs contemporary critical debate. It is not that earlier scholars have deliberately perpetu-
ated the past; that they did so simply dramatizes how completely and
invisibly the psychologized "reality" of Romanticism has determined
our understanding of ourselves and of our writing. With the Romantic redefinition of the self as a mind that grows, writing became an
expressive index to that growth—the product, as we still understand
it, of a developing creative imagination. I argue that this imaginative
mind is not a timeless producer but a culture-specific product, not
knowledge discovered in the course of mankind's inevitable progress,
as Wordsworth and Keats claimed, but knowledge made at a particular point in time. As it traces the transformation into natural truths of
these historical concepts of self and behavior, this book performs the
inevitably political task of relating the production and reproduction
of that Romantic knowledge to the workings of economic, social, and
professional power.

A different kind of understanding requires a difference in critical

3

kind; this is a new literary history. By calling it new, I am not celebrating the argument's "originality," my "creativity," or our profession's
inevitable "development"; in fact, one of the goals of this study is to
put such Romantic claims in their historical place. It is new in that it is
*form*ally innovative, because our place, in the last quarter of the
twentieth century, is within an era of conceptual and thus generic
transition. As we read and write, the interrelations among inherited
forms of discourse are rapidly shifting. Literary history had functioned to help make the subject matter of English studies: history
construed as developmental narrative—for example, the "rise of the
novel"—canonized certain texts as "literature." Now, interrelated
with the theoretical features that have penetrated the entire range of
academic disciplines, "Literary History," as one major university pub-
lisher has advertised, "Returns."[2]

Its increasing prominence in the hierarchy of scholarly genres is
keyed to its increasingly theoretical nature. A new literary history
need no longer focus on the canonical ordering of particular works,
but can instead provide us with procedures for identifying and understanding problematic areas of literary study.[3] In a time of change,
making sense of change becomes just such an area, and literary history is being revived as the formal means of doing so.[4] Acknowledging, in fact foregrounding, its own status as a genre, literary history
now counts among its objects of inquiry its own prior incarnations—
the previous efforts to make other *kinds* of "historical" sense. Writers
in this kind thus find themselves historicizing the very knowledge they
have been trained to produce.

The need to do so becomes evident when we examine recent
events in the study of Romanticism. Two hundred years after Wordsworth's birth, that body of work reached an apparent turning point
with the 1971 reissue of Geoffrey Hartman's *Wordsworth's Poetry,
1787–1814* and the debut of M. H. Abrams's *Natural Supernaturalism*. The former, with its triumphant retrospective essay, capped
the efforts of the "consciousness" school that the first edition of the
book (1964) had helped to inaugurate. The latter similarly solidified
the "secularization" arguments initiated by *The Mirror and the Lamp*
(1953).[5] So weighty and inclusive were the generalizations and critical
bibliographies of these texts that many established Romanticists, such
as Harold Bloom and E. D. Hirsch, joined Hartman in turning from
the early nineteenth century to till the less cultivated soil of contemporary theory. For a younger generation of critics, however, this "culmination" was an opportunity. Beginning with Thomas Weiskel's *The*

Romantic Sublime (1976), Frances Ferguson's study of *Language as Counter-Spirit* (1977), and David Simpson's *Irony and Authority in Romantic Poetry* (1979), a decade of work inquiring into the linguistic theories and rhetorical strategies of Romantic writers displaced "Visionary Imagination" with "Revisionary Language," and "Organicism" with "Irony."[6]

Although these were not specifically historical studies, both the displacements themselves and the assumptions about Romanticism they have left untouched, have focused our attention on a historical issue: the Romantic nature of criticism written about the Romantics. The closer the displacers looked, the more clearly they saw in Romanticism originary parallels to their own deconstructive assumptions regarding language and meaning. The past mapped out by such new landmarks as Wordsworth's interpretative uncertainties, Coleridge's theolinguistic ruminations, Blake's formal ironies, and Byron's abysmal satire came, uncannily, to resemble the present. "I believe," wrote Simpson, "that the Romantics were aware of exactly the problems we now discuss under the heading of 'hermeneutics' and that they used the paradoxes implicit in them to fashion a discourse based on transference, repetition, and the 'double bind' " (9). Just as the earlier, "organic" Romanticists had tended to valorize and to employ the criteria (intensity and depth) and procedures (close reading)[7] of the very texts they were supposed to interpret, so their "ironic" successors have found themselves authorized by the very writing they sought to analyze. The displacements of the last decade of criticism have not moved the past out of the present, but have confirmed the ongoing power of a discourse that synchronically embraces the organic *and* the ironic, and diachronically has written its own critical fate.

No issue is more central to today's Romanticists than clarifying their historical relationship to their subject matter. Reviews of recent scholarship have repeatedly referred, still in mostly approving fashion, to resemblances between the interpretation and that which is being interpreted. James Butler, for example, concludes his review of Jonathan Wordsworth's *Borders of Vision* by exclaiming that when the author

> at last brings his book to the same circular reiteration of its beginning that was employed to such fine effect by his ancestor in *The Prelude,* this reader is inclined to feel about *The Borders of Vision* much as Coleridge felt (and wrote) on first hearing the entire *Prelude* in January, 1807.

Although more modest, in not flattering herself with such comparisons, Aileen Ward is certainly as mesmerized by visions of the present as past when she writes that Helen Vendler

> at her best [in *The Odes of John Keats*] writes in the spirit of Keats's
> marvellous meditation on reading "a page of full poesy or distilled
> prose": let the reader "wander with it and muse upon it and reflect
> from it and bring home to it and prophesy upon it and dream upon it—
> until it becomes stale—but when will it do so? Never." Her own prose
> offers and even challenges the reader to such a "voyage of conception"
> as do the poems she studies.

Also in the same issue of *The Wordsworth Circle,* Paul Jay is criticized
for constructing *Being in the Text: Self Representation from Wordsworth to Roland Barthes* according to a "Coleridgean metaphor" of
organic growth, whereas Anca Vlasopolos in *The Symbolic Method of
Coleridge, Baudelaire, and Yeats* is praised because the "intricacies"
of her "argument in tracing the Coleridgean legacy of symbolic
method mirrors [*sic*] the structure of the works she analyzes." Even
the journal's annual tribute to a distinguished contemporary Romanti-
cist can only conclude by conflating the present with the past: "And
'Romantic' may be the appropriate note on which to end: perhaps
with Tom McFarland as Coleridge."[8]

The need to engage those resemblances as a critical problem has
surfaced explicitly in Jerome McGann's *Romantic Ideology* and Morris Eaves's and Michael Fisher's collection *Romanticism and Contemporary Criticism.*[9] Doing so, of course, requires one to clarify what is
meant by "Romantic" and provide an alternative. In McGann's case,
as I shall show at greater length in chapter 3, the strategy employed to
perform the former task—defining an "ideology"—problematizes accomplishing the latter: in condemning others for conforming to his
notion of a "Romantic ideology," McGann affirms the profoundly
Romantic-sounding quest to "return poetry to a human form" (160).

Offering the creative human subject as a "solution" to cultural
problems also appears repeatedly in the edited transcripts of ques-
tion-and-answer sessions found in the Eaves and Fisher collection.
When Northrop Frye, for example, is asked, "Would it make sense to
describe your critical theory as Romantic?" he replies affirmatively,
crediting the "Romantic movement" with trying to reach the positive
goal of "unify[ing] the mental elements in the creative process." From
that perspective, Coleridge's criticism, and, by implication, that of his

fellow Romantic, Frye, is more valuable than Samuel Johnson's, since it gives us "some sense of the autonomy of the creative person" (32).

M. H. Abrams reacts far more defensively to queries regarding "Romantic positives" and "tendencies" in himself and his work. Both of his responses, however, turn to his "sympathy" with the "enterprises" of "selected writers." In one instance secularization is hailed as the "great Romantic undertaking" in response to "social, cultural, and moral crisis and demoralization"; in his other answer, the Romantic turn "to a belief in an imaginative transformation of the self" is affirmed as "a good thing" (166–67, 178). For W. J. T. Mitchell the more immediate crisis is nihilistic tendencies in deconstruction, and the "cure," to use the editors' word (10), is Blake. Asked if he would consider himself "a Romantic critic," Mitchell replies affirmatively, concluding that "Romantic criticism ought to be a practice of struggle and fierce contention as well as confession and self-criticism" (94–95).[10]

If that prescription sounds like criticism's conventional description of the 1805 *Prelude,* we should not be surprised, for this volume's interrogators, in repeatedly asking the critics to try on a label, are certainly onto something: the connections between primary Romantic texts and secondary, critical ones. For our present purposes we can rephrase the question in more specific terms: what *kind* of writing is a literary history that plots change developmentally as problem and solution, sickness and cure, and psychologizes its agency as the imaginative efforts of "great" Authors? To answer that it is a Romantic literary history is not to diminish the value it has had and, therefore, to deny the substantial achievements of the critics we have been discussing. Nor is it to deny anyone the right to sympathize with or admire anyone or anything. It is, however, to question the *present* function of the kind and the utility of its features. Can they help us *at this historical moment* to learn about, and from, the past and thus profitably address the problem of change?

This book is a new literary history, then, in that it participates in the present theoretical work on that issue by taking and making the opportunity to alter its kind. Its features and procedures are intended to help us clarify the scope of our entanglements with the past. I show that whenever we designate certain texts as "literature," or valorize that distinction in terms of "creativity," "imagination," or "expressiveness," or analyze those qualities as variables of individual development, we have joined Wordsworth in taking the "mind of

Man" to be the "main haunt and region" of our "song." The traditional six-poet, 1798–1832 Romanticism of the anthologies and most
criticism is itself a product of that haunting: a transformation of
history into a short, and therefore sweet, developmental narrative. I
show that it tells the same story of creative epiphany and world-
weary despair that we have also employed, on a smaller scale, to
make Romantic sense of the canonized poems and the lives of the
poets. My purpose in using the label "Romanticism" is to detach it
from that tale and thus make it an effective tool for understanding
rather than replicating the past.

I do not psychologize such replication as the fixation of individual critics, for it is a formal problem. The mixture of lyrical with
narrative features that has characterized almost a century and a half
of Romantic literary histories invariably plots the critic's tales into
conclusions that may have once functioned as solutions but now constitute evidence of impasse. For Matthew Arnold, for example, the
surgical lyricization of Wordsworth into the Great Decade cured the
poet and institutionally authorized the ongoing production of doctors
of literature. But when today's "doctors" cannot help but repeat that
procedure—even in criticism that claims to be new—then we need to
reassess its value and those claims.

In *The Self as Mind,* for example, Charles Ryzepka refers to a
range of recent criticism, including Ferguson and Simpson, so that he
can offer a new understanding of the Romantic conception of self and
its effects upon the poetry.[11] But what do we find as the conclusion to
a Wordsworth chapter offering some useful insights into the poet's
rhetorical strategies? As with effort after effort before this one, vari-
ant interpretations serve only as prelude to the same old story: "The
stars in Wordsworth's poetic firmament thin out considerably beyond
the publication of the *Poems* of 1807, as we near the western horizon
of his life" (98). Notice how the metaphors naturalize what is supposed to be an aesthetic judgment into an inevitable truth. Ryzepka
presents the judgment so that he does not have to justify it, because
he never actually makes it: it was written for him as it had been
written for Arnold. As I argue in chapter 5, the Wordsworth of the
Great Decade is but the most blatant victim of that very myth of
creativity *he* helped to articulate. In accordance with that myth, we
have fragmented his career into the creative and critical, and have
celebrated the "lyric" brevity of the former as a sign of divine inspiration; the "Great Half Century" is Romantically oxymoronic.

The logic of that oxymoron is what leaves Ryzepka helpless to conclude his chapter in a manner fully consistent with what came before. Not only is there the startling increase in the naturalizing organic figures, but his diction shifts toward the personal and nonanalytic ("My own feeling," 98), and there are changes in the frequency and function of quotations from Wordsworth. Rather than being presented so that they can be interpreted, they surface in increasing numbers to carry the entire weight of the argument: "Wordsworth felt less urgently the need to seek refuge in visionary solipsism, until finally that 'celestial light' faded into' the light of common day' " (98). The chapter's final image is the same Arnoldian one that mesmerized Geoffrey Hartman in *Criticism in the Wilderness*[12] (see my chapter 3):

> By the end of his middle years Wordsworth had learned to content himself with the role of priest, rather than prophet, of the imagination. He had come down from the mountain; he had a congregation to look after now. (99)

This complex of assumptions—the poet as prophet; his activity as imaginative; the imagination as a "high"; and the critic as a fatherly "low"—links Wordsworth with Arnold with Ryzepka, confirming the repetitive continuity of Romantic literature and Romantic literary histories. In Ryzepka's version of the latter, the image formally functions as explanation; in a new literary history, it is a feature to be explained. Thus when I use the Great Decade syndrome as a touchstone throughout this book, it is not to argue about what is "really" great but to demonstrate how such arguments can be a blind to what is actually at stake: an understanding of the formal and conceptual limitations of different kinds of literary histories.

To write a kind that does not have to end in a Great Decade, I have turned from the concept of periods, for it has come to carry an assumption of abrupt beginnings and endings that has led almost all critics to write Romanticism off as of the second or third decade of the nineteenth century. However, that was precisely the time at which the constructs and strategies of Romantic texts became normal for the entire culture, not only constituting the new formal and thematic criteria of literariness but also—as the newly charged literary institution took up the cultural work of defining "real language" and the "common man"—transforming the prosaic self into what we now think of as the modern subject. My vocabulary of change is thus of eras of transition (such as the late eighteenth and early nineteenth centuries, as well as the late twentieth and early twenty-first centuries), and of variations within and innovations upon changing norms.[13]

To avoid reifying the history of norm change as yet another developmental tale, I have turned to a classification system that avoids absolutes. Failure to do so, as in the previously described effort to use Language to deconstruct Organic Romanticism as Ironic Romanticism, has resulted only in substituting one absolute (Revisionary Language) for another (Visionary Imagination). More productive has been the emphasis on linguistic transformation that takes writing and reading to be social processes of encodation and decodation. But that critical approach generally ignores or misconstrues exactly the same concept that the Romantic privileging of imagination first left behind as constraining: form. As Ralph Cohen has observed, the language codes hypothesis misconstrues

> the relation between language and genre. Although genres are language structures, they are not reducible to language nor are they merely reflections of changes in the language code. Because every text is an instance of a genre (at least one), genre as a structure always includes features that have continuity with the past—whether these are compositional or metrical or thematic, etc.—and features that are innovative. Genre by this definition is constituted by linguistic codes that are inconsistent in their implications.[14]

Given that inconsistency, as well as other difficulties with linguistic and more traditional approaches (see chapter 2), I have chosen to write a *generic history,* one that is different in kind from a *history of genre* defined in any essentialist terms. A history of genre imposes a historical narrative on single forms, treating each one as an independent, organic entity evolving naturally toward greater sophistication. The result is usually a Romantic developmental tale such as *the* Novel's rise or *the* Lyric's flowering. A generic history, however, uses genre to construct history rather than the other way around. Understood as a family concept, genre can address both change *and* continuity, for it categorizes every text as a member both of an ongoing kind and of a synchronically distinct set of relationships among different kinds. From this perspective, a genre rises not through a hierarchy of absolute aesthetic values, authorized by and authorizing literary critics, but according to its increasing visibility in the changing hierarchies of all other forms of writing with which it is always interrelated. Thus Romanticism is an age of lyric in that the hierarchy of genres was, at the end of the eighteenth and beginning of the nineteenth centuries, lyricized; that is, what we have come to identify historically as lyric features and their effects, such as the turn to the reader and spontaneity, were incorporated with increasing frequency in increasing numbers of forms. To treat spontaneity in this manner, as a formal and historical concern, is to be able to detail the textual construction of the "mind of Man" without naturalizing its informing characteristics.

The relevance of this mode of inquiry to literary criticism in general, as well as to studies in Romanticism, becomes evident when we acknowledge what I have been stressing in this introduction: that criticism itself is a form of writing whose functions are historically determined by its hierarchical interrelations with other forms. I show that criticism has helped to perform what I call, in chapters 4 and 5, the work of Literature, establishing itself as an institution by helping to perpetuate the Romantic myth of culture—a myth which assigns to a set of primary "artistic" texts, and their "creators," the power of psychologically transcending the everyday without unduly interfering with it. The secondary critical texts written to access that power have thus become valuable as the means of standardizing the levels of literacy that ensure the developmental significance of an individual's "love of literature." I pursue this type of inquiry through interdisciplinary as well as intergeneric comparisons, in order to establish the historicity of the boundary lines between that literature and other fields of knowledge.

The same reclassification and valorization that establish literature as such a field also function to make a kind of self that can and wants to produce and consume it. That is why my generic literary history explains the conceptual shift by which man reconstituted himself as the modern psychologized subject: a mind, capable of limitless growth, that takes itself to be the primary object of its own inquiries. In generically detailing how that self was written, I take such constituent parts as imagination, creativity, and development to be neither ahistorical ideas nor psychological truths, but formal features and strategies—parts that interrelate historically to produce a culture-specific whole. In each of this book's three sections I analyze the synchronic and diachronic functions of key parts, producing the following argument: the first section clarifies the need for a new literary history that can establish how Romantic discourse, past *and* present, writes up and valorizes the behaviors that configure the psychologized self; the second demonstrates that this self is written, intergenerically, as something that grows; and the third explores the political significance of that self's developmental desires.

Chapters 2 and 3 follow the generic procedure of tracing the functions of key formal features. Both focus on what I call the "lyric turn," that feature by which creative and critical narratives, from the past and from the present, veer from the generic and historical to the natural and transcendent, metamorphosing all analysis into claims for Imaginative vision. I examine its presence and function in late eighteenth- and early nineteenth-century texts, as well as in some of the most notable landmarks of contemporary criticism of the Romantics. Although I do address the critics by name, my emphasis is on critical *kinds,* and the variety of ways in which the turn operates within them.

I begin the book's next section with an extended example of historical work that does not take that turn. To do so I isolate yet another feature, personification, this time analyzing the difference in its functions within the georgic-descriptive hierarchy of forms of the early eighteenth century as compared to the lyricized hierarchy that follows. I relate those differences to the writing up of a new *developing* self, identifying a shift that established isolated individuality as the natural state of that self, posited social relations in terms of the psychological conformity necessary for "sympathetic identification," and centered the ability to communicate—literacy—as the means and measure of social power. I conclude intergenerically, by using the turn from personification as it also occurred in the novel, to explore the role of the politics of feeling in the inventing of the literary institution—specifically, how Literature was empowered as a discipline by the rewriting of moral imperatives into aesthetic ones.

Chapters 5 and 6 examine the self configured by those imperatives, identifying as its distinguishing characteristic that which remains to this day one of the most apparently natural and ahistorical, and therefore powerful, elements in Romantic discourse: development. Rather than regarding it as a psychological truth, I argue that development is an all-encompassing formal strategy underpinning middle-class culture itself: its characteristic way of representing and evaluating the individual as something that grows. In other words, this section examines the profound shift from the self as static, metaphysical, and inherited to the rounded, psychological, and self-made subject, one that is capable of the limitless self-improvement valorizing and valorized by an "open" society and a "free" economy. By examining development generically, as a strategy, I can once again address change in terms of shifting functions, first establishing its historicity by demonstrating its connection to the specifically Romantic "work" of revision, and then emphasizing the synchronic interrelations among the different lyricized forms in which the strategy appears: Wordsworth's "expressive" poetry, Austen's "realistic" novels, Marx's "class" history.

The three chapters of the final section explore the politics of developmental desire in regard to a trio of now familiar objects: money, sex, and drugs. Using a variety of nonliterary materials, particularly Malthus's essays on population, which explore the problematics of development in all three areas, other tracts on economics, and medical treatises, I show that such desire is, in Michel Foucault's sense of the term, inherently disciplinary. Like him, I assert that modern power is exerted not through the repression but the production of knowledge. Thus a self-made mind, full of newly constructed depths, is an object of the new knowledge of those depths and therefore subject to professional power. The self configured by the desire for ongoing revision, in other words, is self-disciplinary: by requiring and expecting unlimited development, it always opens deeper depths to surveillance and invites more and more specialized intervention.

The advantages of a generic history are evident in each chapter as I treat the eighteenth-century debate over high wages in terms of the concept of mixed forms, identify sexual characteristics as formal features and thus sexual difference as a written construct, and analyze addiction as a historical narrative. By illuminating the historicity of the literary institution, a generic approach enables me to detail the roles of what appear to be *only* literary concerns and truths—Blake's and Wordsworth's high arguments regarding the value of their work; the paucity of Romantic women writers; Coleridge's flawed genius— in the naturalizing of apparently nonliterary cultural behaviors. Such interconnections, in turn, clarify our present stake in understanding the discursive power of the Romantic past.

That power is the reason why this book, even as it reaches across generic, canonical, and disciplinary boundaries, does engage at significant length the texts of the best known male poets. I give those writings such attention, however, not in order to preserve their present dominion over late eighteenth- and early nineteenth-century studies, but to effect a change in our relationship to them, one that will not dismiss them, but will help to put into the past some of their extraordinary power over our professional and personal behaviors.

To "break open" the canon without doing this first is to make the political mistake of being blind to that power, and of thus facing the inevitable prospect of reproducing, with the new material, Romantic relationships that have not yet been written to an end. The kind of history I am writing, with its present proportion of the familiar and unfamiliar, is designed not to ignore but to take advantage of its particular historical moment—a moment of transition which, strategically engaged, can provide opportunities for other kinds of work using other kinds of works. I look forward to reading and writing them.

I wrote this book, then, to provide examples of the theoretical features and strategies of a new literary history. Its value lies, finally, in setting the formal stage for more work that, in examining the transition to the Romantic norm, will help to construct the next one. Because literary history is a relatively small area of inquiry, we can more easily produce within it new formal behaviors, ones that will eventually be acculturated as the "natural" ways of thinking and acting within other realms of experience. The manner in which a self written by the literary innovations of a Wordsworth[15] became normal for Darwin, Freud, and every "developing" individual indicates what is at stake.

2

The Un-Kind Imagination

This riddling tale, to what does it belong?
Is't history? vision? or an idle song?
Or rather say at once, within what space
Of time this wild disastrous change took place?

S. T. Coleridge

Allegories of Reading started out as a historical study and ended up as a theory of reading. I began to read Rousseau seriously in preparation for a historical reflection on Romanticism and found myself unable to progress beyond local difficulties of interpretation. In trying to cope with this, I had to shift from historical definition to the problematics of reading. This shift, which is typical of my generation, is of more interest in its results than in its causes.

Paul de Man[1]

This chapter is about causes—not in the sense of assigning absolute origins, but in terms of identifying interrelations among texts. Its purpose is to clarify the need for a new literary history that does not "end up" transcending itself. What de Man calls a "shift" is a feature of particular forms, and not only has he understated its typicality, but his emphasis on "results" is a blind to its function. Ever since Wordsworth began *The Prelude* by confessing to a swerve from conventional epic expectations into extended self-revelation, what I call the "lyric turn" has played a central role in creative *and* critical narratives. The writer first indicates his intention to write within a received form. This social gesture is then followed by an abrupt turn presented as a personal confession of the writer's *need* to proceed in a more private direction: form and history are implicitly condemned as restricting or inadequate and are therefore internalized and transcended under the guise of individual (to use de Man's word) "progress."

In *Allegories of Reading,* historical and formal *difference* is transcended by "a theory" that describes kinds of writing with absolutes
such as "forever" (19), but in other texts the same turn is made by just
recasting history itself in transcendent terms. Whereas de Man begins
by confessing to an inability to do history, Tilottama Rajan in *Dark
Interpreter* ends by admitting to an inability to do without it: "Although a historical discussion of the evolution of Romanticism has
not been one of my purposes, it seems appropriate to conclude by
suggesting that such an evolution did occur" (265). As with de Man's
aversion to causes, Rajan's reference to what "seems appropriate"
elides the reasons her narrative must end on an "evolution[ary]"
note: the history she describes is a "psychological sequence," one in
"which the later Romantics have *moved beyond* their predecessors"
(emphasis mine; 262, 265). Whether situated at the narrative's start
or finish, the lyric turn shapes it into an affirmation of transcendence
as "naturally" appropriate.

The resulting shape of Rajan's "biography" of the Romantic
imagination" (262) is not an unfamiliar one. The progressive tale that
it tells adds a deconstructive model to the long list of kinds of Imagination drawn up by other Romanticists: Visionary, Creative, Confes-
sional, and so on. By titling this chapter "The Un-Kind Imagination,"
I have tried to highlight the formal significance of that list. But I do so
not to extend it, and thereby present the list and the "faculty" it
describes as "something evermore about to be"; rather I wish to call
into question the very features, such as the lyric turn, that authorize
it, and to suggest that the profession's recent interest in genre and
history indicates that we are now in a historical position to ask different kinds of questions of the late eighteenth and early nineteenth
centuries—questions for which this list, however long, holds no answers. By "Un-Kind Imagination," in other words, I am referring not
to an Imagination that fails to work sympathetically, but to the way in
which critical fascination with Imagination as an actual (physiological?) faculty of mind, or psychological truth, or locus of discursive or
tropological activity, has led to scores of articles and books evaluating
literature according to kinds of Imagination, rather than analyzing
imagination as a historical *construct* having specific formal functions
within literary kinds.

Before addressing de Man's contribution to this list in more detail, it would be useful to examine some of the more traditional
entries. In *The Creative Imagination,* for example, James Engell presents an evolutionary narrative in the extreme; he unabashedly cele-

brates the "triumph" of Imagination by constructing a progressive "history" from a formidable array of sources. He does so without considering, as his reviewer in *Criticism* points out, the forms of writing from which he plucks his quotations. The passage cited compares Akenside and Wordsworth:

> *The Prelude* is a vindication of the attitude that imagination permeates life. And without this personal testament we would miss a closing link in this history of the idea. *The Prelude* does not, in a specifically philosophical or critical sense, say much more about the idea of the imagination than Akenside's *Pleasures*. But the individuality and the connected experiences in *The Prelude* are among the reasons why it is far greater. The idea becomes humanized.[2]

Imagination's lamp, as presented by Engell, shines so brightly that it washes out the formal distinction between a didactic poem and an autobiographical narrative, subordinating questions of function to an assertion of progressive continuity. This Imaginative neglect of form, I maintain, masks a characteristic critical maneuver of conventional histories: in the absence of a formal understanding of literary change, difference is invariably described in *qualitative* fashion. While it may be easy to assent to the canonical force of such evaluations, and nod approvingly when told that *The Prelude* is "far greater" than the *Pleasures of Imagination,* doing so is not an innocent demonstration of taste but a transformation of history into developmental narrative. Evaluation functions within this kind of critical writing to domesticate difference as evidence of a humanizing continuity.

To present this activity as a matter of ignorance or ineptness would be more naive than rude. For doing so fails to acknowledge criticism as a form of writing with functions that can change. To call into question a former function, such as humanization through textual canonization, is not to assert an "evolutionary" superiority over the distant or recent past; it is to de-naturalize the conceptual limits of that past and thus establish the possibility of different classificatory procedures and hence different kinds of knowledge—knowledge that will, of course, be subject to other limits. In a time of accelerated change, as I suggested in the introduction, saving the past is a less practical alternative than historicizing it. Rather than domesticating difference in a creative or supposedly theoretical embrace, one of criticism's new social functions can be to help us learn to recognize and distinguish kinds of change and comprehend their workings.

Thus to avoid what I would argue is *now* a less valuable, as well as repetitive, fate of writing "critical" developmental narratives to praise "creative" developmental narratives, we do not need to evaluate differently (Akenside over Wordsworth), but to use the generic differences elided by such praise as a framework for historicizing both the text's features and procedures and our own Romantic origins. What Engell calls the "humanization" of Imagination in *The Prelude,* for example, is not a matter of authorial greatness or of the inevitable evolution of an idea, but of literature's generative and exemplary role in the recasting of what late eighteenth-century English culture first takes to be human. An individuality grounded in "connected experiences" has been, since that time, so effectively *naturalized* that Engell cites it as an absolute human value somehow missing or inadequately expressed in Akenside. At issue from the point of view of a generic history, however, is the changing value placed upon such continuity and the shifting methods of asserting it. In fact, *The Prelude* becomes, in Wordsworth's own words, a "trac[ing]" of Imagination (1805, XIII.172), precisely because that feature's narrative function in the chronological chaos of lyrical autobiography is to produce the effect of transcendent continuity. It does so in concert with "development" ("The Child is father of the Man"), which, as I show in section II, is no more of an ahistorical psychological "truth" than Imagination, but rather a contemporaneous formal strategy for naturalizing social and literary change. Together, these constructs of a culture in radical transition redefine the "real" in an attempt to make such change make sense.

Those critics who accept that redefinition, either by heralding it as truth triumphant or by taking it for granted, necessarily privilege Imagination, neglect form, and produce Romantic literary histories rather than literary histories of Romanticism: developmental tales of individual and social epiphanies that replicate the narrative turns of the texts they canonize. Even critics who are overtly concerned with formal issues, such as Romanticism as an age of lyric, generally conform to this ahistorical in-formality by conducting their inquiries less on generic grounds than on thematic ones. The themes, centering obsessively upon the workings of Imagination, characteristically turn critical attention toward the mental and emotional activity of the individual poet. As Cyrus Hamlin has observed, "Traditional criticism of English Romanticism has entirely neglected the question of form and interpretation has long been preoccupied with the role of poet as author in a biographical or psychological context."[3] Its more recent preoccupation with the critic as reader in a rhetorical context is but a variation on the same turn.

Both preoccupations explain why the developmental contours of Romantic literary histories conform so closely to the critical biographies conventionally constructed for individual Romantic poets. Discussions of Wordsworth's originality, achievement, and "anti-climax"—his lyrical flowering—for example, have effectively functioned as arguments for the origin (*Lyrical Ballads*), character (greater Romantic lyric), and duration (short) of Romanticism. In each case, issues that appear to invite inquiry into genre—the mixing of kinds (lyric and ballad), the nature of lyric, the viability of experimental forms—have been turned into evaluative debates over Imaginative intensity with only one sure outcome: lengthening the list of kinds of Imagination I mentioned earlier. To see this turn in action is to recognize both how un-kind the Imagination can be and how a history lacking kindness has little to say about difference.

The Mayo debate over *Lyrical Ballads* is a striking example, since difference is ostensibly its major concern. Responding to claims that *Lyrical Ballads* was something totally new, Mayo found in the magazines of the time ample evidence of ballads at least somewhat similar in both form and content. For some critics that was sufficient proof of continuity and the unoriginality of the volume. But for others, Mayo included, this discovery only complicated the question of difference. To their rescue came the lyric turn. In his conclusion, Mayo's terms switch from the generic and historical to the natural and transcendent. Quoting extensively from Coleridge, he assumes the position of cultural critic to distinguish hierarchically two kinds of reading. In the "casual," *Lyrical Ballads* "would tend to merge with familiar features of the literary landscape." The "careful" reading, however, "would give suddenly a tremendous impression of clarity, freshness, and depth." This more "critical" look reveals, of course, Wordsworth's "true genius," which operates in another "dimension" than historical "combinations of 'fixities and definites.'" To think it did operate there "would be to confound the superior powers of imagination with the inferior powers of the fancy."[4]

Almost every study of *Lyrical Ballads* has followed roughly the same course, submitting even the most impressive examples of historical research to the tyranny of this lyric turn in which all analysis seemingly metamorphoses into claims for transcendent readings of special texts. I say "seemingly" because this is no "natural" tendency but a formal feature of the critical kind I have been describing: the developmental history that (Romantically) posits innovation in terms of (creative) originality. To argue that *Lyrical Ballads* is more or less "new," according to the mere presence or absence of subject matter or form in the previous literature, is to ignore the crucial question of their shifting *functions* within diachronically distinct generic hierarchies. By analyzing the interrelations of the features and forms within a particular hierarchy, we can identify their normal functions at that hierarchy's historical moment. If those interrelations are ignored, and change is engaged without a sense of continuity, difference is Romantically posited as creative originality. When continuity is engaged without a sense of change, difference is Romantically dissolved into transcendent development. A generic approach, however, allows us to address both change *and* continuity, for it categorizes every text as a member both of an ongoing kind and of a synchronically distinct set of relationships among different kinds. The question of originality is thus reformulated by generic analysis into a systematic inquiry into kinds of change: variation within or innovation upon a norm.

To place such conceptual and methodological weight upon the term "genre" is, I realize, to risk having one's work misread as a conservative return, perhaps in reaction to the supposed excesses of contemporary theory, to some sort of outmoded formalism. But it is the inadequacy of much of what claims to be theory that I am addressing. And I do so *not* to disclaim it, but to write its interrelations with other kinds of writing. A similar concern with the formal future of criticism, often accompanied by increasing interest in matters of genre and historical difference, has recently been evident in such efforts as Hošek and Parker's *Lyric Poetry*. Its subtitle, *Beyond New Criticism,* as well as its familiar list of prestigious contributors (Culler, de Man, Fish, Chase, Jameson, and others), suggest an effort to link "progress" in theory to the redefinition of a literary kind.[5]

It is not, however, until Jonathan Arac's "Afterword" that the premise of progress is directly addressed:

> Grant that these essays betray no stale fatigue, none of the derivative belatedness Frank Lentricchia has found *After the New Criticism* (1980), it is still possible that many of them do not so much surpass New Criticism as renovate it through revision: less "Beyond the New Criticism" than a "New New Criticism." From Culler's contrast of Cleanth Brooks and Paul de Man on Yeats's "Among School Children," it emerges clearly that the new new criticism shares with the old

> New Criticism an emphasis that is textual and technical, more con-
> cerned with method than with scholarship, and fundamentally
> unhistorical, especially in its confidence about the extensive applicabil-
> ity of its operative terms. (*Lyric Poetry,* 346)

Doubling the adjective denominates attempted innovation as variation. Not only do these efforts share how to know; they also share
what not to know. Among the works they "agree to ignore," Arac
lists texts by Alistair Fowler, Rosalie Colie, and the early 1970s publications of Geoffrey Hartman (*Beyond Formalism* and *The Fate of
Reading*). What these have in common, although Arac does not precisely specify it, is exactly what one would expect to be of prime
interest to the contributors to this kind of volume: a historical concern with genre.

It is not that such a concern is absent from the essays, but that its
presence is visible primarily through suggestions posed in a relatively
private terminology. Cynthia Chase, for example, is aptly questioned
by Arac for her problematic use of the phrase "patterns of rhetoric"
to describe the intertextual connections she deems necessary for literary study:

> Why then does her paper depend upon quotations attributed by name
> to the most famous poets in English—Shakespeare, Milton, Words-
> worth? Why not just make up appropriate patterns of rhetoric out of
> the language environment? (*Lyric Poetry,* 349)

These questions correctly identify the problem as a canonical and
thus a literary historical matter. Literary history, I am arguing, needs
to be understood in terms of changing classification systems. The
canonical restraints upon Chase's new new criticism indicate how
such systems delimit the proper objects of knowledge as well as the
kinds of inquiries to which they are subject. In this light, we need to
understand the "language environment" not as an organic given, but
as a system of speciated interrelations capable of change.

To take those species to be "patterns of rhetoric" presents three
problems. First, as with the "language codes" I discussed in the introduction, doing so fails to acknowledge the different functions that a
particular pattern can have when included in different forms and in
different hierarchies of forms. Second, statements about rhetorical
patterns are themselves parts of a text and therefore need to be
understood as features of that text's genre. Like the de Manian

"modes" of rhetoric I address later in this chapter, pattern statements within "theories of reading" or "new new" criticism function as absolutes that shape literary history into an essentially cyclic repetition. Third, the "patterns of rhetoric" approach cannot define an alternative shape without taking into account its own historicity; it must be able to place itself within the history that it constructs. Genre theory can do so because of the large body of texts that attempt or refer to generic classifications. Those efforts, even if we judge them inadequate, should not cause us to consider genre theory "discredited" (Jameson).[6] In fact, they are a major reason why the concept of genre is so suited to the writing of a new literary history: they make it clear that, in Ralph Cohen's words, "genre concepts in theory and practice arise, change, and decline for historical reasons. And since each genre is composed of texts that accrue, the grouping is a *process* not," as with a mode or pattern of rhetoric, "a determinate category. Genres are open categories" (emphasis mine).[7]

The denial of essential generic traits is the key to the viability of any contemporary genre theory. Cohen shows that Jacques Derrida's argument for the "need *and* futility" (emphasis mine; 204) of genre is launched from the assumption that genre has to do, in Derrida's words, with a "mark of belonging" that cannot really belong.[8] Generic grouping based on such a mark is an attempt to fix an indeterminate text within a determinate class. The resulting "law of genre" is that the making of a class is necessarily the beginning of its unmaking. But this is a paradox only if we assume that genre study is a study of closed categories rather than of the process of categorizing. The latter study is necessarily historical, addressing the issue of difference in the manner Derrida characteristically avoids—diachronically. Genres exist only in competitive or complementary relationship to each other, and the system or hierarchy constituted by those relationships is always subject to temporal change.

The temptation to take the lyric turn and dehistoricize those changes so that they can be offered as "laws" has overcome not only Derrida but many constructive critics as well. Alastair Fowler's massive effort to analyze *Kinds of Literature* ends with a Romantic flourish that could earn the book the subtitle, "The Kindly Imagination."[9] Because he links the "range of genres" to the "variety of imagination," he can use the latter's informing metaphor of "internal/external" to naturalize a distinction between "generic" or "literary" change as opposed to "social change" and "changes of sensibility." Genre, circumscribed in this manner, "is best thought of, perhaps, as a collective or group creative process" (275–76). The "laws of genre" governing that process are thus psychologized absolutes that turn history once again into cyclic repetition: "One such law might be that of compensation, as in the alternating preference for long and short forms" (233–34).

William Elford Rodgers provides yet another variation on the turn in his effort "to preserve the concept of 'genre' as interpretive concept."[10] After beginning *The Three Genres and the Interpretation of Lyric* with useful analyses of the shortcomings of earlier theories, particularly E. D. Hirsch's and Paul Hernadi's, Rodgers constructs his own classification system. Its informing distinction between the "mind of the work" and the "world of the work" is presented as "a function of the *interpretive* act" (55). What Rodgers calls "genre" enters the picture in terms of the ways in which readers find themselves interpreting works, so that, for example, "the fundamental technique of works interpreted epically is *point of view*" (179). He argues that this model can bring us "toward a literary history" by articulating "the felt differences [between poems] in terms of different modes of reciprocity between mind and world, with particular attention to the differences in tropes" (242). What we get, then, is not a new literary history addressing changing classification systems, but a single classification system, with obvious Romantic origins, promising a consistent literary history of tropological patterns. For our purposes, the historical significance of that effort lies not in its results, but in its status as yet another recent text that posits an interrelation of history and genre as a solution to contemporary critical problems.

Cynthia Chase's article in *Lyric Poetry* ends in that position. Mimicking Keats's "rhetorical pattern," she concludes with a suggestion that, to borrow her description of Keats, "leaves us hanging":

> And perhaps one should also reread Keats's letters, looking not at the familiar thematics of "Negative Capability," or "the Vale of Soul-making," but rather at the fleeting comments on the conditions of writing—the condition of writing poems in *letters,* for instance: "I know you would like what I wrote thereon—so *here* it is—as they say of a Sheep in a Nursery Book."[11]

The poem is "On Seeing a Lock of Milton's Hair." Keats recounts, in the sentence before the one quoted by Chase, how Hunt had "surprised" him "with a real authenticated Lock." Both the way Chase raises the issue, "poems in *letters,*" and the way Keats does, a playful simile (sheep/sheared:Milton/delocked) with a "Sheep *in* a Nursery

Book" (emphasis mine), point to this being a matter of generic interrelations: the inclusion of one species within another kind. One of the
effects of this particular inclusion, however, has been to steer critical
attention away from genre and toward psychologized biography,
since the poem is taken to be an event in the creative author's life.
But if we recognize our knowledge of that life to be itself textual, then
genre comes back into view. Since this book is organized to provide
different views of Romantic generic interrelations, I will provide a
brief chapter-by-chapter version of the "rereading" Chase suggests.

    First, and most obviously, this inclusion of lyric features within
another form is not an isolated phenomenon but can be related
synchronically to other lyricizations such as Wordsworth's experiments with "lyrical ballads." As more forms incorporate more lyric
features, the lyric rises within the generic hierarchy. In turn, the
relative importance of every other form alters according to the extent
that it has incorporated parts of the newly dominant form. This is
important to our understanding of past texts, because the functions of
the newly interrelated features and forms change.

    Within a hierarchy dominated by georgic and satiric forms, as
we find through the late seventeenth and much of the eighteenth
centuries, the use of letters is keyed to didactic description. By
formally bridging the conversational and the formal, the private and
the public, the immediate present and the recollected past, the letter
functions to constitute difference as evidence of a stabilizing moral
uniformity and continuity. Whether in the personal efforts of Dorothy Osborne to maintain the correct relationship between "kindness" and "reputation,"[12] or in the novelistic efforts of Richardson
to craft a Christian tragedy, or in the courtesy efforts of Lord Ches-
terfield to re-produce a gentleman, the social and temporal differences the letter highlights substantiate, and are substantiated by, the
universal truths being conveyed.

    The letter as found in Keats, on the other hand, conveys heuristi-
cally rather than didactically; it centers not upon particular epigram-
matical truths, but instead is supposed to enact, through the turn to
lyric, the expressive truthfulness we still call sincerity. As with the
other examples of the lyric turn addressed in this chapter, this one
does not substantiate difference but psychologizes it. The poem's
abrupt appearance suggests transcendence of the prose's day-to-day
history, producing a developmental narrative in which progress is
signaled by the punctuation of lyric epiphanies. That punctuation
calls attention to the writing as writing, producing the depth effect of

self-consciousness, which, as I point out in chapter 3, we have valorized as evidence of creativity. The abruptness of the turn and the fragmentation it produces suggest the spontaneity and intensity that have also been written into our concept of the creative.

Since generic mixing is a social as well as a literary activity, Keats's juxtaposition of informal prose and formal poetry (an ode) makes the same argument for revamping hierarchy that Wordsworth does in the Preface to *Lyrical Ballads*. The valorization of the "common" man and of the poet as "a man speaking to men" is also formally implicit in Keats's act: writing a letter and writing a poem are presented as parts of the same common activity of self-expression—anybody can do it. Or, to be more precise, as I am in chapter 4, anyone who is literate can. Thus in the new hierarchy, with its new cultural myths, the ability to communicate—literacy—becomes the means and measure of social power.

The myth of the individual within that culture depends on the primacy of synecdoche: each person is both whole and part. As shown in chapter 5, this is Wordsworth's fundamental formal argument. Each poem can and should stand both alone *and* as part of a larger whole that is the poet's oeuvre (the gothic church argument). Embedded as it is, Keats's ode is a whole unto itself and also a fragment of the whole letter. The surrounding confessionary prose functions, as I show of other poets' extratextual material, to discipline the reader by making conformity through sympathetic identification a condition of "true" literacy. This particular letter, featuring an ode placed in the middle, is an especially apt illustration of this formal phenomenon. If we take the whole letter as a Pindaric-type ODE, then the ode on Milton becomes an epode, the chorus's still moment of meditation on the historical and personal past, surrounded by the prose "turnings" of a strophe and antistrophe that provide an event-by-event recounting of the present.[13]

Placing an epode with that theme in the middle is a characteristic procedure of Romantic developmental narratives; they turn to the past (the child) as an explanation of—not, as in the eighteenth century, as a model for—the present (the man). Development, as I show in tracing the lyricization of the novel in chapter 6, makes change make sense, and that kind of sense is precisely what the letter, the figure initiating the mix, and the poem dramatize. Keats's letter is a progress report, marking the passage of time ("Twelve days have pass'd," *Letters*, 52) in terms of the prospect of transcendence ("more goes through the human intelligence in 12 days than ever was written," 52). An epiphany (the poem) followed by a negative transition ("perhaps I should have done something better alone and at home," 55) suggests, as does the same feature in "Tintern Abbey," that there is always "something evermore about to be." The figure of the "Sheep in a Nursery Book" introduces the poem as part of childhood and therefore both imaginative and capable of development. The poet is similarly placed within the poem, his development thematized, as elsewhere in Keats's verse and letters, as a progress in forms:

> Lend thine ear
> To a young delian oath—aye, by thy soul,
> By all that from thy mortal Lips did roll;
> And by the kernel of thine earthly Love,
> Beauty, in things on earth and things above,
>   When every childish fashion
>   Has vanish'd from my rhyme
>   Will I grey-gone in passion,
>   Give to an after-time
>   Hymning and harmony
> Of thee, and of thy Works and of thy Life.
>   (*Letters*, 54)

As in the movement from simple romance to complex tragedy laid out in "Sleep and Poetry"(ll. 96–154), developmental progress is linked to progress through a formal hierarchy: "childish fashion" is displaced by adult "Hymning and harmony." This procedure links biological maturity to poetic maturity, naturalizing the latter and granting aesthetic value to the former.

The eruption, or "spontaneous overflow," of poetry within the prose figures this formal transcendence. No literary forms and, thematically, no social categories can contain in their fixedness the developing poet. The three categories against which Keats measures himself in this letter and elsewhere are the same ones that inform the last three chapters of this book: poverty ("that unfortunate Family," 52), sex (*"Why should Woman suffer?"* 52; "Men should bear with each other," 53), and sickness (Tom's "Spitting of blood" 55). Like an inspirational lyric inserted within a letter full of bad news,[14] the poet's function in society is to provide consolation by psychologizing limitation. Imagination can then be written up as the cultural means of escape. Such escapes, however, are only temporary, as clarified by the letter's generic interrelations. Since the poem is only an interruption surrounded by prose, the narrative of developmental transcendence tells a tale of addiction: a mutually reinforcing, and thus compulsive, series of poetic highs and prosaic lows. To understand the generic historicity of Romantic discourse is to recognize the remarkable potency of Keats's injection of lyric into his, and eventually our, everyday experience.

The lyric turns we have located in contemporary criticism are evidence of that addictive power. Its hold is particularly strong in the best known effort to characterize Romantic form: M. H. Abrams's "Structure and Style in the Greater Romantic Lyric." Here, as in Mayo, historical difference is at issue, since Abrams can define the Romantic only by making an argument for change:

> In Bowles' sonnets, the meditation, while more continuous [than the "eighteenth-century local poem"], is severely limited by the straitness of the form, and consists mainly of the pensive commonplaces of the typical late-century man of feeling. In the fully developed Romantic lyric, on the other hand, the description is structurally subordinate to the meditation, and the meditation is sustained, continuous, and highly serious.[15]

Notice that conventional form, in this case the sonnet, is *assumed* to be limiting, whereas its Romantic replacement is "fully developed" precisely because it has been "subordinate[d]" to the Poet's mental activity, his "meditation." This is, in other words, yet another lyric turn in which generic concerns are trivialized as the Poet's expressiveness *naturally* transcends inherited form.

Accepting this hypothesis not only skews literary history in favor of "highly serious" Romantics as opposed to their "pensive[ly] commonplace" predecessors; it also perpetuates, under the guise of interpretation, the central Romantic myth of the artist as creative genius. Within that myth, distinctions between the creative and the critical, and between the individual and society, authorize spontaneity and originality as imaginative means of transcending the supposed limitations of conventional form. But those means, as we saw in regard to the "spontaneity" of Keats's outbursts, are themselves but *effects* of specific *formal* procedures. I discuss them under the rubric of "revision" in chapter 5, indicating that the synecdochic part/whole relationship within the lyrical hierarchy of forms is mutually *interpretative:* each part revises the meaning of the whole, while the whole simultaneously revises the (transcendent) meaning of each part. And just as such interpretation always seeks a final clarification of meaning, so the wished-for end of Romantic revision is a Unity that transcends difference.

When we speak of the Romantic lyric in terms of subordinating form to expressive unity, we are trapped within the discourse of that desire. Romantic revision has done its work so well that the *sense* of "natural" spontaneity and creative unity it produces blinds us to its pervasive presence in not only the actual rewriting of texts, but also in the initial composing, prefacing, and classifying of them. The notoriously abrupt and negative transitions of "Tintern Abbey," for example—"If this / Be but a vain belief, yet, oh!"; "Nor perchance, / If I were not thus taught"—signal that each verse paragraph is not solely a part *added* to the others to produce a sum that is the whole. Rather, each part is itself potentially a whole (i.e., "*This* is what I owe to 'Tintern Abbey' ") that, when placed in revisionary relationship to the others through the use of negatives and qualifiers, both reinterprets them ("That may not be what I really learned") and is itself reinterpreted ("This may not be either"). The abrupt reversals produce the effect of spontaneity, and the repeated reformulations suggest transcendence—that there actually is "something evermore about to be." What is most characteristically Romantic about this "greater Romantic lyric," then, is not, as Abrams's psychologized history argues, the Poet's "high seriousness," but the way in which the supposedly organic text shows itself to be a product of a characteristic form of revisionary behavior.

Even the very notion of a "greater Romantic lyric" needs to be called into question when we realize that Abrams's psychologizing has produced a historical treatment of genre rather than a generic treatment of the problem of history. In the former, as I have argued, a given form of history dictates the generic findings. Thus in Abrams's developmental narrative a genre is organically described, amid metaphors of "blackberries," as a "species" with "a capacity to survive." He can explain how the georgic "becomes" the Romantic lyric only by implying the Imaginative superiority of the latter and suggesting a "parallel," within a "tradition," that cannot be "drive[n] . . . too hard." When genre is prioritized to help us historicize, however, change need no longer be described as one form mysteriously metamorphosing into another, but can instead be posited in terms of how the functions of shared features and procedures shift as the forms they constitute enter into different hierarchical relationships.

"Tintern Abbey," from this perspective, is a lyricized ode containing features that appear in later texts, but it does not, as a whole, constitute a significant model for them. To assert that claim requires an argument as circular as *The Prelude*'s. Having identified a "kind of poem" from a list of features, Abrams reasons that the presence of some of those features in subsequent texts is evidence that the kind has "engender[ed] successors" and is therefore, in fact, a distinct and fertile kind. But I would argue that "Tintern Abbey" in many ways is formally an experimental dead end for Wordsworth, and that if we are looking for a formal model for Romanticism, along the line of the couplet for the early eighteenth century, we need to turn, as John Rowlett has suggested, to the sonnet.[16] To do so, of course, is to suggest generic continuities that require us to rethink the myths of the Great Decade and six-poet Romanticism— two examples, as I argued in the introduction, of how un-kind thinking substitutes Romantic literary histories for a literary history of Romanticism.

The editorial and pedagogical repercussions of a *generic* rethinking of the Great Decade problem would be particularly evident to Wordsworthians in the controversy over the 1805 and 1850 *Prelude*(s). In a recent issue of *The Wordsworth Circle*,[17] Jeffrey Baker forcefully criticized the Norton editors for using the scholarly device of footnotes to enforce their predilection for the supposedly "humanistic" superiority of the earlier version. Robert Young then skillfully criticized Baker for his essentialistic view of poetry and cautioned all critics against "fruitless and unresolvable attempts" at evaluation. But to follow his suggestion that we instead examine what the "multiplicity" of *Prelude*(s) means, we need more than the assertion that poems "are made of words." Any debate over changes of words, over the relationship between Romanticism and language, will face an ahistorical dead end until we add that writers use words to behave linguistically, and such behavior, "Imaginative" or otherwise, is not restricted by form but is itself inevitably *formal.* "Multiplicity" could then be discussed as a formal strategy within a particular historical norm that valorizes rewriting as evidence of developmental growth. The 1850 *Prelude*'s "conformity" could similarly be seen, as I demonstrate in chapter 5, not in terms of a specious link between conservatism and "good" or "bad" poetry, but as a specific index of the text's relationship to that developmental norm.

The debate over the quality of the poet's later work needs to be similarly transformed. To argue over the early and late poetry by claiming that "this is the language really spoken by the real Words-

worth" and "that is the inane phraseology of a comfortable elitist" is
to echo the procedure Wordsworth himself employed in the Preface
to *Lyrical Ballads*. Such sympathy and judgment make, as Robert
Langbaum pointed out years ago, an inseparably Romantic pair,
grounded, I might add, in the subject/object psychology of the mind
that this book tries to historicize. Together, they produced for Wordsworth a progressive history justifying his own exertions in terms of a
notion of absolute naturalness accessible only through endless critical
revision. A history that must transcend itself by thematizing the act of
reading[18] remains, even today, the only *kind* of history the subject/
object dichotomy *can* offer, as de Man's confession, cited in this
chapter's epigraph, inadvertently confirms: "I *had* to shift from historical definition to the problematics of reading" (emphasis mine).

In "The Rhetoric of Temporality," of course, de Man claims to be no
longer "trapped," as he argues Abrams and Earl Wasserman have
been, in the "pseudo-dialectic between subject and object."[19] Because de Man believes that this dialectic "originates . . . in the assumed predominance of the symbol as the outstanding characteristic
of romantic diction," he posits freedom in terms of denying the truth
of that assumption. Truth is then characteristically presented as a
matter of critical misreading: "Does the confusion originate with the
critics, or does it reside in the romantic poets themselves?" (198).
Blaming the critics requires only the discovery, through rereading, of
allegorical as opposed to symbolic texts.
        De Man finds what he thinks he needs in one example from
French literature,[20] citing "the puritanical, religious element" in Rousseau's *La Nouvelle Héloïse,* and in one from English literature, turning to Wordsworth. There, he first sets up Abrams's argument in the
"Greater Romantic Lyric" essay, claiming that in it

> the distinction between seventeenth- and late eighteenth-century po-
> etry is made in terms of the determining role played by the geographi-
> cal *place* as establishing the link between the language of the poem and
> the empirical experience of the reader. ("Rhetoric," 206–7)

But, de Man argues, Wordsworth often problematizes the meaning of
a site, leaving the "geographical significance . . . almost meaning-
less." His main piece of evidence, the source of which is identified not
in the text but in a footnote, is a prose quotation:

Raising the question of the geographical locale of a given metaphorical object (in this case, a river), Wordsworth writes: "The spirit of the answer [as to the whereabouts of the river], through[21] the word might be a certain stream, accompanied perhaps with an image gathered from a Map, or from a real object in nature—these might have been the latter, but the spirit of the answer must have been, as inevitably—a receptacle without bounds or dimensions;—nothing less than infinity." ("Rhetoric," 206)

De Man's un-kind treatment of this passage is most obvious in his misrepresentation of the question(s) being asked. They are not about the "geographical locale" or "whereabouts" of the river but the nature of its destination: " 'Towards what abyss is it in progress? what receptacle can contain the mighty influx?' " The answer "infinity" is not a displacement of the name of an actual river or a renunciation of the symbolical diction entailed by the act of inscribing meaning in a particular location; it describes a kind of receptacle—just as it had earlier described, for the same child asking these questions, a kind of source. The whole passage is a psychological study of the "unappeasable inquisitiveness of children upon the subject of origination." Far from this being an example, as de Man claims, of "allegory" that "designates primarily a distance in relation to its own origin . . . renouncing the desire to coincide" (207), its whole point for Wordsworth is that "origin and tendency are notions inseparably co-relative."

Given the fact that de Man is interested in genre—he pronounces, for example, which texts "can no longer be classified with the locodescriptive poem" (206)—it is all the more extraordinary that he does not acknowledge that the Wordsworth passage is part of an essay on genre that defines a specific form: the epitaph. Place naming is a feature with different functions in different forms, a point Wordsworth emphasizes by beginning the essay with a sentence declaring that an epitaph is a poem that requires a particular place in a very particular way—it needs to be written on it: "It need scarcely be said, that an Epitaph presupposes a Monument, upon which it is to be engraven" (*Prose,* II, 49). Only as part of this specific object does the epitaph provide spatial particularity, a local description, to what de Man calls the "void" of absolute temporal difference. Like the essay as a whole, the river/receptacle passage does not describe the allegorical displacement of "specific locale[s]" by a new "typology" ("Rhetoric," 206); it affirms as the "perfection" of a *particular form,* the inscribing in a particular place of "particular thoughts, actions, images" (*Prose,* II, 57). De Man's poor choice of examples is due to the confused conflation of two different classification systems: generic on the one hand, and de Man's personal version of rhetorical on the other.

Those rhetorical classifications are remarkably simple and heavily normative. Tied to the subject/object dialectic is the symbol, which is a "seductive" illusion because it denies the "truth" of the subject's relationship to nature and its own "destiny" ("Rhetoric," 206). That truth lies in an "authentically temporal predicament" that is the domain of allegory and irony: the "two faces of the same fundamental experience of time." The former presents time as changing and the subject as stable, whereas the latter reduces time "to one single moment" causing difference to reside in the subject. What de Man has done is translate subject/object, with its familiar distinction between the "egotistical sublime" (subject stable while objects change) and "negative capability" (subject changes while objects remain stable), into subject/time. Notice what side of the dialectic survives the translation unchanged: the subject. It is the element common to all the equations.

De Man's own description of what he takes to be Coleridge's actual, but misread and ignored, position on the symbol is ironically applicable here: distinctions among types of figural language are of "secondary importance" to a recognition of "the reference . . . to a transcendental source." "The Rhetoric of Temporality," with its appeal to a "true voice" (207), provides us with the "self" as just such a reference point. This may seem like a harsh judgment, especially since de Man repeatedly refers to "de-mystification," but his actual target is not the self but those relationships (the "illusory identification with the non-self," 207) that prevent it from getting "closer to *the* pattern of factual experience" (emphasis mine; 226). The self that conforms to "the" pattern is an essentially stable and ahistorical self, for the very possibilities of diachronic difference are reduced to variations on the rhetoric of that pattern: "The dialectical play between the two modes [allegory and irony], as well as their common interplay with mystified forms of language . . . make up what is called literary history" (226). Such a history is an epiphanic tale of allegorical and ironic insights into the "fundamental" and "authentic" experience of a subjectivity that manifests itself in such familiar Romantic forms as the "divided self" (226).

I emphasize the disciplinary nature of this ahistorical subject in section III, but de Man's diction already makes the connection evi-

dent. The accession into demystified selfhood is described in the puritanical language he associates with allegory: "renunciation," "loss,"
"error," "pain" (206–7). It is a diction that is often applied to, but is *not*
a part of, a poem that his essay has helped to keep central to the study
of Romanticism:

> A slumber did my spirit seal;
> I had no human fear:
> She seemed a thing that could not feel
> The touch of earthly years.
>
> No motion has she now, no force;
> She neither hears nor sees;
> Rolled round in earth's diurnal course,
> With rocks, and stones, and trees.

To argue that this poem is allegorical as opposed to ironic, de Man
must assert that "the *difference* does not exist within the subject,
which remains unique throughout," but is "spread out" over the poem's temporality. With this maneuver, de Man feels free to fill the
gap between the stanzas with the puritanical diction Wordsworth
avoids. We move, de Man argues, from "error" to loss to a "painful"
knowledge that—and he is assertively coy here—"could be called, if
one so wished, a stance of wisdom" (224–25).

But, as John Rowlett points out, if knowledge is gained by the
second stanza, it is knowledge of a different *kind* than that found in
the first and of "little consolation with respect to what is lost." Replacing the metaphysical diction of the philosophic/psychological poem, is
the diction of Newtonian nature poetry in the form of a " 'scientific'
inscription." This change calls our attention to the fact that the subject is not, as de Man puts it, "unique throughout," for "the 'spirit' [if
'spirit' = 'She'] makes it across the stanzaic gap, but the 'I' (the poetic
speaker) does not—at least not in this poem."[22]

To understand what kind of poem formulates that crossing, we
need to turn not to a rhetorical classification system but to a generic
one. Rowlett posits the stanzaic disjunction as a "*generic* identity
crisis," showing the coupling of the ballad stanzas to be a formal step
in the "uncoupling of the georgic-descriptive couplet"; "A Slumber"
was originally two heptameter couplets (Rowlett, 165, 172). Wordsworth's experiments with the ballad stanza, and his variations on a
William-and-Margaret/Mary/Lucy ballad line popularized by Percy's

Reliques, are presented as parts of an effort to find "the necessary generic features and combinations to enable a sufficient poetic procedure for further composition rather than cyclical repetition of outmoded possibilities." The sonnet, claims Rowlett, with its "radical discontinuity *and* radical continuity" provides a formal model that "recognizes no break or division of the subject in terms of its external structure, but it displays disjunction in the subject in terms of internal structure of perception" (158–59). De Man's allegory (subject as continuous) and irony (subject as discontinuous) are thus not the "two faces of the same fundamental experience of time" (note the organic synecdoche and the ahistoricity of "fundamental"), but are two interrelated features of historically specific genres with culture-specific functions.

If variations on the sonnet and on its constituent parts, the octave and the sestet, play such a central role in Wordsworth's overall poetic production and in the production of the poets who follow him (see chapter 5), then why has criticism from Arnold through de Man focused almost exclusively upon less generative formal models such as "Tintern Abbey" and the Lucy poems? Because Romantic discourse has been normal for so long, and the reality it constructs and valorizes, as we have seen, offers incompleteness and struggle as evidence of an ongoing transcendence. We have gloried in the gaps, such as the one between the stanzas of "A Slumber," and have written off all else, especially those texts whose forms of completeness historicize the incomplete, as overly conservative and (therefore) aesthetically boring. I use the past tense in order to emphasize that we are now at a historical moment when we can begin to recognize and examine those tasteful limitations as artifacts of a different kind of criticism.

Let me conclude this chapter, then, by briefly commenting on a poem written at the very time when Romanticism is conventionally depicted as drawing to a close:

Phantom or Fact
A Dialogue in Verse

AUTHOR

A lovely form there sate beside my bed,
And such a feeding calm its presence shed,
A tender love so pure from earthly leaven,
That I unnethe the fancy might control,
'Twas my own spirit newly come from heaven,

Wooing its gentle way into my soul!
But ah! the change—It had not stirred, and yet—
Alas! that change how fain would I forget!
That shrinking back, like one that had mistook!
That weary, wandering, disavowing look!
'Twas all another, feature, look, and frame,
And still, methought, I knew, it was the same!

FRIEND

This riddling tale, to what does it belong?
Is't history? vision? or an idle song?
Or rather say at once, within what space
Of time this wild disastrous change took place?

AUTHOR

Call it a moment's work (and such it seems)
This tale's a fragment from the life of dreams,
But say that years matured the silent strife,
And 'tis a record from the dream of life.

The similarities between this effort by Coleridge (ca. 1830) and Wordsworth's "A Slumber" are striking. A description of a "spirit" that is free from the "earthly" is abruptly followed by an announcement of change. Here there is no gap between stanzas, but there is a metrical break. The initial six lines constitute a sestet with interlocking rhyme (*aabcbc*), while the exclamations of change are presented in three end-stopped couplets.

This poem, however, extends beyond the paradox of difference: "all another" yet "the same." Just as the sonnet can close the "Slumber" gap by embodying the continuity and the discontinuity of the subject, so the dialogic structure here formally realizes the Coleridgean metaphor of the "friend": someone who is not us and yet is like us. In both cases the generic procedure functions to produce the effect of (psychological) depth by dramatizing the limits of (didactic) description. That effect is multiplied here by breaks between speakers and breaks within speeches; the internal break in the first stanza is reproduced in the following two heroic quatrains, each consisting of two distinct couplets.

Since the Friend's questions are literary critical inquiries into a Romantic text, we should not be surprised to find that his quatrain is informed by the very distinction examined in this chapter. The first couplet inquires into genre, seeking to classify the Author's tale. But the concluding couplet insists ("say at once") upon a turn to the perception of time. The Author's response mirrors his Friend's critical priorities. The naming of kinds is subordinated to the psychological matter of how something "seems" to a subjective consciousness. Since the something is time and the subject is Romantic, the poem concludes with a de Manian rhetoric of temporality: time as a moment produces ironic "fragment[ation]" whereas time "spread out" ("Rhetoric," 225) gives an allegorical "record" of how the subject "matured," that is, experienced loss. This conclusion, in other words, enacts the lyric turn from genre and history that we have been discussing: the evaluation of literature according to "fundamental" kinds or figures of imaginative experience (allegorical and ironic) rather than an analysis of such experiences as formal constructs. Such evaluation characteristically involves the centering of a subject's dialectical relationships in terms of the mind's role in figuring reality. That mind's transcendence is formally effected by the positing of alternatives ("Phantom or Fact"/allegory or irony), negative transitions ("But say . . . "/"Yet the two modes," 226), and syntactical mirroring ("life of dreams"—"dream of life"/"the illusion of a continuity that it knows to be illusionary," 226). Keats has provided us with a particularly condensed and well known version: "Was it a vision, or a waking dream? / Fled is that music:—Do I wake or sleep?" The answer, of course, does not matter, since the point was to naturalize the problem in terms of states of mind.

Coleridge's poem reaches the same dreamlike end, its turn naturalized as part of a conversation among friends. Critical conversation has followed the same course, extending the dialogue along the same Romantic lines. De Man's turn from history and genre has, in fact, been "typical" for so long that it is *now* more interesting in its "causes" than in its "results." In saying this, I am not trying to be unkind, but to exercise kindness as a principle of critical behavior: to acknowledge, in other words, the different historical functions performed by different forms of criticism.

3

Creative Criticism

But, indeed, Ion, if you are correct in saying that by art and knowledge you are able to praise Homer, you do not deal fairly with me, and after all your professions of knowing many glorious things about Homer, and promises that you would exhibit them, you only deceive me, and so far from exhibiting the art of which you are a master, will not, even after my repeated entreaties, explain to me the nature of it. You literally assume as many forms as Proteus, twisting and turning up and down, until at last you slip away from me in the disguise of a general.

PLATO[1]

The present volume . . . attempts rather a survey of cultural topography, those areas of paradox and poetico-philosophical function out of which arise the twin peaks of originality and imagination. It circles these masses, sights them from varying perspectives, ascends or tries to ascend them by likely-looking paths. The range from which they rise is that of *a priori* human domain, and it is one that has been located and trodden by many others, coming from different directions, laden in different ways, faced with different contours of ascent. All report the same; no two record exactly the same forms.

THOMAS MCFARLAND[2]

Slipping up and away in the disguise of a mountain climber can be presented as a worthwhile effort only if mountains are classified as forms worth climbing. Then, as with the disguise of the general, the professional "reader" of literature can command respect by assuming that form. A reclassification of mountains, from forbidding scars to sources of sublimity, did occur in eighteenth-century England. As part of a conceptual change that redefined nature and the natural, that shift coincided with the formation of McFarland's twin peaks. He

37

portrays the altered status of originality and imagination as an inevitable "*rise* to prominence" (emphasis mine) governed by what appears to be a natural law of the conservation of "ideas": "as 'soul' became weaker, they became stronger." Because they rise from an "*a priori* human domain," their single, ahistorical purpose is to convey a "human intensity" (xi, xii). All the "areas of paradox and poetico-philosophical function" (xiii) that McFarland explores are bound within that domain and yield records confirming that intensity.

Erased by the seamless continuity and unity that such a history demands and the metaphor implies, are *formal* differences in function entailed by new sets of disciplinary and generic interrelations. "Poetico-philosophical" is not a label that should justify ignoring those differences, but one that should draw our attention to the reclassification of information and thus the redrawing of disciplinary borders. I speak of borders, of course, not to deny the interrelation of disciplines but to assert its inevitability. Understood in nonessentialistic terms, such markers help to establish the relative importance of the historically variable mixtures that define a culture's range of knowledge. In this case, as originality and imagination appear with greater frequency as features of *literary forms,* the new mix that constitutes literature appropriates certain functions from philosophy and religion.

Within this new set of interrelations, those two features become particularly integral to discussions and examples of the lyric, such that specific formal effects of procedures identified as lyric[3] are labeled and valorized as "original" and "imaginative." That process furthers, and is furthered by, the making of a categorical distinction between texts that have those qualities and texts that do not—the distinction between the creative and the critical that informs the modern literary institution and the concept of the human that it has been professing as "*a priori.*" To psychologize the concept and the distinction as matters of "intensity" is to make the generic and historical links between particular behaviors or emotions and particular activities function as natural description: for example, the passionate expressiveness of the creative writer as opposed to the cool analytics of the critic; the spontaneous creativity of the child versus the chastened wisdom of the man. These are the tales that, since the "rise" of the twin peaks, have configured the possibilities of selfhood in its professional as well as personal, psychological as well as physiological, moral as well as genetic, manifestations.

This chapter, then, is about the disguises worn by the Romantic writers, creative *and* critical, who tell those tales. It relates the protean forms they assume to the forms they "record." To understand the historicity of what they record, I look at how they record it. The point is not to dismiss the value of these texts, but to identify the kinds of values *they* formally insist upon. My literary history, structured around comparisons between late eighteenth- and early nineteenth-century texts and late twentieth-century ones, draws attention to diachronic continuity and discontinuity. In addressing McFarland's creative philosophizing, Geoffrey Hartman's creative criticism, and Jerome McGann's creative politics, I highlight the hierarchizing function, both literary and social, of the Romantic creative/critical distinction.

For McFarland, the law of conservation of ideas presides over a developmental tale he calls "the historical progress of thought." Thus, in response to questions regarding the "enormous acceleration . . . of the sense of imagination's importance," he can

> *boldly* present an answer in its largest outline: imagination became so important because soul had been so important and because soul could no longer carry its burden of significance. That significance was an assurance that there was meaning in life. (emphasis mine; 151)

Since history conceived as "progress" necessarily plots its own telling as evidence of its ongoing validity, we should not be surprised to find the book concluding with a reassurance. After citing a physicist's anxiety about a "pointless" universe, McFarland ends by proclaiming, "It is against this encompassing darkness that originality and imagination hold aloft their flickering torches" (200).

This is criticism with a mission, just as with McFarland's previous book on Romanticism, in which he denominates the types of "great" art that can alleviate the "burden of incompleteness, fragmentation, and ruin."[4] Consolation through the identification and preservation of the best cultural artifacts is, of course, not an unfamiliar critical activity, and I do not question his personal zeal, individual motives, or substantial achievement. But an inquiry into how the authority of such a cultural critic is formally constituted can help us to identify the power, as well as gauge the historicity, of Romantic discourse.

Within that discourse, as I argue in detail in chapter 5, the model for all histories of progress is the tale of individual development. Because the latter is understood to be biologically inevitable, all examples of the former are taken to be naturally appropriate. Thus

McFarland's propensity for quoting from his own earlier work is not a matter of egotism, but a feature by which the "natural" development of his own thinking formally rationalizes the writing up of his data as "the historical progress of thought." The macrohistory of *Originality & Imagination,* in other words, is already generically inscribed by the microhistory of individual change alluded to in its preface and carefully detailed in its second chapter:

> My statements of 1969 and 1974 thus constitute a parataxis whose structure will serve to introduce the larger body of cultural concerns I am addressing at this juncture. On the one hand, the intensified statement of 1974 obviously arose from the statement of 1969 and in a certain sense can be fully accounted for simply as a broadening of a current of thought—as a widening of the river of my mind. On the other hand, the intervening five years had seen the beginning of the revolution I noted above. In particular, two books had appeared that were already changing the critical scene and that generated lateral currents that flowed into my own, or perhaps, to improve the metaphor, lateral winds that caused my own coals to glow more brightly. (34)

The metaphors serve a crucial, explanatory function here, since they organically ground his understanding of change in a subject/object model of personal development we know quite well from a previous five-year retrospective: "Tintern Abbey." The self psychologized as mind naturally widens under the influence of external objects.

No de Manian confession of a turn from history occasioned by personal need is necessary here, for this history is itself derived formally from a personal tale. McFarland's lyric turns toward absolutes are thus features *of* his history; they occur not only when that narrative intersects with the personal, but also when it engages the external objects that excite it. The number of such objects confirms McFarland's reputation as a scholar of "immense erudition,"[5] and the manner of engaging them indicates the kind of knowledge such erudition produces. As in Coleridge's *Biographia Literaria,*[6] references to other texts supplement and pace the narrative of personal development. Catalogued as a "Key to Brief Titles Cited," placed between the preface and the first chapter, and printed in full-size type, the references also function as extratextual material (see my chapter 5) intended to alter the reader's behavior by constituting the writer's authority in nondidactic fashion: truths are not insisted upon, but we are put in the company of truth-tellers.

When it comes time to tell and the brief titles are placed within long footnotes, the assembled voices cause McFarland's to resonate with what appears to be the wisdom of ages. But if we examine how the chorus is assembled, we can identify the function of that kind of footnote and gauge the historicity of its wisdom. In a section on Harold Bloom, for example, McFarland criticizes

> Bloom's devaluation of individual experience as the basis of poetry. His half-truth is that poems take shape as resonances from earlier poems, and that no one would become a poet were there not prior poets to serve as models. But the other half of the truth, which his system cannot accommodate, is that it is an individual's unique experience that makes him feel like a poet in the first place, and that it is his distillation of that experience that provides him the essence of his poetry. The entire course of Keats's development, poetic, intellectual, emotional, documents this truth, and indeed demonstrates that the uniqueness of individual awareness must always occur and be distilled before there can supervene the phenomena of intra-poetic relationships.[53] (57)

Footnote 53, printed in small type, fills up half a page with references to Benjamin Haydon, Leibniz, and Proclus. The quotations are intended, of course, to support McFarland's truth at Bloom's expense, and at first glance they appear to do so quite effectively. After all, if essentially the same argument has been made by painters and philosophers as well as critics for hundreds, even thousands, of years, then it must be truthful.

But the key adjective ("same") and imperative ("must") of that assumption are generically bound. They make sense only when functioning within a narrative that takes all differences in kind and in time as evidence of a transcendent sameness. For McFarland those differences do not raise questions of conceptual change; they attest to the harmonious variety of the "historical progress of thought." A generic history, however, can address change because it looks to identify the different functions that apparently similar features play within different forms and different hierarchies of forms. It attempts to account for the verifiable fact that information about an "essential" poetic self, for example, appears in a personal diary at one moment in history and in a philosophical tract at another. Amassing evidence about such a self without such an accounting is tantamount to a turn from the study of diachronic difference. The irony of this kind of footnote within this kind of literary history, in other words, is that, rather than substantiating historical understanding, it constitutes a lyric turn from it.

The purpose of the following analysis of McFarland's footnote, then, is not to denigrate it but to classify it as characteristic of a kind. Within that kind there is no fix; no one could do it better without undermining the assumptions of McFarland's enterprise. He begins the footnote by setting up the quote from Haydon with an initial assertion: "It was not prior poems, but intensity of experience, that generated the poetic genius of Keats." The distinctions assumed here are both temporal and categorical. Looking to identify what causes "genius," McFarland claims that immediate "experience" deserves temporal precedence as a first cause over the effect of prior poems. But that argument implies a categorical distinction that takes "experience" to be in some way essentially different than the reading of, or some other form of exposure to, poems. Rather than turning to Keats to collapse the distinction, as the poet does by combining natural objects with "passages from Shakespeare" in a list of "real" things (*Letters,* 73), McFarland gives us Haydon's description of Keats's relationship only to the former: " 'Keats was in his glory in the fields!', testifies Haydon. 'The humming of the bee, the sight of a flower, the glitter of the sun, seemed to make his nature tremble! his eyes glistened! his cheek flushed! his mouth positively quivered & clentched!' "

This statement says nothing at all about the priority, temporal or categorical, of "experience" over "prior poems." Are we to assume that Keats had not read poetry before entering the fields, and that such contact, or even more indirect means of acculturation, did not play a role in the "glory"? Is this testimony to Keats's "individual" and "unique" genius, or to the historical fact that at this historical moment a new set of behaviors toward natural objects, such as "splendour in the grass" and mountain climbing, were for the first time becoming *normal* for the entire culture? Does the "intensity" of such behaviors generate the poetical, or does a particular historical concept of the poetical authorize and instigate being intense? McFarland appears to assume, since the description places Keats out in nature, that what it describes is ahistorically "natural." Is it not important to ask why Keats was out in the fields in the first place? And why his reactions were thought worthy of being recorded? And why they were recorded in the personal diary of another artist as evidence of artistic temperament? And why such personal diaries have been published and construed to be sources for the production of scholarly knowledge?

Since Bloom would never deny that Keats felt with intensity, this first quote from Haydon poses no threat at all to his argument. But this type of footnote always depends for its force on re-creating in miniature the "historical progress of thought" that it is supposed to substantiate. Thus the footnote continues with a movement backward in time and over in genre:

> The unity and intensity of experience that precede and give meaning to the discursive techniques of poetry are signalized by Leibniz, who of all philosophers most unequivocally asserts the fullness and priority of individual knowledge. Even before Locke's essay appeared, Leibniz urged almost mystically that "it is a bad habit we have of thinking as if our souls received certain forms as messengers and as if it had doors and windows. We have all these forms in our own minds, and even from all time, because the mind always expresses all its future thoughts and already thinks confusedly of everything of which it will ever think distinctly. Nothing can be taught us the idea of which is not already in our minds, as the matter out of which this thought is formed. This Plato has excellently recognized when he puts forward his doctrine of reminiscence. . . . Aristotle preferred to compare our souls to tablets that are still blank but upon which there is a place for writing and maintained that there is nothing in our understanding that does not come from the senses. This conforms more with popular notions, as Aristotle usually does, while Plato goes deeper."

Because McFarland is trying to counter Bloom's argument that "no one would become a poet were there not prior poets to serve as models," we would expect a quote supporting his belief in the "uniqueness" of the "individual." But McFarland's footnote formally leads him back into a century in which those concepts do not interrelate as they have for us since Keats's time. For the past 150 years, the concept of individuality has been valorized by assertions of uniqueness within discussions of the nature of the "mind of Man" that have been *literary* discussions. In looking for discussions of the mind prior to the late eighteenth century, McFarland finds himself out of the literary and in the philosophical, where he provides us with a text that, far from asserting the "fullness and priority of *individual* knowledge" (emphasis mine), emphasizes instead what all men have in common through "all time": "forms" and "idea(s)" that precede experience (not, as McFarland would have it, experience that precedes discourse). Since philosophical texts of Leibniz's time employ assertions about the mind to naturalize uniformity rather than particularity, Leibniz's argument provides no means for accounting for and valorizing "uniqueness of individual awareness." Bloom, I am sure, would be most willing to provide a modern, literary supplement to that older philosophical argument—one that would make the latter more compatible with his, and McFarland's, emphasis on select, strong poets—whatever the source of that strength.[7]

The latter part of the quotation, dealing with Aristotle and Plato, functions to extend the footnote backward one more, final time, thereby completing a minihistory that links the ancients and the moderns. By addressing the former first through Leibniz, the sense of historical continuity is heightened: if Leibniz can adopt their wisdom and we can adopt his, then, according to the footnote's logic, the Ideas at issue must transcend any conceptual differences between the classical and the contemporary. Diachronic change is decentered even further by the focus on what is meant to be understood as an ongoing synchronic opposition—one that is posed here in spatial and social terms as Plato's, and supposedly McFarland's, "deeper" truth versus Aristotle's "popular notions." But Plato's truth hierarchizes forms of knowledge (innate over sensory); it does not, and it conceptually and generically cannot, address the Romantic experiential interaction between an individual's innate psychological faculties on the one hand, and natural objects on the other, that is the informing concern of McFarland's spousal criticism: "though it may have been the reading of earlier poems that made Wordsworth write verses," asserts McFarland immediately after footnote 53, "it was his personal experience of the orange sky of evening that made him a great poet" (58).

Noting this gap between the text's argument and the one made by the footnote highlights the manner in which the footnote's internal, generic logic produces the final turn to *A Commentary on the First Book of Euclid's Elements*:

> Compare Proclus: "According to the tradition, the Pythagoreans recognized that everything we call learning is remembering, not something placed in the mind from without, like the images of sense pictured in the imagination, nor transitory, like the judgments of opinion. Though awakened by sense-perception, learning has its source within us, in our understanding's attending to itself. They realized too that, although evidences of such memories can be cited from many areas, it is especially from mathematics that they come, as Plato also remarks."

Leibniz drops Plato's name and Proclus picks it up. If we take seriously the only directive we are given—"compare"—we realize the importance of this nominal connection. It must bear the weight of the comparison, since Proclus's emphasis on the uniform apprehension of innate forms of knowledge has much more in common with Plato than it does with the anti-Bloom argument for "the uniqueness of individual awareness" and the importance of "personal, monadic experience" (58). In fact, what Proclus's act of commenting on Euclid's laws formally enacts as important is not differences among individuals, either in their faculties or in their experience, but the disciplinary interrelations among kinds of order, particularly the mathematical and the metaphysical.

Since the early nineteenth century, the *literary* order of lyrical development has dominated the disciplinary interrelations of our educational institutions, producing scholarship that documents developmentally conceived truths by assembling facts and sources into developmental narratives. The lyric turn taken by McFarland's footnoting is an example of how that maneuver generates an apparently weighty but profoundly circular argument. We begin with a poet such as Keats, who, as we saw in chapter 2, writes up himself and his work in terms of a biological development thematized as a development in forms. We then "interpret" him and his works by using those same procedures to reproduce the identical kind of order that his own texts first imposed on themselves. Then we document the truth of our "findings" by transforming all of the past into a developmental prelude to our present.

What remains unfound can best be seen by briefly examining McFarland's reading of Coleridge on imagination. He begins by wittily observing that

> a favorite question on viva voce examinations was a request to distinguish Coleridge's conceptions of primary imagination, secondary imagination, and fancy; and the ritual answer, which invariably satisfied the examiners in full, was simply to repeat the puzzling words. (90–91)

We should, of course, be able to do something more with those definitions than repeat them, and McFarland himself provides a very useful analysis. But we must not gloss over the repetition with a knowing smile, lest we miss the irony of its historical function: it is in that repetition and not in any explication, no matter how skillful, that the power of those definitions lies. Fascination with the nature of the distinctions naturalizes the terms being distinguished. In worrying about degrees we authorize the kind, just as to argue that a drug does or does not have an effect upon *the* imagination, as I show in chapter 9, is to authenticate the concept of imagination. McFarland's examiners were satisfied in full by repetition not only because they themselves might not have been able to do any better, but because repetition was the right answer to their inquiry. Like all Romantic inquiries, its goal is sympathetic identification. As the examiners repeat Coleridge and the student repeats the examiners, the entire oath-taking process testifies to the ongoing power of the rhetoric of imagination to delimit the conceptual range of literary studies and to write the politics of the profession.

The feature of the oath that helps to clarify those politics is the casting of the hierarchical division between primary and secondary in terms of a kind/degree distinction. Instead of letting Coleridge's text determine our critical activities, so that we inevitably join him in elaborating the definitions authorized by that feature, a new literary history inquires into the function of that feature. In doing so, we can identify interrelations among apparently disparate texts that provide a basis for making statements about diachronic similarity and difference. Rather than asking, "What are the differences between the primary and the secondary imaginations?" we can ask, "What do we make of the fact that key concepts in texts of this historical moment are characteristically defined using divisions justified by the collapsing of kind into degree?" As I show in the next section of this chapter, statements ranging from Blake's on the Incarnation to Wordsworth's on the nature of the poet share this procedure. In each case it functions to naturalize the transformation of hierarchy from a structure based on inherited, unchanging distinctions to one that posits an initial equality subject to psychological and developmental difference. The latter, of course, is the democracy of the modern subject—an order in which inequities are rationalized as the inevitable product of the realization of the individual.

Poets and men, to use Wordsworth's example, are of the same kind, but they differ in the degree of their innate skills ("endued with more lively sensibility") and their acquired skills ("greater knowledge of human nature") (*Prose,* I, 138). Defined in the same manner, imagination becomes both the ever-present link we all share (primary), *and* a means of establishing natural hierarchy (secondary). Texts understood as the products of this imagination can be similarly

classed together and tastefully subdivided under the rubric of Literature. Such imaginative works are supposed to have universal appeal,
but the dissemination of them, as products of different degrees of
imagination that are to be consumed by similarly ranked readers, has
been understood to require professional mediation. A kind-and-
degree notion of imagination, in other words, does more than point
symbolically, as McFarland offers, toward "reality" and "deity" (141–
42, 149); it functions as a rationale for the making of a literary institution manned by unique, creative geniuses and specially trained critics.
As teachers, to extend the metaphor just a bit, the latter dispense to
developing students the extra degrees necessary to valorize the
former.

For the dispensing to be anything other than haphazard, what is dispensed must be systematically ordered. Thus the institutionalization
that arose from kind/degree categorizations helps to explain the increasing interest in literary theory.[8] The incorporation of theoretical
features within the generic hierarchy has, in turn, unsettled "normal"
lyric interrelations, producing a sense of collapsing boundaries. That is
a major reason why the structuralist and poststructuralist work of the
late 1970s and early 1980s occasioned such strong reactions both inside
and outside academia, even eliciting responses in the pages of the *New
York Times,* the *Washington Post,* and *Newsweek.* The form that has
proved most threatening is that of the creative critic: the writer, to
those who find the label oxymoronic, whose efforts are a violation of
kind and who therefore deserves an unkind reception. My purpose
here is to historicize those efforts and that reception by engaging them
as generic matters informed by our understanding of Romantic discourse. Distinguishing variation within, from innovation upon, that
discourse is an essential step in assessing the present process of literary
change.

Because the creative/critical distinction is so central to the literary institution and to the culture in which that institution is centered,
the literary skirmish over who gets to be creative is, in fact, but one
manifestation of a larger cultural anxiety over the status of this theologically and politically charged concept. Public television, for example, sent Bill Moyers to track it down and capture it on film. Not only
our concern over creativity's continued presence but our democratic
aspirations have been soothed by such books as D. N. Perkins's *The
Mind's Best Work: A New Psychology of Creative Thinking,* which
assures us, according to Harvard University Press, that "Nabokov

wrote *Lolita* the same way you make macaroni."[9] Geoffrey Hartman, in his book-length study of creative criticism, confesses to using a "personal and macaronic procedure" which involves treating critical works as primary texts in order to demonstrate that "all criticism entails a rethinking, which is itself creative, of what others hold to be creative."[10] His purpose, in both *Criticism in the Wilderness* and in an article on the same subject in the *New York Times,* was to assert criticism's right "not to be fobbed off as a secondary activity, as a handmaiden to more 'creative' modes of thinking like poems or novels."[11] What does Hartman hold to be creative? In the *Times* article we find the following: "It is *creative,* that is, within literature rather than outside of it and merely looking in. . . . an inventive feat, a 'creative' rather than 'definitive' answer" (*NYT,* 24). Hartman refuses to assign a static definition to the term, arguing that "the relation between creative and critical must always be reenvisioned" (*CIW,* 19). His assumption about creativity will thus be most visible, albeit indirectly, in his descriptions of its *effects* on criticism. Three major relationships appear to be at issue:

1. Criticism and the reader: creative criticism "demands of the reader a rigor like that which the writer expended on his work" (*NYT,* 25).
2. Criticism and the work of art: "a reversal must be possible whereby this 'secondary' piece of writing turns out to be 'primary'" (*CIW,* 201).
3. Criticism and form: "does the essay . . . and the literary essay in particular, have a form of its own . . .?" Can it be an "intellectual poem?" (*CIW,* 191, 195–96).

Taken as effects, these relationships provide perspectives that are, in order, psychological (the creative is "demanding"), political (creativity is a question of hierarchy), and formal (creativity is poetic) on what Hartman considers "creative." But the resulting viewpoint, I would argue, is not personal but cultural. These are *assumptions* that have become dear to all of us over a period of time; to understand them, we need to historicize them by treating creativity as a culture-specific behavior (literary and nonliterary) that is comprehensible in terms of a characteristic hierarchy of interrelated forms. Hartman repeatedly points us in the right temporal direction in *Criticism in the Wilderness* by noting "the falsification, even repression, of *Romantic* origins in Arnoldian and much New Critical thought" (emphasis

mine). That repression has been exposed, he argues, by the creative
critics he collectively dubs the "Revisionist Movement": "The term
revisionist, in fact, is perhaps most appropriately applied to the rethinking of literary history now going on, which questions a periodization that has given 'modernity' a polemical and prestigious life separated from Romantic origins." This "better understanding and higher
evaluation of Romantic writing" has shown them to be "clairvoyant
rather than blind precursors of later movements that tended to dis-
own them while simplifying the radical character of their art" (*CIW,*
9, 44–47).

Jonathan Culler has used this kind of progressive ("better" and
"higher") history to transform a very unwilling M. H. Abrams into a
blind rather than clairvoyant precursor of the very Revisionists he has
so vehemently opposed during the past decade. Abrams, says Culler,
succeeded in *The Mirror and the Lamp* in demonstrating "that a
whole series of critical concepts, including those that one had thought
of as antiromantic, had in fact been formulated by Coleridge and
other Romantic critics." He did so, however, only by adopting a
methodology (examining "systems of metaphor") that implicates him
in "a tradition of writing that explores the peculiar logic of theoretical
discourse and whose recent exponents include, for example, Jacques
Derrida."[12] Thus Abrams the humanist described an Organic Romanticism that accounts for criticism through the New Critics. As an
unwitting deconstructionist, however, he "pointed the way" toward a
very different set of Romantic "roots" for what was supposed to be a
very different kind of criticism. Culler cites Frances Ferguson for
pursuing Abrams's suggestion that Wordsworthians pay adequate attention to the "Essay upon Epitaphs." He considers her *Wordsworth:
Language as Counter Spirit* to have been the first step toward identifying "what in Romantic theory and practice lies beyond the mirror
stage" (162–63).

The problem in construing this as a progress ("beyond"), as I
pointed out in the introduction, is that Romantic discourse has always
synchronically embraced the organic *and* the ironic. Both lead us
toward the *same* conception of creativity: the organic does so by
highlighting the intensity of our desire for the presence of the Creative; the latter's celebration of the play of language helps us discern
the formal strategies that produce the effect of creativity. Desirable
effects—what the creative text *demands* of the reader—are Hartman's concern, when he expands on his psychology of creativity by
taking a de Manian turn toward an absolute theory of reading:

> Criticism differs from fiction by making the experience of reading ex-
> plicit: by intruding and maintaining the persona of editor, reviewer,
> reader, foreign reporter, and so forth. Our struggle to identify—or not
> to—with imaginative experience, usually in the form of a story, is what
> is worked through. Both paradigmatically and personally the critic
> shows how a reader's instincts, sympathies, defenses are now solicited
> and now compelled. The psychological drama of reading centers on
> that aroused merging: a possible loss of boundaries, a fear of absorp-
> tion, the stimulation of a sympathetic faculty that may take over and
> produce self-alienation. (*CIW*, 50)

The critic, Hartman maintains, makes us self-conscious about what
happens when we read. The plot of reading is then presented as a
timeless tale, but its vocabulary betrays its historicity: the reader's
identification with the *imaginative* depends upon a *sympathetic* faculty.

Hartman is following Wordsworth in premising his author-reader
relationship upon a reciprocity between the author's creative imagination and the "co-operating *power* in the mind of the reader."[13] The
creative text thus demands, to borrow Wordsworth's phrase, that the
reader be "prompt / In sympathy" (1805 *Prelude*, I.645–46). James
Beattie's 1778 dictum that "the philosophy of sympathy ought always
to form *a part* of the science of Criticism"[14] (emphasis mine) clarifies
the generic interrelations at issue. The literary appropriation of philosophical discussions of the "mind" psychologized the acts of reading
and writing, thereby redirecting authorial strategy toward consideration of individual emotional response. Thus Coleridge and Wordsworth's initial conversations during the very first year of their friendship (1797) turned upon, in Coleridge's words, "the power of exciting
the sympathy of the reader."[15] To address the function of that turn, I
will briefly analyze two texts composed within five years of each
other: Blake's *THERE is NO Natural Religion* (a and b) (1788) and
Godwin's *Caleb Williams* (1793).

Blake casts the theological and epistemological into densely
metaphorical aphorisms which he arranges in progressive patterns of
opposites, engraves, and touches up with watercolors.[16] The result
is a "literary" text[17] that translates one form of worth into another
and thus is largely cast in a language of quantity, value, and possession: the language of economics. The problem with Lockean economics, according to Blake, is that it is a closed system: "From a
perception of only 3 senses or 3 elements none could deduce a

fourth or fifth." Given the limited kinds of perceptions and therefore desires possible (solely "organic"), quantity and value are necessarily in inverse proportion[18]: "The same dull round even of a uni-
ver[s]e would soon become a mill with complicated wheels." Blake's
solution is to provide external, that is to say non-Lockean, stimulation. The innate "Poetic or Prophetic character" is an imaginative
power that "creates" excess value by allowing man to perceive and
desire "More!" But if demand were to outstrip supply, the system
would collapse into "despair." The "Infinite" is therefore made available to man, who is transformed by a perfect purchase: "The desire
of man being infinite the possession is infinite & himself Infinite."
Blakean economics thus achieves an eternal equilibrium expressed
in the tract's conclusion as the reworking of the central Christian
mystery into an image of sympathetic identification: "He who sees
the Infinite in all things sees God. He who sees the ratio only sees
himself only. Therefore God becomes as we are, that we may be as
he is." It is this absolute exchange that guarantees the *value* of
Imagination; unsecured by sympathy, the Poetic character's creative
activity is merely inflationary. The Romantic nature of this system of
valuation is evident in the way in which inherited hierarchy is undermined: the distinction of kind between God and man collapses into
a distinction of degree as the traditional doctrine of incarnation
becomes proof of Blake's most unorthodox assertions of human
divinity.

In *Caleb Williams* this transformation of hierarchy of kind into
hierarchy of degree is thematized as a nightmare of sympathy gone
awry. Whereas Blakean sympathy has the force of faith, Caleb is
compelled to collapse the distinction of kind between himself and the
aristocrat Falkland by sympathy in a less respectable guise:

> The spring of action which, perhaps more than any other, charac-
> terised the whole train of my life, was curiosity. . . . this produced in
> me an invincible attachment to books of narrative and romance. I
> panted for the unravelling of an adventure, with an anxiety, perhaps
> almost equal to that of the man whose future happiness or misery
> depended on its issue. I read, I devoured compositions of this sort.
> They took possession of my soul; and the effects they produced, were
> frequently discernible in my external appearance and my health. My
> curiosity however was not entirely ignoble: village anecdotes and scan-
> dal had no charms for me: my imagination must be excited; and, when
> that was not done, my curiosity was dormant.[19]

Value again requires the pairing of imagination and sympathy. Both are aroused by Falkland, for he is presented as a character right out of a book "of narrative and romance": "Among the favourite authors of his early years were the heroic poets of Italy. From them he imbibed the love of chivalry and romance. . . . The opinions he entertained upon those topics were illustrated in his conduct, which was assiduously conformed to the model of heroism that his fancy suggested" (10).

In keeping with the Romantic thematizing of reading, both of the text's central characters construct themselves out of characterizations from other texts of a specific kind. Their fate is tied to the fate of that kind—romance—in the new set of literary interrelations being written at the turn into the nineteenth century. Individual, private response is thus cast as an aesthetic, literary matter of proper writer/reader relations: in his sympathetic admiration of Falkland, Caleb serves by the author's design as a reader surrogate. The novel cannot work, argues Godwin in his 1832 Preface, unless "every reader should feel prompted," like Caleb, "almost to worship him for his high qualities" (337). Falkland proves, however, to be a vengeful god, adverse to any form of incarnation that threatens his social status. As persecutor, he transforms his victim into an outcast increasingly incapable of sympathetic identification with any member of society. Caleb's failure is clarified as a "literary" failure as language becomes his last repository of value and hope for relationship: "Why have we the power of speech, but to communicate our thoughts? I will never believe that a man conscious of innocence, cannot make other men perceive that he has that thought" (171). Sincerity has no positive communicative value in a society without proper sympathy, or to an audience that cannot sympathize in the proper manner.

In Godwin's original ending for the novel, the inadequacy of language breaks Caleb. He finally confronts Falkland in court and speaks his piece, only to be told by the magistrate, "Be silent!" (330). His final connection to reality severed, Caleb goes mad. But, as Frances Ferguson has observed of Wordsworth's linguistic conceptions, language is presented within Romantic discourse as tending to be too little *and* too much.[20] In the novel's published conclusion, words do work, but the results are equally devastating. Falkland hears his accuser, repents, and dies; sympathy undermines the hierarchy on which he based his identity. Similarly, Caleb's sympathetic curiosity rebounds in the form of guilt, robbing him of himself: "I began these memoirs with the idea of vindicating my character. I have now no character that I wish to vindicate" (326). Blakean incarnation, in what Godwin calls the "corrupt wilderness" of "things as they are," produces not value but absence.

With the voiding of Romantic characters, Godwin's novel thematizes its own formal difficulties. The problems in a mix that juxtaposes characterization drawn from traditional romance with a plot configured by didactic description surface most obviously in the narrative struggle to produce a conclusive wholeness out of what Godwin himself called "many flat and insipid parts" (341). In terms of the eventual normative "solution"—the "creative" ordering of parts within Romantic developmental wholes that I cover in section II—this text is a transitional experiment. It demonstrates that both the supposedly personal "macaronic" ordering of parts highlighted by Hartman and the Harvard University Press, as well as Hartman's psychologized understanding of creativity as a matter of interpersonal sympathy, are *constructs*— ones that illustrate the historical connection between formal innovation and newly "normal" human behavior.

That connection clarifies the reason why a generic "experiment" in exciting the reader's sympathy, such as Wordsworth's *Lyrical Ballads,* receives prefatory material that is distinctly disciplinary. The material insists, for example, that readers revise their "pre-established codes of decision" to be receptive to "common language," so that there is a language in common, as well as be in a "healthful state of association," that is, not corrupted by things as they are (*Prose*, I, 116, 122–26). The "philosophy of sympathy" can then function as it does within Blake's heavily normative tractates, to enhance the value of the creative imagination *and* those who possess it. It is, in other words, essential to the late eighteenth-century cultural centering of art and the artist for which Wordsworth's Preface is one of the key documents. The politics of the Preface are thus not suprisingly those that we saw in Blake: the collapsing of distinctions of kind into distinctions of degree. Eliminating kinds makes sympathetic identification possible; positing degrees makes it desirable. Poets can speak to men, for example, because they are of the same kind. The men *want* to listen because the poet is more sensitive.

This is the same politics of creativity seen in Hartman. The Revisionary critic does not challenge hierarchy by making the secondary text primary, but by eliminating kind through intertextuality.[21] He then ranks all texts by degree according to the other criteria of creativity. In addition to the demand for sympathy, the creative is characterized, says Hartman, by poetic form. Not only does he argue that the essay should aspire to be an "intellectual poem," but he also claims that it is a "secret relative of the Romantic 'fragment'" (*CIW*, 193–94). By associating creativity with a particular type of a particular form, he illustrates how behavioral norms are always formal propositions. In this case the form of creativity is the Romantic poetic fragment. Increasing the creativity of a particular form therefore inevitably raises the issue of the manner in which forms interrelate: how can an essay, for example, become more like a poem? Hartman is notably and significantly vague on this important problem. In fact, his familial metaphor ("secret relative") and favorite participle ("blurring") imply not only that forms can be but *naturally* are pure and unmixed. What, then, is pure lyric? Or for that matter, pure creativity?

The alternative to essentialistic definitions that deny change, as I argued in the introduction, is to posit interrelation not as "transgression" or "promiscuity" but as "characteristic." What features in late eighteenth- and early nineteenth-century interrelations can we call lyrical? To say they are those features that are "creative" is only to emphasize, as I have been doing, the historicity of all forms of behavior. We need, then, to turn to contemporary usage and classification, such as Wordsworth's in the 1815 Preface: "The Lyrical,—containing the Hymn, the Ode, the Elegy, the Song, and the Ballad; in all which, for the production of their *full* effect, an accompaniment of music is indispensable" (*Prose*, III, 27). At first glance, this may appear at best an irrelevant, at worst an unrealistic, etymological effort: the lyric requires the lyre. But if we pursue the issue further into the Preface, we find the following disclaimer:

> Some of these pieces are essentially lyrical; and, therefore, cannot have their due force without a supposed musical accompaniment; but, in much the greatest part, as a substitute for the classic lyre or romantic harp, I require nothing more than an animated or impassioned recitation, adapted to the subject. Poems, however humble in their kind, if they be good in that kind, cannot read themselves; the law of long syllable and short must not be so inflexible,—the letter of metre must not be so impassive to the spirit of versification,—as to deprive the Reader of all voluntary power to modulate, in subordination to the sense, the music of the poem;—in the same manner as his mind is left at liberty, and even summoned, to act upon its thoughts and images. (*Prose*, III, 29)

Wordsworth raises the traditional issue of musical accompaniment not to revive an outmoded practice but, characteristically, to identify what he found to be the essentially poetic, that is the lyrical, in terms of reader response. The text's quality is paradoxically depicted in terms of inadequacy: it cannot read itself. That weakness is a strength when conceived of as an invitation to the reader to act. In musical terms, the text is a score that invites performance. Strength in the form of inflexibility, however, deprives the reader of "power" and "liberty."

Wordsworth's definition of lyric thus clarifies its role as the form of Romantic creativity; it undermines the inherited distinction of kind between poet and reader by inducing the sympathetic participation of the latter in the supposedly liberating act of "making" the poem. Romantic lyrical features, then, can be understood as those features intended to produce in specific interrelations, through strategies of inadequacy *or* excess, an effect of fragmentation experienced by the disciplined reader as a call for interpretative activity. These include: flexible blank verse, measured stanzas, economy of language, multiplicity of metaphor, seriality, deliberate fragmentation, negative transitions, apostrophes, reader surrogates, and framed narration. Their cumulative effect is ultimately self-referential because, in their appeal to the reader, they call attention to the discourse they constitute. Romantic poetry, it has often been noted, is poetry about poetry.

Creative criticism is criticism about criticism because criticism is a form and, in efforts such as Hartman's, it is being lyricized. Like the novel in the nineteenth and twentieth centuries, as I show in chapter 6, criticism is presently aspiring to rise in the generic hierarchy through the incorporation of lyric features. That many current critical debates seem to echo the problematics of Romanticism should therefore not surprise us. Wordsworth's preoccupations in the Preface to *Lyrical Ballads,* the efficacy of language and the workings of reader response, still loom large today. Instead of a Lake School led by the poet of the egotistical sublime, we have had a Yale School comprising critics frequently charged with the same crime. The linguistic self-consciousness which Culler describes as the central feature of that group's Revisionary Romanticism has not led us from what he calls the "mirror stage." The importance of irony for Revisionists, for example, has been but a reflection of New Critical ambiguity and the Romantic celebration of obscurity for the sake of sympathy: "That which can be made Explicit to the Idiot," says Blake, "is not worth my care" (*Blake,* 676).

What sinks from view in this multiple mirroring is an understanding of the historicity of forms. *Criticism in the Wilderness,* for example, begins in a manner with which we should now be quite familiar: a confession. Rather than producing a "systematic defense" of literary studies or a traditional "argument," Hartman says he will offer a personal book of "experiences" with the aim of justifying creative criticism. It is the turn that tells us how. The un-kind lure of creative criticism for Hartman is quintessentially Romantic: the "blurring of boundaries" signifies for him the transcendence of Form. Assuming Wordsworth's retrospective posture in "Tintern Abbey," he says that he will tell us what art "has meant to me." In the next part of the book, again like Wordsworth, he offers personal "experiences" of critics in the form of a developmental history. A turn to the reader ("The Work of Reading"), paralleling Wordsworth's turn to Dorothy in "Tintern," opens the concluding section, which finishes with a comparison of "Past and Present" that serves as an occasion for speculating, as it does for Wordsworth, on the future. The "polemical pieces" are banished, also in Wordsworthian fashion, to an extratextual "coda."[22] The resemblance to "Tintern Abbey," I hope I have shown, is no accident. To make criticism "creative" according to a lyrical standard of creativity is to perpetuate Romantic procedures. Not that a return to the Wye is unenjoyable; Hartman's voice resounds with a depth of pleasing echoes. But the creative critic has remained fixed on that spot, and we are now in a historical position to recognize that what purports to be a Revisionary description of growth entails repetition.

What is wrong with such repetition? Jerome McGann, who appears to share my interest in identifying Romantic criticism of Romanticism, has described *The Romantic Ideology: A Critical Investigation* as an effort "to persuade scholars that criticism ought to be trying not to reify, or recuperate, or repeat Romantic interests and experience, but to use them for clarifying and criticizing our own immediate interests and experiences."[23] The assumption is that the past and the present differ, and that the failure to recognize this difference alters the present and therefore the future. Describing the nature of this difference is thus an absolutely crucial step in any literary history, and that is where McGann's kind and mine part ways. The parting is political, in that it turns upon the social function of professional power.

The language in which McGann presents that function often echoes the language which his model, Heine, used when comparing "literature" to a "huge hospital" (*Romantic Ideology*, 35–36): "I have tried," writes McGann, "to free present criticism from the crippling illusion that such a [Romantic] past establishes the limits, conceptual and practical, of our present and our future" (3). As with Wordsworth's insistence upon "healthy" readers, McGann's call for uncrippled critics naturalizes departures from the "normal" in terms of diseases and cures, and casts the professional as a healer.[24] Throughout the book, his tone tells a tale not of changing kinds of criticism but of deviation. With the medicoreligious fervor of a faithhealer, he scolds those critics he thinks are still suffering from illusions, upbraiding them not "to misuse words shamelessly, to violate the mind and encourage confusion of thought: the last result being, let me say, the mortal sin of every form of criticism" (31). For McGann, what is wrong with repetition is not just the delimitation of present and future possibilities; it is wrong to repeat, because something was and is wrong with *what* is repeated. The act spreads a disease that needs to be cured.

As with McFarland's work, this is criticism with a mission. Since its purpose appears to be much closer to mine, it is particularly appropriate to inquire into how this kind of critic formally constitutes his prescriptive authority. The terminology McGann uses to administer to the past is that of ideology. Although he admits the term is "deeply problematic" (3), he prefers " 'ideology of poetry' to 'theory of poetry' in order to emphasize the broad social and cultural determinations which are involved in the assumption of an intellectual position, particularly in the period when the concept of ideology was born" (10–11). I have already argued the connection between the contemporary prominence of theory and "the assumption of an intellectual position" within the modern literary institution. Presenting ideology as an alternative to theory, I would add, belies the fact that the former is now a feature of the discourse of the latter.

Questions of that kind are not McGann's concern, however, since two progressive histories occupy his attention. One is in the form of a personal confession, not of the need to turn from history but of the desire to turn to it as repentance for his own earlier, "misleading" criticism (137–38). Participation in the second history, the development of the idea of ideology beyond its Romantic childhood, is supposed to help correct that error in "judgment." Defining what "we would now call 'ideology'" as "a coherent or loosely organized set of ideas which is the expression of the special interests of some class or social group" (5), McGann aligns himself with the conventional view that "ideology will necessarily be seen as false

consciousness when observed from any *critical* vantage." His intended improvement on how that view is exercised by "some Marxist
critics, like Althusser," is to identify their tendency to "separate poetry and art from ideology" as "a latent idealism" (12). The remedy is
to turn from the analytic detachment of the "idea of literature-as-
text" in order to echo the Wordsworthian theme of "distance from
the Kind" ("Elegiac Stanzas," 54): poetry must be "return[ed]" to "a
human form" (159–60).

McGann sprinkles his book heavily with the word "human," and
repeatedly invokes it synecdochically with references to such parts as
the work's "soul" (11). Thus, despite the book's combative tone, its
methodology is one of open arms, since the humanizing of ideology is
clearly an effort to reconcile the apparent opposites of traditional
humanistic criticism and of radical, ideological critiques. But as
Foucault's analysis of the notion of ideology has shown, the conceptual gap between humanistic and ideological assumptions has never
been very wide. His three reasons for finding it difficult to make use
of "ideology" map out its common ground with the supposedly more
conservative tradition it is intended to critique:

> The first is that, like it or not, it [ideology] always stands in virtual
> opposition to something else which is supposed to count as truth. Now
> I believe that the problem does not consist in drawing the line between
> that in a discourse which falls under the category of scientificity or
> truth, and that which comes under some other category, but in seeing
> historically how effects of truth are produced within discourses which
> in themselves are neither true nor false. The second drawback is that
> the concept of ideology refers, I think necessarily, to something of the
> order of a subject. Thirdly, ideology stands in a secondary position
> relative to something which functions as its infrastructure, as its mate-
> rial, economic determinant, etc. For these three reasons, I think that
> this is a notion that cannot be used without circumspection.[25]

Within McGann's type of history, the ideology of Romantic
works is "a body of illusions" (12). Although he is careful to emphasize in the book's conclusion that "no criticism, not even literary
criticism, can invoke a conceptual privilege for its activity" (159), the
concept of a true reality against which he measures ideological illusion has certainly held a privileged place in criticism since the Romantics. Speaking of Wordsworth's displacements of "realities," McGann
explains that the poet "imprisoned his true voice of feeling within the
bastille of his consciousness" (91). Emotion is privileged as a form of

deep truth repressed by conscious thought. In other words, even as the ideological perspective calls for the condemnation of Wordsworth as a member of "what Hans Enzensberger has called 'The Consciousness Industry,'" it also furthers the psychologizing of individual poems, Wordsworth's career,[26] and as I shall show shortly, literary history.

McGann's access to the procedures that make and valorize psychological depth is the translation of what he sees as Heine's dialectical movement between the poles of past and present into a movement "between the shifting poles of judgment and sympathy which criticism is *always* obliged to negotiate" (emphasis mine; 38–39). The negotiation is inherently disciplinary with sympathy being an *invitation* to judgment[27]: the former overcomes differences in kind, and the latter replaces them with differences in degree. As we saw in the last section of chapter 2, such psychologized evaluation characteristically entails the centering of a subject/object dialectic that "explains" the role of the "mind of Man" in figuring reality. As in my previous examples from Keats, Coleridge, and de Man, that mind's transcendence is formally effected in McGann's work by features such as syntactical mirroring: the proper "critical dialectic is only possible if the historical uniqueness of subject and object is carefully preserved. To do this means that the critic must be as much 'subject to' the judgment of his critical 'object' as that object is subjected to his criticism" (56).

As the effort to return poetry to a human form moves from an absolute "oblig[ation]" to an "only possib[i]l[ity]," it tells Foucault's tale of ideology: the recovery of truth from illusion is the (sympathy/judgment) task of a subject whose work is a "reflex" of its "social and historical realities" (132). Foucault finds the tale "difficult," of course, because he takes truth, the subject, and reality to be historical constructs—discursive representations that take on the nature of Nature. By producing knowledge of that Nature, the subject becomes its own object, disciplining and reproducing itself. In returning to a human form, with an emphasis on "concrete, human particulars" (11), McGann's kind of knowledge reproduces a particular form of the human. Whereas my effort to historicize Romantic discourse details the formal construction of that discourse's conception of the human, this history with a human face takes the Romantic turn from form by averting its gaze from criticism "as fruitless and arid as *any* type of formal or structural or thematic criticism" (emphasis mine; 160). Even calling a "literary work of art" a "text," according to McGann, leaves it "fetishized—frozen, immobilized, abstracted—into an arrangement of words" (159).

In asking us to turn instead to the study of "*works* . . . of specific men and women" (160), is McGann claiming that knowledge of such specifics exists unarranged and outside of language? Arrangements, in the frequency of their use, in their interrelations with each other, and in the resulting differences in function, have specific histories; they enable diachronic knowledge. The possibility of such knowledge is precisely what is at issue, when McGann argues that

> we are . . . accustomed nowadays to hear Romantic literature charac-
> terized as a "poetry of process" and to accept this sort of formulation
> without serious demur. But when we recall that the same term has been
> applied to the work of Pound and Charles Olson, and that a process
> model has been equally employed to explain Chaucer, Spenser, Mil-
> ton, and Marvell, and to distinguish Medieval from Renaissance poetic
> methods, we recognize the poverty of such a concept when it is used to
> define some special quality in Romantic literature. Whatever else it
> involves—whatever its usefulness in various, often excellent, critical
> discussions—this idea cannot serve to *distinguish* the literary phenom-
> ena of Romanticism. (28–29)

The ubiquitous use of a particular "concept" within a particular kind of writing is precisely the type of linguistic arranging that a literary history should be able to account for and use, rather than just dismiss, as McGann does here, through a diagnosis of "loose critical thinking" (29). In this case the kind of writing is literary criticism, and if, as McGann himself urges, we historicize it and thus come to recognize the ways it mirrors Romanticism, we should not be surprised to find Romantic features and procedures repeatedly employed as explana-tory devices—even in regard to texts written well before or after the late eighteenth and early nineteenth centuries. Thus the fact that many critics of Shakespeare have followed Coleridge in valorizing and analyzing the plays in terms of characterological "development" does not lessen development's utility as a historical marker; in fact, the extent to which it has been used, ahistorically and thus inappropri-ately, within traditional literary criticism is evidence of its own histori-city and the ongoing power of the discourse of which it is a part.

McGann's emphasis on the "individual work" as the work "of specific men and women"[28] is itself a concept whose modern func-tion appeared, as did the copyright laws, during the eighteenth century. It leads him into a crucial misinterpretation of L. J. Swingle's argument that "to get into the poetry successfully, what is needed is not so much a theory of Romanticism but a theory of Romantic poetry."[29] McGann argues that this entails the "general position that our concern as scholars and critics must ultimately lie with the individual work rather than with our procedures for dealing with those works" (60). Swingle's formulation does not displace the word "theory" with "reading an individual work" or some concept that opposes theory to "practice." He is instead concerned with shifting theoretical attention from an originary psychological context ("state of mind") to the poetic "manipulations" within the texts themselves. In that gesture he joins Ferguson, Simpson, de Man, and others who have sought a stylistic or rhetorical theory of the workings of Romantic poems. McGann adds the turn to the "individual" work and the opposition to "procedures," thereby suggesting that the former has some transcendent status distinct from our historical "dealing[s] with" it. Such a gesture, by reproducing the Romantic distinction between the creative and the critical, mystifies the work and thereby enhances the critic's value as the respectful and therefore respectable keeper of the mystery.

The "historicizing" of Romanticism in terms of individual works returned to a human form, without recourse to a theory that can address either the changing forms of the human or the shifting functions of features shared by interrelated works, takes on the disciplinary nature of a sobriety test: some works are intoxicated with Romantic ideological illusions, some are not, and those which test positive can be grouped according to the "natural" states of intoxification— from initial euphoria to the self-conscious despair of the hangover. "Not every artistic product in the Romantic period," argues McGann, "is a Romantic one" (19). Of the works that are Romantic, the "primary" ones do not question their own ideology of displacement, whereas the "secondary" ones are "self-critical." In addition, there are "three different phases" of " 'primary' (visionary) and 'secondary' (or revisionary) relationships" (108–10). McGann suggests, on the one hand, that these groupings are historical: poetry "which is the reflex of circumstance" (117) in the late eighteenth and early nineteenth centuries follows the period's "realities" of Revolution and Reaction. On the other hand, the logic of "revision" requiring a primary "vision" is absolute. As McGann applies it to specific poets, in fact, that logic describes personifications of psychological states:

> Byronic Despair is the reflex of an Ideal attachment in precisely the
> same way that Shelleyan Hope is the reflex of his Idealism. This is the
> structure which governs their ideological commitments. (127)

The temporality of that structure has been so thoroughly psychologized that the changes it describes are fundamentally ahistorical sequences of "natural" reactions. The potential for repetition and the
implied universality of what becomes a natural history of ideology
account both for McGann modeling his effort to historicize English
literature of the nineteenth century on a nineteenth-century German
text, and for his arguing that "the literary criticism of Romantic works
will justify itself . . . when it is seen to have followed the example"—
secondary "unmask[ing]" of primary "illusions"—"of the poetry itself"
(136).[30]

The creative/critical politics of this call to follow examples can be
clarified by examining that procedure's function within this kind of
history. Criticism unmasked, we discover, shows how the patterned
reflexes of the poets' unmaskings "define what is *valuable* in their
work" (emphasis mine; 127). With such definitions as their purpose,
the "instances" of applied criticism that occupy the latter part of *The
Romantic Ideology* thus assume the form of appreciations. Long quotations are strung together using strong critical adjectives ("splendid," "subtle," "cool . . . urbane," "brilliant and witty," "dazzling,"
"splendid," 139–43) as historical specifics blend almost imperceptibly
into absolute, and very familiar,[31] aesthetic judgments: in reaction to
the "special circumstances" of early nineteenth-century history, a
burned-out Wordsworth "fell asleep" (116), whereas a "high energy"
Byron produces "greatness" out of "Despair" (127). Sober Jane Austen, of course, would never fail a sobriety/drug test, so she becomes
the primary example of a non-Romantic writer of the Romantic period. But this cannot be done without valorizing her, in historically
telling fashion, as a (Romantic) outsider going against the grain: "the
greatest artists *in any period* often depart from their age's dominant
ideological commitments" (emphasis mine; 19).

My point is not to echo Francis Jeffrey, as McGann does, and proclaim that "this will *never* do" (emphasis mine; 20). It has been done,
done well, and for quite some time. But to say that historicizing
enables the past to be of value to the present is no longer to be forced,
by the Romantic logic of sympathy/judgment, into fetishizing that
past into parts with various inherent values. Nor does it mean that the

critic's job is to stabilize the market for those values by offering literary products as the culmination of a "progress," as objects of critical desire, or as examples of (self-critical) ideological rectitude. My remaining chapters offer possibilities for a kind of knowledge that historicizes its own disciplinary procedures within an analysis of the literary institution's production of value. To do so, it examines the formal construction of the human form, acknowledging the kind/ degree displacement as a means of constituting the social function of professional power. As critics serving the creative, our sympathetic turn from kind has made us the arbiters of degree—the degrees of cultural literacy that naturalize the social hierarchy by psychologizing difference as a matter of developing minds. At stake in writing a *generic* history, therefore, are both specific literary critical issues, such as Austen's Romantic status, and the tests by which status is established and preserved.

II

*Parts and Wholes:
The Strategy
of Development*

4

Inventing Literature

But who, ah! who, will make us feel?

MATTHEW ARNOLD

With those words, Arnold confirmed Wordsworth's cultural status and his own. His strategy was, simply, to do what Wordsworth had done: locate power in past sublimity so as to make continuity, or its apparent failure, the central concern of the present. Just as the creative child, within the developmental tale of the "Immortality Ode," evokes the adult's "primal sympathy" and "deep" thoughts, so, within the literary history of "Memorial Verses," great poets invite the sympathy and judgment of great critics. To accept that invitation, however, is, as we have seen, to psychologize diachronic differences in kind into an absolute hierarchy of degree. In this chapter I will offer an alternative way of relating the past to the present which does not take that lyric turn.

At stake are our assumptions about what we study and why. For Arnold, as for Wordsworth, writing that is valuable, real literature, is that which can "make us feel." Both men offered that formula as a cure, but a new literary history can provide a second opinion. The prescription can be reread, I am suggesting, as something less salutary and more coercive: for roughly two centuries we have had no choice *but* to feel. In the late eighteenth and early nineteenth centuries, the self was *made* to feel by being re-made into an active agent— one whose primary activity is feeling and whose cultural status is as high as that feeling is deep. A significant depth signals a consumer of literature (and vice versa); a self even more profound, of course, can produce it. Literature as the discipline we study and know, in other words, invented and was the invention of a self that both uses it to establish hierarchical difference and requires it as a cure.

Since those acts of invention entailed acts of writing and rewrit-

ing, changes in the use of specific formal features, such as personification, were not merely matters of aesthetic preference that, at best,
reflected a changing reality; they were among the means by which, at
the end of the eighteenth century, man reconstituted himself as a
different type of "person." My methodology in the first part of this
chapter, therefore, is to isolate personification as an exemplary feature and trace its shifting *functions* in mid- and late eighteenth-
century poetic texts by Gray, Collins, Goldsmith, Smart, Cowper,
Blake, and Wordsworth. Unlike Frye and Abrams, as well as Hartman, Bloom, and de Man, I do not try to transform a favored Romantic trope into a theoretical system applicable to all of Western literature. Nor do I try to colonize the eighteenth century with developmental tales of Romanticism qualitatively culminating (pre-Romanticism)
or superseding in stages (the Age of Sensibility) all that has come
before. Instead, I use the trope to read the cultural reorganization of
England in the late eighteenth and early nineteenth centuries, arguing that those changes in social behavior had to be written to become
"real." I show how this rewriting entailed a fundamental shift in
representational strategies that valorized literacy and Literature by
replacing the earlier fiction of community as the basis for communication with the later fiction of communication as the basis for a new
human community.

In the chapter's second part, my analysis of that valorization
departs from the monogeneric norm of most literary histories, particularly those that engage Romanticism, to focus on personification's
functions in the novels of Sensibility. This intergeneric perspective
helps me to explain the literary institution's marginalization of late
eighteenth-century texts—fifty years' worth garners sixty-two pages
at the very end of volume I of *The Norton Anthology*—in terms of
what I call the "politics of feeling." I relate the turn from personification that occurs not only in poetry, but also in the novel, to a shift in
the workings of social power. The changes in the interrelations of
forms that occasion that turn empower the literary institution by
rewriting and psychologizing moral imperatives as aesthetic ones:
"make us feel."

Given the preponderance of personification in early and
mideighteenth-century poetry, and Wordsworth's denunciation of it
in the Preface to *Lyrical Ballads*, the shift in its function may at first
seem to be a matter of mere presence and absence. But such an
explanation not only wrongly reduces the issue to a matter of autho-

rial preference for an unchanging feature; it also fails to account both for prolific personifying by Blake and others, and for the Wordsworthian proclivity for casting the objective world in the mold of the human subject. Various functions of personifying, in other words, are present and even strengthened during the turn into the nineteenth century, for only one in particular was found essentially problematic: Wordsworth attributed it to personification of abstract ideas.

To understand the difficulties it raised, consider the following examples from Pope's *Essay on Man* and Johnson's "Vanity of Human Wishes":

> Modes of Self-love the Passions we may call;
> 'Tis real good, or seeming, moves them all;
> But since not every good we can divide,
> And Reason bids us for our own provide;
> Passions, tho' selfish, if their means be fair,
> List under Reason, and deserve her care;
> Those, that imparted, court a nobler aim,
> Exalt their kind, and take some Virtue's name.
> (II.93–100; written 1730–32)

> With distant voice neglected Virtue calls,
> Less heard and less, the faint remonstrance falls;
> Tired with contempt, she quits the slipp'ry reign,
> And Pride and Prudence take her seat in vain.
> In crowd at once, where none the pass defend,
> The harmless Freedom and the private Friend.
> The guardians yield, by force superior plied:
> By int'rest, Prudence; and by Flatt'ry, Pride.
> Here beauty falls betrayed, despised, distressed,
> And hissing Infamy proclaims the rest.
> (ll. 333–42; written 1749)

The personification of abstract human faculties or attributes requires the transplantation of a part of the body of the individual (e.g., each man's reason) to the body of the community (e.g., Reason as a standard faculty shared by all). Personifying and generalizing are, in that sense, interrelated processes. In rhetorical terms, personifications of this sort function as a metonymic affirmation of community; the parts personified stand for the uniformity of their wholes.

However, personification not only affirms the presence of community within the poem; it also confirms that community as the stabilizing moral Presence. Goldsmith's definition of personification as "the representing [of] moral virtues, or inanimate beings as rational *agents*" (emphasis mine)[1] indicates how the pervasive use of that trope produces a passive poetic voice in which the possibility of action is displaced from the speaker or character to the "figure" of speech. In the Johnson passage "Virtue *calls*," "beauty *falls*," and "Infamy *proclaims*." What happens to the individual in these texts—his destiny—is thus determined by the action of those personified characteristics he shares with all men. But since those same personifications help generate the sense of community within the poem, that destiny is ultimately community. In Gray's "Ode on a Distant Prospect of Eton College," for example, the fate of the speaker and of all the students, no matter how much each individual deviates from the other, is determined by the rogue's gallery of personifications that occupies the poem's central stanzas to ensure that everyone ends within nature's norm: "All are men, / Condemned alike to groan, / The tender for another's pain; / Th' unfeeling for his own" (ll. 91–94).

The didactic power behind those closing lines needs to be explained. How does a speaker who leaves action to personification and shuns the later Romantic tactic of self-description and justification establish such authority? The eighteenth-century option of apparent self-effacement has been described by David Simpson as a willingness to be "content to insinuate the unquestioned verification of the perceiving subject by never describing it, never suggesting that it might be responsible for what it sees. It exists as an unspoken but implicitly central presence" (*Irony and Authority*, 138–39). In other words, the eighteenth-century speaker paradoxically asserts his presence by his absence. As a purveyor of truths sanctioned by uniformity, he owes his authority to his anonymity. Overt efforts at self-definition would only tend to undermine his claim to be a representative observer.

Instead, that claim is made implicitly through the use of particular figures who function as surrogates. Thus the thread again leads back to personification, this time as a specialized form of metaphor. "Metaphors speak of what remains absent," argues Karsten Harries. They "imply lack."[2] From an intentional standpoint, then, they are the trope of desire.[3] In personification, the procrustean poet desires to fit all things to a specific conception of the human. The result is a transformation of potential chaos into uniform human community that then reflects back upon the speaker as an expression of who he wants to be. As the supposed maker of the trope, the speaker constitutes himself as the center of the community—the abiding presence who is its Spokesperson. In that capacity, of course, he speaks with the authority evident in the characteristically didactic conclusions of eighteenth-century poetry. No overt identification or list of qualifications need clutter the text.

The reader's response to that authority is supposed to be passivity, since he is being told truths he already knows and accepts by a speaker whose voice he identifies through community as his own. However, the more extensive and intricate the use of the figurative language that shapes this writer-reader relationship, the smaller the potential readership becomes. As Ted Cohen has argued, in comparing metaphors and jokes, the use of particular types of figurative language can restrict community because it "can be inaccessible to all but those who share information about one another's knowledge, beliefs, intentions, and attitudes."[4] The Mob, in other words, can be shut out.[5] Thus proliferation of this type of personification is an essential tool in assembling the specifically eighteenth-century fictions of individuality and community. It helps to figure both the sense of a universal human community, whose uniformity is the basis for all communication, and the sense of a select literary community that is grafted upon it. Such grafting functions to ensure social stability by representing the strategies of exclusion as natural outgrowths of the principle of inclusion. Thus, the logic of Gray's dictum, "the language of the age is never the language of poetry," is that preservation—of those natural truths that define our common humanity—requires mediation of an uncommon, established elite.

Eighteenth-century systems of patronage, political as well as literary, rationalized in similar fashion the society's inherited web of patriarchal bonds and loyalties. The threat to community posed by wide discrepancies of income was minimized by overlaying that vertical hierarchy with a horizontal hierarchy of "interests": the "various trades, industries and professions," writes historian Harold Perkin, "represent[ed] through their leaders all levels of society from the squire, great merchant or industrialist down to the humblest labourer, seaman or handicraft worker." Those interests did not compete directly, but in a profoundly conservative manner, lobbying the "great landowners and their friends" for patronage of their particular policies.[6] Not until the end of the century did the modern concepts of class and class struggle become viable replacements for the older model of inherited privilege and patriarchal power.

If, in gauging personification's role in that change, we see it and the other features and forms of language as *reflections* of a reality

determined by economic conditions and political events, we are missing the literary historical point. The reality at issue here, as with any
reality, is a matter of representation—a construct of changing discursive practices that define the "nature" of experience in culture-
specific terms. This is not to deny that what we refer to as "circumstances" or "events" effect change, but to assert that we never experience such change outside of discourse. As I show of the effects of
opium in chapter 9, and as the "war" on drugs and the "epidemic" of
AIDS make clear today, what are construed as effects, how they are
understood to work, and why they do, are always formal matters. The
outcomes of those effects, the actions they elicit and the results of
that activity, are neither inevitable nor arbitrary, but written within a
historical range of generic possibilities.

We lose sight of that range when we thematize change within
histories of "ideas" (Uniformitarianism to Individualism) or of authors (Gray's elitism versus Wordsworth's democratic genius). The
former gives abstractions lives of their own, implying an inevitable
development to the better or more powerful, while the latter invites
ahistorical psychologizing and absolute aesthetic/political judgments.
Both mystify the workings of change by turning it out of the forms in
which it was experienced. To turn it back in is to recognize that, if
personification helped to configure the fictions of community in the
eighteenth century, then it also helped to configure the ways such
fictions were to change. In Goldsmith's "Deserted Village," for example, the collapse of community constituted through personifications
can only be represented by their dispersal:

> I see the rural virtues leave the land:
> Down where yon anchoring vessel spreads the sail,
> That idly waiting flaps with every gale,
> Downward they move, a melancholy band,
> Pass from the shore, and darken all the strand.
> Contented toil, and hospitable care,
> And kind connubial tenderness, are there;
> And piety with wishes placed above,
> And steady loyalty, and faithful love.
> And thou, sweet Poetry, thou loveliest maid,
> Still first to fly where sensual joys invade.
>
> (ll. 398–408)

What Raymond Williams terms the "negative identification" between the poet and society—"the exposure and suffering of the writer,

in his own social situation, are identified with the facts of a social history that is beyond him"[7]—is a specific corollary of using this type of personification to write up change. The reason that "Poetry" flies, and the poet can offer society no literary cure, is not that Goldsmith is a pessimist or lacks Wordsworth's genius, but that, within personification's configuration of communities, the breakdown of the uniform human community inevitably entails the collapse of the elite literary community grafted upon it; community was not understood to be the product of communication, but its prerequisite. Without those natural bonds, even the most productive mid- and late eighteenth-century poets (Goldsmith, Gray, Collins, Cowper, etc.) read themselves as helpless. For *us* to read their bleak descriptions of poetry's present and future as evidence of personal failings—madness, lack of genius, inferiority complexes—is to indulge in ahistorical psychologizing.

To psychologize in that manner, you need a psychologized subject; after all, to find hidden mental flaws, you first have to construct the mind as a hiding place. Thus when, as another formal corollary to the breakdown of the uniform and literary communities of personification, the poets just mentioned turn for refuge to the self, we must recognize that the self being presented is *not* as we now know it. It is neither privatized nor developmental, but representative and stable, for it is *still* constructed by the use of personification even as such usage increasingly produced, in Goldsmith's words, "the anxiety of disappointment."[8] Enacting what Martin Price identifies as the informing theme of mid- and late eighteenth-century poetry, "the poet as his own subject,"[9] entailed not the abandonment, but the deployment of personification.

The poets' most common strategy entailed actively making sense of their situation. Personifications thus proliferated, since, as we have seen, they are the texts' active agents. The individual self is formally and thematically a consequence of that activity and not its author. Thus it is only after the personifications desert Goldsmith's village that the self's passivity becomes the apparent virtue of stability: the speaker retreats into a "self-dependent power" to "defy" time. That is also its only possible function in "The Traveller." There, the reality of change is once again a product of invoking a sense of community through personification *and* critiquing that community by problematizing the personification:

> Thine, Freedom, thine the blessings pictured here,
> Thine are those charms that dazzle and endear;

> Too blessed, indeed, were such without alloy,
> But fostered e'en by Freedom ills annoy:
> That independence Britons prize too high,
> Keeps man from man, and breaks the social tie;
> ·
> Nor this the worst. As nature's ties decay,
> As duty, love, and honour fail to sway,
> Fictitious bonds, the bonds of wealth and law,
> Still gather strength, and force unwilling awe.
>   (ll. 335–40, 349–52)

In keeping with the eighteenth-century ideal of nature as balance, the problem with personification here is not desertion but excess: "Freedom" "foster[s]" too much. With personifications and their actions as much a curse as a blessing, since they too easily engender change, the self bereft of the proper ties is left to itself and a "Vain, very vain . . . search" for "bliss" (ll. 423–24).

The rustic poet of Gray's "Elegy" is also an ineffective victim; his life and death blend in anonymity. Who or what victimizes him? A squad of personifications: "Fortune," "Fame," and "Science" ignore him, "Melancholy" marks him, and "Misery" takes from him "all he had" (ll. 117–23). Narratives that temporally displace such activity into the future, back to the past, or out of time altogether thematize this helplessness. The poet's final vision in "The Bard" is of a large cache of personifications that cannot belong to him, but are the property of future poets:

> 'The verse adorn again
> 'Fierce War, and faithful Love
> 'And Truth severe, by fairy Fiction drest.
> 'In buskined measures move
> 'Pale Grief, and pleasing Pain,
> 'With Horrour, Tyrant of the throbbing breast.'
>   (ll. 125–30)

Without those figures there is no uniform community to speak for, and no literary community to speak to. The self as representative Spokesperson is, in this situation, no self at all.

The speaker of the "Ode on the Poetical Character" is similarly negated by temporal change represented by the actions of personifications. In fact, the very personifications—"Fancy" and the personification of divinity, "He"—that had acted to produce the "rich-haired

Youth of Morn," act in the present to abort the possibility of repeating that achievement:

> And Heaven and Fancy, kindred powers,
> Have now o'erturned the inspiring bowers;
> Or curtained close such scene from every future view.
>
> (ll. 74–76)

The repetition of a single personification keeps the possibility of such a negative change out of Christopher Smart's "Song to David." Helplessness there assumes the posture of prayer as the self seeks transcendent community with God through the action of one central figure: "ADORATION" as the fully capitalized personification of the act of worship.[10]

When the personifications appear in each of these poems, the self becomes the subject of their authoritative activities and not an active, authoritative subject. At the time, of course, the writers do not pose their situation in those terms, but they do, as Steven Knapp points out, increasingly share an "ambivalent interest in figurative agency." In a text such as William Collins's "Ode to Fear," that ambivalence is translated into "poetic theme and structure."[11] The sublimity of the poem's central personification is signaled by the abrupt apostrophe and the dramatically elaborated description:

> THOU, to whom the world unknown
> With all its shadowy shapes is shown;
> Who see'st appalled the unreal scene,
> While Fancy lifts the veil between:
>   Ah Fear! ah frantic Fear!
>   I see, I see thee near!
> I know thy hurried step, the haggard eye!
> Like thee I start, like thee disordered fly,
> For lo what monsters in thy train appear!
> ·
> Who, Fear, this ghastly train can see,
> And look not madly wild, like thee?
>
> (ll. 1–9, 24–25)

The logic of the text, "Like thee I," appears to be that the more elaborated the personification as the trope of desire, the more coherent and authoritative the speaker it constitutes. Fear is particularly desirable for its power to invoke and connect human and literary communities; it is praised in the epode and antistrophe as both a universal feeling and an aesthetic response. Thus for the speaker to speak for those communities, he must establish the proper relationship with personification. Shakespeare appears as matchmaker:

> O thou whose spirit most possest
> The sacred seat of Shakespeare's breast!
> By all that from thy prophet broke,
> In thy divine emotions spoke,
> Hither again thy fury deal,
> Teach me but once like him to feel;
> His cypress wreath my meed decree,
> And I, O Fear, will dwell with thee!
>
> (ll. 64–71)

The active agent is still personification, which must "Teach" the poet, but Shakespeare's presence provides a variation in the configuration of community. It can occur now only through a web of transference. Fear lives in Shakespeare. Therefore if the speaker becomes "like" Shakespeare, he also will "dwell" with Fear, and the three can then live fearfully ever after. Within this dramatic thematizing of figurative agency, in other words, personification's function of making community must be *acted out* in the form of sympathy. The speaker, however, cannot act, except in the sense conveyed in the epode of "know-[ing]" Fear as a reader of *Oedipus at Colonus*. The self's helplessness appears here, then, as the inability of the reader to become a writer.

The difference between the two informs Cowper's "Castaway," a poem with far fewer personifications than the preceding examples, but one which clearly illustrates that figure's eighteenth-century function. After describing the castaway's death, Cowper writes:

> No poet wept him, but the page
>   Of narrative sincere,
> That tells his name, his worth, his age,
>   Is wet with Anson's tear.
> And tears by bards or heroes shed
> Alike immortalize the dead.
>
> (ll. 49–54)

Cast as a passive reader in relationship to Anson's text, the speaker must justify acting as a writer:

> I therefore purpose not, or dream,
>   Descanting on his fate,
> To give the melancholy theme
>   A more enduring date;
> But misery still delights to trace
> Its semblance in another's case.
>   (ll. 55–60)

The "I" that opens the stanza, however, cannot act on its own as a personalized subject. Only when it is displaced by the personification that constitutes it as a representative observer, does writing take place: "misery" acts to outline the uniformity of its metonymically configured human community.

Such displacement is *not* the "reason" Wordsworth and other late eighteenth-century writers turned from personification of abstract ideas. The very first sentence of the Advertisement to *Lyrical Ballads* casts the choice of stylistic devices as a matter of poetic content. Since the "materials" of poetry "are to be found in every subject which can interest the human mind," then poems can be written about, and in the language of, "the middle and lower classes of society" (*Prose*, I, 116). Devices such as personification, which were canonically understood to "elevate" style, were set aside as part of a "family language" that was different in kind from "the very language of men." There was no need to "censure" personification as long as that difference was acknowledged; "they may be well fitted," emphasized Wordsworth in the 1800 Preface, "for certain *sorts* of composition" (emphasis mine; *Prose*, I, 130–31).

If personification had performed only one function, and if the "real" linguistic and psychological behaviors of social class had been ahistorical givens, then the sorting out of personification would have been but a technical adjustment in the angle at which poetry reflected reality. If, however, we engage reality as a construct, the inadequacy of reflection theory becomes evident. In this case we see that the newly real behaviors were being written at the same historical moment that the multiple effects of personification's removal were altering what and how men and women wrote. In the call to conform writing to reality—as with Wordsworth claiming to use the real language really spoken by real men—a different reality was formed. The privatized, active self was thus not a solution offered by Romantic geniuses to problems posed by inadequate predecessors, but at least in part a consequence of actions aimed at other ends.

Producing that self required more than the presence of the first-person pronoun, or the use of any *single* formal feature, for change is a matter of historically specific interrelations; a shift in the hierarchy of all features alters the functions of each of them. Thus in Gray's ode the "I" who "feels"upon his return to Eton College may at first appear to us to be personalized, but its function, in conjunction with the dense grouping of "elevating" personifications at the poem's core, is, as we have seen, to speak as the eighteenth-century generalized observer. But in "Tintern Abbey" the first-person pronoun—returning, like Gray's, to a place from its past—is not met with personifications of abstract ideas, but with features we now identify historically as lyrical. If we think of the poem, as Wordsworth suggested, as a lyricized ode, then this middle section is an epode structurally equivalent to other odic turns such as the one to "earliest Greece" in the "Ode to Fear." There, the timelessness of personification set up the past as an absolute model for the present, so that change had to be construed as decline. Without such personification the center of "Tintern Abbey" describes the past, as I argued in chapter 2, as an *explanation* of the present, so that difference can be narrated as development punctuated by different kinds of lyrical highs.

The features that displace personification include: repetitive diction that produces the effect of depth ('All thinking things, all objects of all thought, / And rolls through all things," ll. 101–2); negative transitions that suggest spontaneity and transcendence ('Nor perchance / If I were not thus taught," ll. 112–13); and apostrophe that socializes the situation without depersonalizing it ("My dear, dear Sister!" l. 121). Such socialization is necessary, because without personification to link the "I" metonymically to others (misery is common to all) the individual's natural state is isolation. In a reversal of the link we observed earlier between the absence of self and the reliance on personification to constitute authority, here, in the absence of personification, the individual self has been rewritten to occupy the center of power; replacing the myth of uniform selves tied to the old hierarchy of "interests," is a myth of individuality that masks the newly drawn inequities of class by emphasizing not what everyone has passively in common, but rather what each person can accomplish actively on his or her own.

Personification, of course, need not be absent to do this; only its stylistically elevating and metonymic functions must be replaced. In fact, the transformation of the "I" that we have been describing can itself be considered a kind of personification: the idea of the individual, which for the eighteenth century was an abstraction of the generalized truth of the human, became a flesh-and-blood person. That individual, in turn, cast nature in its own mold. Its new function was thus to form an authoritative identity. Capitalizing on personification as the trope of desire, for example, Blake interrelated prolific personification with a privatized diction—the "Persons & Machinery" of *Jerusalem,* he proclaimed, are "intirely new to the Inhabitants of Earth" (*Blake,* 697)—and extended narrative to constitute his speaker as the spokesperson of a desire that he claimed was naturally Infinite. For Wordsworth, however, man's desire was a violation of nature's calm, as in "Nutting," and personification as the trope of desire was therefore a poetic sin. Wordsworth thus constituted his speaking voice by overtly describing its characteristics in the text, a task he undertook with such relish that one eventual product was the fourteen-book *Prelude.* As with Blake, the speaker's "creative productivity" confirmed his personal status as the authorial stabilizing Presence.

How that subject embodied and directed some of the major changes in circumstance in the mid- and late eighteenth century is engaged in some of the later chapters. The rise in population, for example, and its relationship to the strategy of development and the concept of class, is addressed in chapter 6. In addition, the naturalizing of rapid economic growth[12] as a matter of "mixing" is analyzed in chapter 7. The major change in the number of readers, however, must be engaged here, for it has already been touched upon: the thematizing of figurative agency in terms of the reader becoming a writer was one of the representations of that change.

During the first eight decades of the eighteenth century, the expansion of the reading public was due primarily to population growth. The literacy rate, in fact, may have actually dropped during that period; Richard Altick believes that "at least we may be fairly sure that by 1780 the national literacy rate was scarcely higher than it had been during the Elizabethan period."[13] Only during the last two decades did it clearly rise, beginning with the founding of the Evangelical Sunday-school movement in 1780. Within seven years there were over 200 schools with an enrollment of over 10,000 children. Although many of the students may not have achieved full literacy, the Sunday schools did "swell the total of the nation's literates, both directly and by sharpening public interest in reading" (Altick, 68). Two hundred thousand copies of Tom

Paine's *The Rights of Man* were estimated to be in circulation within a year after its publication in 1792. Even if somewhat exaggerated, that figure would be far beyond the previous mark of 80,000 in four years (70–73).

During the initial rise of literacy through population growth, the increases, in writers as well as in readers, were represented not as improvements or opportunities but as threats to stability. In declaring his age the "Age of Authors," Samuel Johnson contrasted it with the past by observing that "the province of writing was formerly left to those who, by study or appearance of study, were supposed to have gained knowledge unattainable by the busy part of mankind."[14] The stability that was understood to be threatened by "busy" readers and "busy" writers was that of the configuration of communities we have been describing. The model of an elite literary community grafted upon the uniform human community no longer seemed to describe a society in which poetry was "almost fallen into disrepute,"[15] its poets finding themselves, in Goldsmith's words, "at the mercy of men who have neither abilities nor learning to distinguish [their] merit." The Golden or truly "Augustan Age" for Goldsmith was therefore "the reign of Queen Anne, or some years before," because "at that period there seemed to be a just balance between patronage and the press." On the one hand, without any booksellers "men were little esteemed whose only merit was genius," but on the other, patronage was necessary to ensure that the final judgments were educated ones; the poet would be protected from the unqualified "middle ranks" because they would ultimately imitate "the Great" and applaud "from fashion."[16]

This literary tale of the 1760s is more familiar to us in its political version, which twenty years later helped make sense of events in France. Just as the writer freeing himself from the limitations of patronage was faced with the prospect of being savaged by an uneducated mob, so the Revolution was written up as offering an inevitable choice between aristocratic oppression and mass terror. In both cases the violence was understood to have been precipitated by the undoing of the "natural" arrangement of elite and uniform communities. Given personification's role in configuring that relationship, the Revolution could be read as a nightmare of that figure's inadequacy.

The Preface to *Lyrical Ballads* certainly seems to tell it that way. Wordsworth's description of the "general evil" in the "life and manners" of society, and of the "great national events" that contribute to it, sets up the writer as a doctor who can cure the "savage torpor." In the very next paragraph—after what seems, if we do not grasp the connection between community and personification, to be an arbitrary turn to "*style*"—the diagnosis appears: personification is not "natural." Society can be cured by rejecting the trope that helped to constitute it both figuratively, *and,* through the blunting of sensibility by its overuse, literally. This rejection is imaged as a generational dispute: Wordsworth has cut himself off from "a large portion of phrases and figures of speech which from father to son have long been regarded as the common inheritance of Poets." He must therefore construct a new poetic family by inviting the audience into the personification gap: "I wish to keep my Reader in the company of flesh and blood, persuaded that by so doing I shall interest him" (*Prose*, I, 128–32). By simultaneously sharing the "company" of "flesh and blood," poet and audience are supposed to develop flesh and blood ties; according to this new fiction of community, they become a family generated by the communicative act.

The Prelude tells essentially the same tale of the Revolution leading to despair over abstract ideas that can be cured only by yielding them up and making community and an audience out of Dorothy and Coleridge. The apostrophe to the former in "Tintern Abbey" was thus but one example of the various strategies by which such community was supposed to be authored through the transference of meaning from the personal to the social sphere. Such strategies became the functional equivalent of personification, appearing as ubiquitously in the nineteenth century as that figure had in the eighteenth. The narrator of *Don Juan,* for example, transforms the tale of his "hero" into Romantic satire by turning from it to address the reader. Those appeals, dramatically voiced in a variation of what Wordsworth called the "language of conversation," are supposed to elicit the sympathetic identification that forges communal norms *and* the possibilities of deviation from them. Making satire thus required a solidifying of community between audience and author in which the present dismisses the past as undesirable abstraction:

> There poets find materials for their books,
>   And every now and then we read them through,
> So that their plan and prosody are eligible,
>   Unless, like Wordsworth, they prove unintelligible.
>   (I.717–20)

Coleridge is also yielded up in despair as a "metaphysician" (I.728) within apostrophes that promise the reader *real* flesh and blood:

> And here the advantage is my own, I ween
> . . . .
> They so embellish that 'tis quite a bore
> Their labyrinth of fables to thread through,
> Whereas this story's actually true.
> (I.1611, 1614–16)

By making the story the validity of the story, these turns thematized themselves. As they did so, associated characterizations such as the Byronic hero came to embody the problematics of community. Although he seems to reject all possibility of union, what that hero longs to do is to make the connections that he believes the past has denied him. Manfred, for example, would eagerly yield his splendid isolation if he could live without guilt with Astarte:

> Oh God! if it be thus, and thou
> Art not a madness and a mockery,
> I yet might be most happy. I will clasp thee,
> And we again will be—
> (I.i.188–91)

Individuality is asserted as a demand for a renewed sense of community. In Wordsworth this paradox appeared as the famous spectacle of the poet who celebrated the "One life within us and abroad" by dwelling upon himself at a length "unprecedented in literary history."

When, in the acting out of that paradox, the reader becomes a writer by writing about becoming one, it is those acts of literacy that are valorized. In the absence of personification, the dwelling *in language* upon the "I" as an active agent constituted the self as isolated and thus established the ability to communicate as the condition for dwelling with others. The literary language of sympathy and the language of the nuclear family came to produce and to reinforce each other.[17] "[Dear] Reader," wrote Blake in the introduction to *Jerusalem*, "[forgive] what you do not approve, & [love] me for this energetic exertion of my talent." When represented as potential family, the influx of readers in the 1780s and 1790s became not a threat to poetry and community but an opportunity.[18] Blake referred to the readers who received his "former Giants & Fairies" with "[love] and [friendship]" as "those with whom to be connected, is to be [blessed]."[19] What made the connection special, of course, was that money and love were now inextricably intertwined within fictions of the self as active subject, and within fictions of community as the product of communication rather than its prerequisite. Poetry was no longer elevated by the figure of personification; that function was now the poet's. The latter, as we noted in relationship to the hierarchies of kind and degree in chapter 3, was now "a man speaking to men." If they listened sympathetically, argued Wordsworth, the rewards were inevitable. Communication breeds community breeds truth: "the Poet, singing a song in which all human beings join with him, rejoices in the presence of truth as our visible friend and hourly companion" (*Prose*, I, 141).

What was valorized, of course, was "joining in," and the reader could only do so if his mind, as Wordsworth put it, was "healthy," that is, just like the poet's. Thus as the cultural representations of community were reconfigured so that the literary community was the new human community, the call to individuality and creativity became a means of asserting a need for psychological conformity. Whereas the patriarchal power of the earlier configuration exercised itself negatively, through exclusion (from an elite) and denial (of the possibility of change), this postpersonification power was apparently positive, valorizing the spread of knowledge and truth (to all) through a sympathetic openness. In order to be open, however, man first had to be opened up, and the cutting was done with (a) "style."[20]

After rejecting personification in the Preface to *Lyrical Ballads,* Wordsworth offered the following sentence as an explanation of his alternative: "I do not know how to give my Reader a more exact notion of the style in which it was my wish and intention to write, than by informing him that I have at all times endeavoured to look steadily at my subject" (*Prose*, I, 131, 133). Personifications of abstract ideas had interrelated describing, as the pictorial representation of surface details (abstraction as concrete image), with narrating, as the ordering of representative events (abstraction as active agent). Once that *kind* of personification was elided in a supposed act of leveling, the heights became the depths: the abstract that could no longer be represented on the surface was spatially mystified as deep and temporally displaced to the past. Within the new "style," description was psychologized as the gaze that looked within, and narration became the dramatic linking of personal present to personal past. Altering the function of personification was thus an essential step in *making* a "subject" to look at. Doing so established isolated individuality as the natural state of the self, posited social relations in terms of the psychological conformity necessary for "sympathetic identification," centered the ability to communicate—literacy—as the means and measure of social power, and helped to coin a vocabulary of visionary activity (from "looking steadily" to "close reading") that naturalized that power's panoptical gaze.

The institutionalization of that gaze—in the work of those creative writers, analytic critics, developing students, and loving readers who have helped to form academic departments, publishing houses, foundations, and governmental bureaucracies—is what I refer to in this section as Literature. The capital letter is not an act of arrogance or affectation but a historical gesture: Literature arose in the absence of the personifications capitalized in eighteenth-century texts. As a feature, in that sense, of Romantic discourse, we need to clarify its functions.

Arnold offered Literature as a cure because he thought its gaze made us feel. It puts us in touch, according to this argument, with the "deep" feelings that are both our most intimate emotions and our primary links to community. In the climactic act of feeling demanded by what are supposed to be the best works of art, every individual, as we have seen, is supposed to identify sympathetically with the work—its imagery or characters or speaker or author—and, inevitably, with each other. As one self becomes like another, conformity to a psychological norm is achieved. Once Wordsworth and others inscribed this capacity to conform sympathetically with the sign of "health," deviation from the norm became a sickness. The advent of Literature as both diagnostic tool and cure thus figured, for the society as a whole, the shift in the workings of power described earlier. In terms of the politics of feeling, the moral imperatives to which human behavior had been subject until the late eighteenth century were rewritten and psychologized as aesthetic imperatives—"make us feel"—and their normative content was naturalized as simple medical matters of good mental and physical hygiene and of taking the cure.

Since the texts tagged as novels of Sensibility have made us laugh as often as they have made us feel, they would appear to have little to do with this change. In fact, we have analyzed Literature so far by looking only at that genre—poetry—and those particular texts that were made a part of it. Doing so, however, is only a first step, for we cannot historicize the making of Literature's canonical boundaries without engaging texts that were marginalized or omitted in the process. Other genres and less familiar texts were essential to the changes that we have been discussing, and they are equally essential to our understanding of how such changes take place. To learn from them, we must stop arguing over whether they are fifth-rate, third-rate, or sometimes even first-rate. The making of such judgments, whether positive or negative, invariably produces, as we have seen, developmental tales—Sensibility as a gloomy afternoon on the way to a Romantic lyrical flowering, or as a detour from the novel's rise between Richardson and Austen—that function as a blind to difference. This domesticating of difference as a step on the way to the "real" thing has been an essential strategy of traditional histories of Literature, since the success of the constructions of Literature and of the deep self—their ability to sustain our belief that they really do nurture and describe human nature as it was, is, and shall be—has required that they be presented as that which was really already there.

It wasn't. One form of difference between the self of feeling of Sensibility and the feeling self with which we are still familiar, is the subject of Gary Wills's book *Inventing America*.[21] By historicizing the texts that inform American political debate—in this case he reads Jefferson's Declaration of Independence as a Sentimental document—Wills illuminates the metapolitics of the debates' limitations. He shows, for example, that the elision of Sensibility from traditional American histories has cast all arguments over "inalienable rights" into a seemingly inescapable tug-of-war between the individual and the state. But that contest becomes inevitable only when we assume that the natural state of the individual is isolation and that its rights are always of retention. Wills shows how those assumptions became truths through the writing off of historical difference. In the Sensibility texts that informed Jefferson's work, individuals are social entities whose pursuits of private happiness are invariably public, because of a natural inclination toward benevolence, and whose basic rights—those that they cannot alienate from themselves—are always ones of exchange. The point for our purposes is not that this version corrects the traditional one, but that it confirms a difference that historicizes both. In doing so, it calls into question those exercises of institutional power that justify themselves through an appeal to the supposedly ahistorical truth of one or of the other.

I bring up Wills's effort here because Literature, like America, is an invention that has obscured its own origins. It, too, has de-

historicized a version of the human, domesticating that self's differences with previous representations with the tales of artistic development cited earlier. Such activities are no less political than those
studied by Wills, but grasping the politics of feeling requires a literary historical inquiry into the interrelations of forms rather than
Wills's more thematic intellectual history of "ideas." In understanding how these different kinds of selves were the products of literary
kinds, we can begin to understand the history of our profession's
role not in the reflecting, but in the prescribing—the writing before—of the real.

From the mix of the dramatic and the georgic-descriptive that
characterizes the novels of Sensibility, emerge selves that exhibit features with which we think we are familiar. "Thoroughly to unfold the
labyrinths of the human mind," wrote Sarah Fielding in the introduction to *The Cry: A New Dramatic Fable* (1754),

> is an arduous task; and notwithstanding the many skilful and penetrat-
> ing strokes which are to be found in the best authors, there seem yet to
> remain some intricate and unopened recesses in the heart of man. In
> order to dive into those recesses and lay them open to the reader in a
> striking and intelligible manner, 'tis necessary to assume a certain free-
> dom in writing, not strictly perhaps within the limits prescribed by
> rules.[22]

Why bother? Why struggle to penetrate the unopened? For us, the
labyrinth within suggests the mysterious intimacy of the individual;
the depths hold private secrets. We would dive in because we do not
know what we would find. Fielding, however, wants to enter precisely because she *does* know what she will uncover—"human nature
in general"—and that, as the Introduction's explicit statements and
numerous personifications make clear, is all she needs to know. Such
sufficiency explains why a character's resemblance to a "real" person
is, for us, a legal matter centering on individual privacy, whereas for
her, as we read in the introduction's concluding disclaimer, the concern is moral in that the "fixing . . . down" into the "personal" may
divert us from universal truth (108).

Thus, although Fielding's language suggests that a recess exists
independent of the failed efforts to represent it, what is found is that
which is *made:* the product of the historically specific combination of
features and strategies being employed. Fielding, in fact, leads up to
the "recesses" passage by specifying the contents of her formal mix:

. . . the puzzling mazes into which we shall throw our heroine are the perverse interpretations made upon her words; the lions, tigers, and giants, from which we endeavour to rescue her, are the spiteful and malicious tongues of her enemies. In short, the design of the following work is to strip, as much a[s] possible, Duessa or Falsehood of all her shifts and evasions; to hunt her like a fox through all her doublings and windings; to shew that, let her imitate Truth ever so much, yet is she but a phantom. (106–7)

This "dramatic fable" lifts, from the latter kind, an allegorical design that encourages a didactic reading of the quotidian action as the moralistic escapades of personifications: Falsehood is the loser as Affectation and Fallacy battle Truth and Simplicity. From the drama comes the strategy of dividing the action into *scenes* played before an "audience" of "allegorical phantoms."

The two formal elements correspond to the twin functions of eighteenth-century literature: in the words that Fielding herself repeats, "to entertain and to instruct" (103). The figuring that produces the audience for scenes of dramatic confrontation with the "mortal persons" primarily serves the former purpose. "The nearer things are brought to dramatic representation," claims Fielding, "the more are you . . . interested in the event of the story" (107). When abstract ideas are personified, however, instruction is the goal. That purpose was, of course, understood throughout the eighteenth century to be the dominant one. Even when not offered, like Fielding's effort, as explicitly allegorical, the novels of Sensibility were intended to personify in their characters the triumph of Virtue. "A large majority," wrote the author of *Female Friendship* in 1770, "especially of the fair sex, have not time nor talents for the investigation of abstract principles in moral and social life; wherefore a lighter kind of study is essential."[23] Writing a novel to teach those universal truths was thus to give fictional body to abstractions; in other words, the novel as a conduct book in the eighteenth century was, conceptually, an act of personification.

That act, though didactic, was understood to be descriptive, for the procedure of description at that time was modeled on Virgil's *Georgics*. As a mixed form interrelating art and politics, the detailing of rural life and the promotion of civic virtue, the georgic-descriptive was *not* governed by our ideals of individual objectivity and deep thoroughness; it offered, instead, a balanced selection of representative details confirming an ordered uniformity within the context of community. This allowed for the presentation, in Addison's words, of "plain and direct instruction."[24] Lest the result be too plain, and thus fail to instruct by losing the reader's interest, dramatic features had to be mixed with the descriptive.

By engaging Sensibility texts in this manner, as mixed forms rather than essentialistically defined "novels," we can avoid dismissing them as poor or sui generis examples of the latter, and analyze instead the social and historical functions of the mix. And by isolating the particular feature of that mix with which we are already familiar, personification, we can make the analysis intergeneric. By doing so, we can see that such formal variations as Collins's use of personification as dramatic allegory in the "Ode on the Poetical Character" were paralleled by Sarah Fielding's effort in *The Cry*. Both engaged personification because it was the nature of the "person" that was at stake. As the literary men and women we usually group (and dismiss) under "Sensibility" whistled the familiar refrain of mixing moral "profit and delight," they took up the cultural work of defining the "natural emotions" and "probable behavior" of "real people": "A true picture," in the words of the anonymous author of *Constantia,* "of human life."[25]

The kind of reality prescribed by Sensibility evokes our somewhat nervous laughter because of the way the picture mixes the Truth, personified, and the truly accurate; the didactic always informs the empirical. For the modern reader, that priority violates the imperative of full and objective disclosure. What appears to be dishonesty is understood to distort reality, amounting to our general sense of "an essential falsity," as J. M. S. Tompkins put it, "which infected the whole cult of sensibility" (111). The feelings portrayed do not seem to grow out of the detailed depths of character and of nature that we expect to find. We look for that kind of truth to the supposed empirical accuracy of an Austen or a Wordsworth, writers whose renderings seem to grow on us—making us, in turn, feel like them.

The formal ability *not* to do that is evident in Sensibility novels such as *A Sentimental Journey*. As in Fielding's effort, Sterne's dramatic devices include both the dividing up of the action into scenes and the positing through personification of an immediate audience. Like Sarah Fielding, he makes the principal character the speaker, but that speaker is also the author, and its multiple turns to an audience not of "allegorical phantoms" but of an individual "Reader" have appeared, to modern critics, to produce a familiar effect. The passage is introduced dramatically as a scene set by the subtitles:

> THE REMISE DOOR
> CALAIS
>
> When I told the reader that I did not care to get out of the Desobligeant, because I saw the monk in close conference with a lady just arrived at the inn—I told him the truth; but I did not tell him the whole truth; for I was full as much restrained by the appearance and figure of the lady he was talking to.[26]

The apparent effect is of an intimate look into an individual's secret psychological depths, and critics eager to be made to feel have taken such passages as evidence that Sterne is the granddaddy of stream of consciousness.

But that stream issues from Wordsworth's "mighty flood of Nile": the "something evermore about to be" (1850 *Prelude,* VI.606–16) that signifies the unlimited depths of the self as transcendent Mind. Sterne, however, suggests depth only to assert universal limitation. Neither he nor the reader can ever know "the whole truth" because man's faculties are permanently imperfect, not continually reaching new heights or depths of perception. The depths are cut off and the limit inscribed in the text by a didactic personification that characteristically displaces the action from the individual "I" to the representative part that universalizes the lesson: the "lady" becomes the product of a "Fancy" that "charm[s]" and "cheat[s]" all of us. Similar personifications, such as those of "Liberty," "Nature," "flattery," and, most emphatically, Sensibility itself as the "great, great SENSORIUM of the world," curtail scene after scene (97, 133, 141). In cutting off the drama of the individual self, they obviate the need for, even the possibility of, personal sympathy in favor of the detached laughter of satire. In terms of the characteristic formal mix of the novel of Sensibility, they function georgically to put the dramatic narrative shenanigans to work publicly and didactically, making us learn from feelings rather than insisting that we learn to feel.

In showing that Sterne is "dismissive" and "assertive," and in that order, J. Paul Hunter observes that "denigration of a [traditional] didactic method does not necessarily equal anti-didactic . . . sentiments."[27] That argument needs to be seen as a fundamental assumption of Johnson's essay on "fiction" from the *Rambler*. For him, the whole point of novels as "lectures of conduct" is that they *can* be better didactic tools than the "solemnities of professed morality."[28] To do so, they must properly discriminate the informing personifications of Vice and Virtue. That is the job of description, since it necessarily entails selection and classification of an unlimited amount of detail:

> It is justly considered as the greatest excellency of art, to imitate nature; but it is necessary to distinguish those parts of nature, which are most proper for imitation: greater care is still required in representing life, which is so often discoloured by passion, or deformed by wickedness. If the world be promiscuously described, I cannot see of what use it can be to read the account. (22)

Such promiscuity is, at best, an aesthetic fault that wastes a reader's time; at worst, it illictly "mix[es]" Virtue and Vice, and thus signals moral failure (24). A bad book, for Johnson, is *bad;* that is, it fails to teach what is good.

Here is the modern literary critical formulation:

> Nevertheless, it is to be noticed that this didactic prepossession [in Sensibility] is always strongest with mediocre novelists and with critics who are reviewing mediocre novels; these they often acquit or condemn wholly on *moral* grounds, whereas before a *good* book they do not indeed forget their function as public watchdogs, but they remember that they have other functions as well, now that there is a chance to exercise them. (emphasis mine; Tompkins, 72)

This is offered as a historical observation, but the only evidence cited is of critics from the late 1700s who repeat the Johnsonian assumption that, to be successful, a novel must make the morality interesting. What is being asserted here is, in fact, a more recent critical line: "good" as an aesthetic judgment is to be applied in inverse proportion to a work's overt concern with moral goodness. The novels of Sensibility, in other words, have been marginalized by the literary institution because they suggest that feeling is *unavoidably* didactic. Purveyors of Literature must take their feeling pure. By thinking of it as detached from that which is now considered time-bound and political, such as standards of morality, they can proffer the capacity for it as an absolute measure of the greatness of works, the normality of readers, the value of critics, and the health of societies.

Describing this change is the task of literary history because, even though it did, as I indicated earlier, alter the workings of social power, the shift itself did not unfold as a conspiracy to do so. It was written by literary arguments generated within late eighteenth-century texts, as the discourse of feeling reproduced and critiqued itself during the latter half of the century. Two of the debates that played important roles in altering the mix of features representing the self and feeling centered on narration and nationality. *A Sentimental Journey,* with its famous digressions and its ongoing concern with the issue raised in its first line,"—They order, said I, this matter better in France—," illuminates both.

Although Sterne has certainly been a personal focus of debate over digressions since *Tristram Shandy*'s chapter on that topic, breaks in narrative continuity need to be seen as an unavoidable point of contention within mixtures of the dramatic and the georgic-descriptive. For the latter form, turns from the details of beekeeping to the machinery of state were "natural." But the dramatic, since it bore within discussions of the novel an Aristotelian stress on continuity of action, took those turns to be interruptions. By the 1780s the mixing of these alternatives was in the hands of third- and fourth-generation English novelists seeking to clarify the identity and heighten the value of what was rapidly becoming a significant body of texts. To those who sought to distinguish the novel from the childish "simplicity" of the fable and the arbitrary "adventures" of the Romance, the dramatic elision of every incident not "forwarding the main story" seemed to promise a "unity" worthy of a higher generic ranking. By thus advocating that the novel be "made to form a whole," Thomas Holcroft and his fellow authors turned upon the georgic turns.[29] In doing so, of course, they indirectly undermined the didacticism of their texts, since those turns had functioned to provide instruction and point out truths. There is thus no need to psychologize the writing off of didacticism as a conscious or unconscious authorial decision; it was, in large part, like the altering of the "I" that resulted from the elision of personification's elevating function, the consequence of a formal strategy tailored to suit other purposes.

The features that had functioned to produce the didactic turns, such as Sterne's personifications of abstractions like "Liberty," were literally in the way of this generic consolidation. Their fate was the same one declared for their poetic counterparts by Wordsworth. As we noted, he banned the personifying of abstract ideas not as an immoral activity but as an unnatural one; it was not a "regular" part of "the very language of men." What now constituted a real man, however, was less immediately evident in his example, a shepherd, than in what surfaced in the novel. With the personifications and other didactic interruptions gone, novels were written in which the probable behavior of a single character was stretched without interruption over a series of continuous actions. The result was a new kind of person: one whose value lay in the capacity to incorporate, by making internal sense of, each succeeding action. Supplying the raw material for this endlessly *developing* self required promiscuous description—a need "to look steadily," as we saw Wordsworth put it in defining the "style" demanded by the absence of personification—that functioned as a penetrating gaze revealing, actually making, the depths within.

For feeling to become the measure of those depths, and thus a sign of health, its strictly didactic function had to be written off. This was accomplished largely through an initial politicizing of feeling along nationalistic lines within Sensibility. The opening sentence of *A Sentimental Journey* sets up the entire novel as a comparison of the accomplishments in Sensibility of England and France. In doing so, Sterne is participating in an ongoing debate over the relative merits of English and French manners and novels that was being conducted within the latter as well as within the reviews and essays of and about them. Yorick's observations largely conform to the general appraisal of French character (and characters) as possessed of highly refined, even superior, sentiments unaccompanied by proper moral decency.[30] His personifications present the French as slaves to Flattery and as insensitive to Liberty.

Although these kinds of comparisons were certainly intended to critique the two nations, they functioned within literary history in a very different manner. What was really at issue was Sensibility itself: the belief in the didactic power of intense feeling. Criticism of the French failure to link refined sentiments with moral behavior was a way of questioning the possibility of that link. That questioning accelerated as the elision of didactic turns in the name of dramatic continuity led the English to read their own links as increasingly arbitrary. By 1785, Clara Reeve referred to "sentiment" as a word in "disgrace,"[31] a condition necessitating a distinction between true and false Sensibility. As sentiment became treacherous, the judgment of the French as feeling intensely *but* behaving immorally was spun into a causal narrative that told of intense feelings *producing* immorality—the narrative that embodied the "lesson" of the French Revolution years before the guillotine drew blood.

Within that narrative and the contemporary critical ones that mimic it, Sensibility had made feelings too easy and too available: in the classic words of reaction, here voiced by a twentieth-century literary critic, "One longs for a little toughness." Feeling was thus rewritten to require "the discipline of great poety" and to serve an audience specifically made to feel.[32] That group was defined intergenerically: critics of Sensibility novels had condemned both the overly refined and the "Cook-Maid [who] talks sentiment"[33]; Wordsworth followed, declaring the elite damaged by their distance from nature and the rustics—in their use of language—in need of being "purified . . . from all lasting and rational causes of dislike or disgust," because they were so much a part of it (*Prose,* I, 124). Feeling became the property of those in the middle.

With didacticism written off as dangerous, and the market properly restricted, a disciplined feeling was able to be revalorized as, quite simply, natural—not that which is good but that which is good for you. By embodying morality in a sixth sense, a moral sense, Sensibility had made being moral a matter of health; Yorick's sentimental journey was a form of exercise paced by the turns to personification. With those didactic elements smoothed out of the narrative, however, the journey no longer described the growth of a moral sense, but of sense itself. The imperative to be healthy remained; stripped of its overt moral purpose, however, it took growth as its end. It was through the telling of the result—the tale of healthy growth and of deviations from it—that Literature rewrote the self and transfigured the workings of power. The didacticism that asserted through prohibitions the moral limits both of the stable self and of what it can know gave way to a positive form of control—one that "produces," in Foucault's words, "effects at the level of desire" (*Power/Knowledge,* 59).

For Literature to make us feel, we must be made to want to feel; feeling must seem to have no strings attached. The novels of Sensibility seem so artificial to us because the didactic strings of feeling are so heavily drawn. But if we stop spending critical time bemoaning apparent defects, we can learn how those strings were formally attached and, more important, *apparently* detached. We will find that long after the novel stopped lecturing us on Sensibility and poetry ceased being elevated and didactic, both types of writing remained, and remain, conduct books of the most sophisticated kind.

5

The Work of Literature

Poets in all ages have claimed that their poems were not willed but were inspired, whether by a muse, by divine visitation, or by sudden emergence from the author's subconscious mind. But as the poet Richard Aldington has remarked, "genius is not enough; one must also work." The working manuscripts of the greatest writers show that, however involuntary the origin of a poem, vision was usually followed by laborious revision before the work achieved the seeming inevitability of its final form.

The Norton Anthology of English Literature, 5th ed., 1986

When, by ignoring diachronic differences of kind,[1] literary study became a discipline devoted to canonizing "the greatest writers" by degree, its conduct lessons became increasingly disciplinary. Attention to individual "genius" has celebrated spontaneity and originality while prescribing the necessity of "work."[2] In other words, just as sympathy has proved to be an invitation to a particular kind of judgment, so the idealizing of subjective "vision" has functioned as a call to "laborious revision." Within the economics of Romantic discourse, the value of the former is underwritten as a loan to be paid off by the latter.

The ongoing power of that discourse is nowhere more evident than in the payments we currently find ourselves making. To historicize the current literary critical situation—what we write about, the way we write, and how, in doing so, we write and rewrite ourselves— we need to make an accounting of visionary and revisionary activity. The problematizing of the object of critical attention, for example, is most dramatically evident in the ongoing publication of the Cornell Wordsworth. Romanticists can no longer write about *The Prelude* without addressing the issue of which one, for when the work of literature is revision, then the identity of the work of literature becomes a matter of editorial and theoretical concern. As more and more of the early products of Romantic revision become generally available, the problem of what to do with these textual riches will become increasingly central to every kind of critical endeavor.[3]

The kinds that have been written over the past decade have already been informed by the imperative of vision/revision. Culler's and Hartman's calls for a Revisionary criticism, Bloom's fixation on revisionary ratios, and McGann's history of "'primary' (visionary) and 'secondary' (or revisionary) relationships," are all payments for debts incurred (sometimes by those very same critics) through the critical celebrations of the Visionary Imagination offered during the 1950s and 1960s. These revisionary payments are presented as demystifications, but they can only demystify the visionary past, I would argue, by historicizing the revisionary present.

To do so is to begin to account for the fascination with self-revision found thoughout our society, from the pop psychology of "changing for the better" to the religious fervor of being "born again." When we take the Romantic subject—that version of the self, as I argued in the last chapter, that invents and is the invention of Literature—to be a text subject to the Romantic logic of vision/revision, then that logic appears in a more familiar guise. The insistence upon rewriting to achieve what *The Norton Anthology* calls a "final form" is translated, in that case, into the necessity of change so that potential can be fulfilled; aimed at the human form, the mandatory labor of revision becomes the imperative of development. By analyzing, in this section of the book, the invention of Literature, its work, and the "natural" results, I can present that imperative not as a psychological truth, but as an all-encompassing *formal* strategy underpinning the society that places Literature at its center: as I shall use it in the ensuing argument, the term "development" refers to our culture's characteristic way of representing and evaluating the individual as something that grows. Understanding how that strategy works is essential to tracing the profound shift from the self as static, metaphysical, and inherited to the rounded, psychological subject capable of the limitless self-improvement valorizing and valorized by an "open" society and a "free" economy.

The first part of this chapter, therefore, establishes the historicity of development by identifying how it interrelates with the specifically Romantic use of revision.[4] Instead of turning immediately to the process of rewriting, which is but one possible guise of revision, I start on fairly familiar thematic grounds, looking to contrast the different ways of conceiving of relationships between parts and wholes and of change and continuity that delimit the historical ranges of revision's meanings and functions. The second part uses texts by Wordsworth to relate the variety of Romantic revisionary strategies to the making of models of developmental order that we continue to valorize. I show that the sense of organic roundedness that comes to characterize "real" people is a complex of effects produced by the manipulation of formal features. Those manipulations are the labor of revision and thus the work of Literature.

Since I am trying to identify a diachronic change in *function,* I have chosen texts not for the obvious differences between them but because of their apparent similarities. Owing largely to the adjective around which its title is centered, Edward Young's *Conjectures on Original Composition* (1759) has been viewed as being similar to, or at least an anticipation of, later texts we call Romantic. But, as we have seen in regard to the use of the "I" in poetry, the mere presence or absence of a single feature is not sufficient evidence for making a literary historical argument; that feature's functional historicity is always a factor of its synchronic interrelations with other features. By attending to shifts in those interrelations, I avoid essentialistic definitions of revision as either a personal proclivity ("Some writers like to revise") or a creative absolute ("Even expressive artists must revise"), and can account instead for revision's suddenly high profile in the texts that historically construct the modern subject.

Mid- and late eighteenth-century poems, as we saw in the previous chapter's analysis of personification's metonymic function, exhibit characteristic ways of writing up and thus furthering change. The increasingly problematic relationship of author to audience, for example, was thematized in poems such as "Ode to Fear" by presenting the speaker as a reader/auditor unable to write. Within the epistolary form of Young's *Conjectures,* this posture of embarrassment turns upon the distinction between public and private that is central to the use of the letter in the eighteenth century:

> How you may relish the pastime here sent you, I know not. It is miscellaneous in its nature, somewhat licentious in its conduct; and, perhaps not over-important in its end. However, I have endeavoured to make some amends, by digressing into subjects more important, and more suitable to my season of life.[5]

Digression functions here as an organizational manifestation of embarrassment, in which the author distances himself from the work of writing by partially disowning his announced theme and only partly engaging his "real" one. Analogous strategies include forgery, for which the late eighteenth century is particularly well known, and other forms of disguised or disavowed authorship.[6]

The *Conjectures* is an especially arresting example of how embarrassment breeds thematic self-denial and authorial deception. Given its title, for example, we should expect Young to provide a definition of "original." But after a few paragraphs our expectations collide with a blunt denial: "I shall not enter into the curious enquiry of what is, or is not, strictly speaking, *Original,* content with what all must allow, that some compositions are more so than others; and the more they are so, I say, the better" (223). The reader's curiosity is transformed into, and dismissed as, a "curious enquiry," leaving the central concept of "originality" unexplored but not lacking in explanatory power. In the absence of truth content, we must remain "content with what *all* must allow" (emphasis mine). Originality, in other words, is not dismissed; it is domesticated as a tool for making hierarchical distinctions by its interrelation with the assumption of the uniform human community whose configuration we analyzed in the previous chapter.

How does its companion noun fare? The advantages of "Composition," understood as reading or writing (222), are listed early in the *Conjectures,* but they actually convey at least as much doubt as certainty:

> If those are held honourable, who in a hand benumbed by time have grasped the just sword in defence of their country; shall they be less esteemed, whose unsteady pen vibrates to the last in the cause of religion, of virtue, of learning? Both These are happy in *this,* that by fixing their attention on objects most important, they escape numberless little anxieties, and that *tedium vitae* which often hangs so heavy on its evening hours. May not this insinuate some apology for my spilling ink, and spoiling paper, so late in life? (223)

Why, we might ask in return, does composition require insinuated apologies? Young's metaphors provide important clues: composition, as a "spilling" and "spoiling," is, like man, burdened with an *Original* Sin. Its morality forever suspect, it must, like the old patriot, be ever prepared to prove its loyalty. "The more composition the better,"

argues Young, as long as one "restriction" is observed: like originality, composition must be hierarchically domesticated into the "real
service of mankind" (222).

All the functions it performs in that service are intended to help
men cope with "life's endless evils." A problem arises, however,
when that one inevitable evil puts an end to all the others; in a
startling turnabout occasioned by his description of Addison's death,
Young ceases his praise of composition, subordinating it as a sign of
genius and a guidepost to immortality to his hero's final, spoken
words: "See in what peace a Christian can die" (248). That one verbal
act so outshines Addison's written achievements, argues Young, that
to commend him only for his composition would be "detraction
now." The magnitude of Young's deception is finally evident and
must be admitted: "This you will think a long digression; and justly; if
that may be called a digression, which was my chief inducement for
writing at all: I had long wished to deliver up to the public this sacred
deposit" (249).

To classify historically a text entitled *Conjectures on Original
Composition,* in which conjecture is a blind for prose elegy, originality is left undefined, and composition is dismissed as detraction, is an
obviously troublesome task. Yet in ascertaining whether the author
of "Love of Fame, the Universal Passion: In Seven Characteristical
Satires" became a "Romantic" at seventy-six, literary historians have
largely ignored how all those features interrelate within the historically identifiable posture of embarrassment. Either/or arguments as
to whether the *Conjectures* was "the first salvo in the battle for Romanticism" or "the last in the battle of the ancients and the moderns,"[7] cannot address it as a particular kind of variation within an
established set of interrelations: one in which, in Ralph Cohen's
words, "efforts are made to bring within the established concept ways
of thinking and feeling that seem no longer variations of the original
innovative concept."[8]

In that light, Young' sense of his own originality—"I begin with
Original Composition; and the more willingly, as it seems an original
subject to me, who have seen nothing hitherto written on it" (222)—
need not be seen as essentially irreconcilable to Dr. Johnson's surprise
at finding "Young receive as novelties, what he thought very common
maxims."[9] Young's combination of emphases—originality, genius, the
self, the mind—may appear novel, in other words, but it is didactically
elaborated to produce maxims that were unarguably "common." Asking, as Sarah Fielding did, "who has fathomed the mind of man?" may

tickle *our* Romantic antennae, for example, but Young pursues the inquiry along Ancient/Modern lines (233), arriving, like Fielding, at generalized truths he calls "golden rules" (234). Similarly, his discussion of "genius" rings with an almost familiar enthusiasm until cut off with a "caution" against setting "genius, not only above human learning, but divine truth" (230).[10] In both discussions, inherited distinctions are psychologized as states of mind,[11] but, as we saw in Sterne's *A Sentimental Journey,* that apparently private turn inward functions, in interrelation with the didactic use of personification, publicly and didactically. Thus in Young's representation of the battle between the Ancients and the Moderns, the possibility of action continues to be displaced from the personalized "I" to a generalized active agent: "Admiration" does "mischief" (235). Young's variation on this historically normal procedure is, like Collins's and Sterne's, strangely compelling to us now—both foreign and familiar—because he thematizes the problems the procedure appears to pose. Personifying "Genius" as "a dear friend," for example, raises the issue of whether "men may be strangers to their own abilities" (234).

The historicity of such a variation is further evidenced by the fact that the *Conjectures* appears in the same year as the second edition (the first appeared two years earlier in 1757) of Edmund Burke's *A Philosophical Enquiry into the Origin of Our Ideas of the Sublime and the Beautiful.*[12] Both texts call attention to "originality" and "origins," suggesting the use of a developmental framework. But their shared conception of development differs significantly from the Romantic one with which we are familiar; the former admits of gaps and insists upon discontinuity. Operating from a view of knowledge that is sensationalistic and experiential,[13] Burke elaborates a system through the *additive* extension of an absolute distinction between pleasure and pain. The meaning of the system lies in the perpetuation of difference: referring to the qualities of the sublime and the beautiful, Burke claims that he is "in little pain whether any body chuses to follow the name I give them or not, provided he allows that what I dispose under different heads are in reality different things in nature."

Burke codifies these differences into natural laws upon the model of scientific investigation pioneered by Newton. But he recognizes as his own the difficulty Newton then faced:

> When Newton first discovered the property of attraction, and settled its laws, he found it served very well to explain several of the most remarkable phaenomena in nature; but yet with reference to the gen-

eral system of things, he could consider attraction but as an effect, whose cause at that time he did not attempt to trace. But when he afterwards began to account for it by a subtle elastic aether, this great man . . . seemed to have quitted his usual cautious manner of philosophising; since, perhaps, allowing all that has been advanced on this subject to be sufficiently proved, I think it leaves us with as many difficulties as it found us. (129)

All inquiries into origins, including his own, insists Burke, are inevitably incomplete: "I do not pretend that I shall ever be able to explain, why certain affections of the body produce such a distinct emotion of mind, and no other; or why the body is at all affected by the mind, or the mind by the body." As we have already seen in poetic efforts contemporary with the *Enquiry,* such a turn to the past, even when it is explicitly represented as "origin," provides *models* of proper behavior—in this case a framework for binary system-building—not causal *explanation.* The latter knowledge is of another kind: the "great chain of causes," concludes Burke, "which linking one to another even to the throne of God himself, can never be unravelled by any industry of ours" (129).

This type of turn to the past thus occasions a particular type of turn to Presence, one that takes the form of an epistemological disclaimer: man's knowledge cannot pierce God's mystery. The resulting gap between the human and the divine appears explicitly and implicitly throughout the interrelated forms of eighteenth-century discourse. Thomson's *Winter* (first edition, 1726), for example, features the following description of a storm:

> Night o'erwhelms the Sea, and Horror looks
> More horrible. Can human Hearts endure
> Th' assembled *Mischiefs,* that besiege them round:
> Unlist'ning *Hunger,* fainting *Weariness,*
> The *Roar* of Winds, and Waves, the *Crush* of Ice,
> Now, ceasing, now, renew'd, with louder Rage,
> And bellowing round the Main: Nations remote,
> Shook from their Midnight-Slumbers, deem they hear
> Portentous Thunder, in the troubled Sky.
> More to embroil the Deep, Leviathan,
> And his unweildy Train, in horrid Sport,
> Tempest the loosen'd Brine; while, thro' the Gloom,
> Far, from the dire, unhospitable Shore,
> The Lyon's Rage, the Wolf's sad Howl is heard,

And all the fell Society of Night.
Yet, *Providence,* that ever-waking *Eye*
Looks down, with Pity, on the fruitless Toil
Of Mortals, lost to Hope, and *lights* them safe,
Thro' all this dreary Labyrinth of Fate.

(ll. 340–58)

The poet-observer surveys the scene through temporal and spatial movements that allow him to intensify the feeling of horror by adding more horror. To control it, he must invoke God, but he does so in a manner that highlights the characteristic gap. "*Providence*" is suddenly introduced by a "Yet," and its essential separateness from man is emphasized by a shift from auditory to visual sensation. The "ever-waking Eye" saves man from the "*Roar,*" "Thunder," and "Howl" by *lighting* him to safety.

The lesson Burke and his contemporaries would draw from this rescue would be not to venture back near the water: "When we go but one step beyond the immediately sensible qualities of things, we go out of our depth. All we do after, is but a faint struggle, that shows we are in an element which does not belong to us" (*Enquiry,* 129–30). Although Young appears to challenge the surf with a combination of emphases that create in us an expectation of innovation, his embarrassments reaffirm Burke's admonition. The digression to Addison's death is the major structural manifestation of the gap: the living man's original compositions can never earn more than "sublunary praise"; only his dying act of faith can *truly* speak of "human nature not unrelated to the divine" (*Conjectures,* 249—50).

The *Conjectures* is a particularly instructive illustration of this gap, because it thematizes it in linguistic as well as in theological terms. Young's view of originality as a form of psychological competition governed by personified mental states forces him to divide linguistic behavior into the consumptive *versus* the productive. That opposition authorizes questions—"Who knows whether Shakespeare might not have thought less, if he had read more?"—which, in isolating reading from writing, point to the same impasse faced by the speaker as reader/auditor in the "Ode to Fear." Addison's death fixes our attention on this gap. The few words that he speaks, and that we are allowed to overhear and repeat, easily outweigh thousands of written ones to earn the "approbation of angels" (248). Thus, just as Thomson's mariner finds himself surrounded by hostile Nature on the one hand, and by an infinitely superior and unknowable Power on the other, so Young's original writer is isolated from both the apparently debilitating activity of reading and the overpowering sound of his own Voice. To revise, within this scenario, is to *add* without the expectation of transcendence. The laborious revision that is of considerable value within Romantic discourse, however, is of a substantially different sort.

That difference is not a matter of a "problem" that is "solved" by later texts, for the change that occurs authorizes not better but different kinds of communicative activity—kinds that have by now exhibited their own historically specific forms of impasse. At issue, then, is a reclassification: changes in the use of one feature, such as we saw earlier in the elimination of the elevating function of personification, occasion a general shift in interrelations that alters the functions of other features, such as the "I" that, in the absence of personification, became an active agent. The kind/degree workings of such a reclassification—the newly active agent is "a man speaking to men"—apply here as well. The gap illustrates a distinction of kind (human versus divine) that would collapse if reconfigured by degree.

What the reconfiguration formally entailed becomes clearer when, instead of spatializing kind/degree in terms of vertical hierarchy, we reconceive it as the relationship betwen parts and wholes. Then Young's text can be seen as proceeding cumulatively; that is, its parts are fragments whose sum approaches but cannot equal the whole. Because this difference in *kind* between parts and whole represents inherent epistemological and ultimately spiritual limitations,[14] the "embarrassment" of the narrative is the failure of all of its parts to connect temporally and generically into a coherent whole. Their didactic functions conflict, producing different "golden rules" on different topics that, as Young put it, "detract" from the intended overall lesson. Each part functions as a digression in kind from the desired transcendence of the whole.

This historical embarrassment of writing, in other words, posed a generic problem: how to remix kinds so that the result would now invite, rather than digressively call into question, further composition. As we saw in chapter 2, different combinations of features could effect a different part/whole relationship: the lyricizing of the ode in "Tintern Abbey," with its negative transitions, as well as the turn to the radical discontinuity *and* radical continuity of the sonnet, produce narratives of transcendence in which parts and wholes are synecdochically interchangeable. Differing only in degree, they enter into a mutually interactive relationship premised neither on an additive principle nor on neo-Newtonian cause and effect, but on simultaneity:

part as whole and whole as part.[15] While Young's addition posits an unknowable future sum and Newton's causation an equally unknowable past origin, later texts such as Wordsworth's[16] provide, not answers, but a conceptual and temporal rearrangement that obviates any need for them. Obscurity of either origin or tendency would prove troublesome for Wordsworth, but he turns their shared obscurity into reassuring doctrine: "origin and tendency are notions inseparably co-relative." The child is part of what the man will be, but at the same time the man is but a part of what the child was. Each epistemologically accesses the other through the positing of growth as continuous revision.

That notion was central to a rhetoric of development that Wordsworth elaborates in verse and prose, through arguments both theological and philosophical, as well as psychological and linguistic. Development has been so thoroughly naturalized into *truth* by that rhetoric, that its historical and formal relationship to the labor of revision has been obscured. Recovering that relationship thus entails historicizing the rhetoric, including the passage that de Man found so compelling (see chapter 2) on the co-relativity of origin and tendency:

> Never did a child stand by the side of a running stream, pondering within himself what power was the feeder of the perpetual current, from what never-wearied sources the body of water was supplied, but he must have been inevitably propelled to follow this question by another: "towards what abyss is it in progress? what receptacle can contain the mighty influx?" And the spirit of the answer must have been . . . nothing less than infinity. (*Prose*, II, 52)

Bridging Young's theological gap—once it is reconfigured in these terms—is kid's stuff: children who "meditate feelingly" upon their own sense of divine origin thus surmise an equally illustrious end. Wordsworth seeks to make these "intimations of immortality" so significant that he places the ode that enshrines them in a category of its own at the end of the collected poems. They also elicit the following confession:

> with me the conviction is absolute, that, if the impression and sense of death were not thus counterbalanced, such a hollowness would pervade the whole system of things, such a want of correspondence and consistency, and disproportion so astounding betwixt ends and means, that there could be no repose, no joy (*Prose,* II, 52)

The religious language in which these developmental arguments are cast should not mislead us into thinking that Wordsworth's supposed turn toward orthodoxy is the sole concern raised by the "intimations." The gospel they proclaim becomes the gospel truth of development, for they describe and exercise the strategies of transcendence that shape all Romantic discourse. Notice, for example, the relationship established in these statements between the "progress" of the "running stream" and joyful "repose." They are linked within a development scheme that posits change as substantial and inevitable (the stream does run), but also robs it of its sting by valorizing it as evidence of absolute continuity (the repose is unchanging). In other words, this rhetoric assumes and establishes a relationship between parts and wholes that we can now define more precisely as essentially interpretative[17]: each part modifies the meaning of the whole while the whole simultaneously modifies the (transcendent) meaning of each part.

That kind of relationship, which we now classify as hermeneutical, informs the Romantic rewriting of the concepts of memory and habit, and is in turn naturalized by them. Remembering, for Wordsworth, is not a passive and arbitrary act of recollection; rather, it becomes an active and highly selective process by engendering its opposite. The poet forges a sense of identity in Books I and II of the 1805 *Prelude* not through perfect recall of childhood events and emotions, but by remembering *and* forgetting:

> . . . if the vulgar joy by its own weight
> Wearied itself out of the memory,
> The scenes which were a witness of that joy
> Remained, in their substantial lineaments
> Depicted on the brain. . . .
>
> (I.625–29)

> . . . the soul
> Remembering how she felt, but what she felt
> Remembering not. . . .
>
> (II.335–36)[18]

As later feeings are substituted for the earlier ones, the sublime forms of nature become "habitually dear" and are "allied to the affections" by "invisible links" (I.638–40). The connections are forged, not through habit understood as enslavement to custom, but through habit *developed* dynamically as part of the process of growth. In terms of the part/whole relationship described above, habit is posited as a continuously modified product of the very experiences it processes. To cast the psychological as the revisionary, is thus to naturalize the latter while rewriting the former as a means of transcendence: Wordsworth understands the habit that plays an interpretative role in the formation of meaning and identity to be essentially *creative*.

In the unpublished fragment on "Morals," probably written in Germany in the winter of 1798, he uses this concept of habitual creativity to combat what he has come to see as "Mr. Godwyn's" over-reliance on reason in moral matters. Operating from the psychological assumption that "in a [?strict] sense all of our actions are the result of our habits," Wordsworth argues that "bald & naked reasonings are impotent over" them; "they cannot form them; from the same cause they are equally powerless in regulating our judgments concerning the value of men & things. They contain no picture of human life; they *describe* nothing" (*Prose*, I, 103). The connections that Wordsworth suggests here among habit, morality, and description are intriguing, but the fragment ends a paragraph later without much further explanation. It is not till two years later that he indicates just how central they are to his poetic enterprise. "The Poems in these volumes," argues Wordsworth in the 1800 Preface to *Lyrical Ballads*,

> will be found distinguished at least by one mark of difference, that each of them has a worthy *purpose*. Not that I mean to say, that I always began to write with a distinct purpose formally conceived; but I believe that my habits of meditation have so formed my feelings, as that my descriptions of such objects as strongly excite those feelings, will be found to carry along with them a *purpose*. If in this opinion I am mistaken I can have little right to the name of a Poet. (*Prose*, I, 124, 126)

Such high stakes deserve our literary historical attention, because the risk Wordsworth is taking is to tie his "name" to the function of a particular formal procedure. To put it in the framework that we established in the second part of the last chapter, the issue here is how description that is no longer georgically didactic still carries a consistently moral significance.

The answer is the work of revision, but not the work that comes after composition; it is the revisionary work of *habit* that earns a

man the "name of a poet" by ensuring that his Imagination is as
naturally ethical as it is naturally productive. "All good poetry,"
argues Wordsworth,

> is the spontaneous overflow of powerful feelings; but though this be
> true, Poems to which any value can be attached, were never produced
> on any variety of subjects but by a man who being possessed of more
> than usual organic sensibility had also thought long and deeply. . . .
> [S]uch habits of mind will be produced [by having our feelings and
> thoughts modify each other] that by obeying blindly and mechanically
> the impulses of those habits we shall describe objects and utter senti-
> ments of such a nature and in such connection with each other, that the
> understanding of the being to whom we address ourselves, if he be in a
> healthful state of association, must necessarily be in some degree en-
> lightened, his taste exalted, and his affections ameliorated. (*Prose*, I,
> 126)

The key to the kind of description that enacts the paradox of moral
objectivity is a complementary relationship between revision and
spontaneity. To be specific, habit's revisionary quality, depicted here
in terms of the mutual modification of thought and feeling, ensures
that spontaneity is a blindly mechanical response productive of descriptive verse invariably exhibiting the habitual moral associations.
The stylistic credo of "look[ing] steadily at my subject"[19] is thus not a
guarantee of "genuine simplicity" (*Early Letters*, 328), but a promise
of what I am terming interpretative activity: to describe without
"falsehood" is to interpret with good intentions. The transparent poet
of nature *is* the disciplinary poet of mind.

    That discipline is exercised, as we saw in the last chapter, as a
matter of "health." In this case, it takes the form of insisting that the
revisionary habits of the reader match the poet's. Why the rhetoric of
development features this need to identify can be clarified by a brief
return to Young. His original writer, we discovered, was left without
an audience: the most important act of communication described in the
Conjectures is between a "deathbed" that "speaks" and a "heaven"
that "read[s]." Discourse has been removed from the human realm,
leaving Young to yearn for the magical means to make the "monumental marble" of Addison's tomb tell the tale: "yet it is silent on a subject,
which (if any) might have taught its unletter'd stones to speak" (250).
The marble is blank as long as description functions as a *turn* from the
particular object to a general truth that the object points toward but
cannot fully embody. But when that function shifts, such that descrip-

tion entails a *steady* look at the single subject, each of those subjects is made to have depth; the gaze (re)produces the deep truth of the whole in every part, so that each contains the other and the interpretative activity between them "naturally" *never* stops. When Wordsworth "describes" monumental marble, neither he nor it are at a loss for words: "As soon as nations had learned the use of letters, epitaphs were inscribed upon these monuments; in order that their intention might be more surely and adequately fulfilled" (*Prose,* II, 50). By establishing the epitaph as the primal form for language, Wordsworth bridges Young's linguistic gap the same way he did the theological one: origin and tendency are reconciled. As Francis Ferguson has observed,

> Wordsworth established the sign of mortality at the origin of language, so that the incarnation of language always seems to involve a gesture not merely towards the feelings which precede language but also towards the disembodied state of immortality which no longer has need of language.[20]

Since the epitaph is both the speech of the dead and the writing of the living, as death ceases to be a sign of discontinuity within Wordsworth's developmental rhetoric, speaking and writing are reconciled. That reconciliation is one of Wordsworth's primary concerns in the comments on language prefacing the *Lyrical Ballads.* Even in the brief Advertisement to the 1798 edition, he argues that the poems "were written chiefly with a view to ascertain how far the language of *conversation* in the middle and lower classes of society is adopted to the purposes of poetic pleasure" (emphasis mine; *Prose,* I, 116). The Preface(s) make it clear that, as in Young, speech is still the ideal, for a poet is a "man speaking to men" and "his situation is altogether slavish and mechanical compared with the freedom and power of real and substantial action and suffering" (*Prose,* I, 138). However, Wordsworth establishes this hierarchy only to challenge it through a characteristically revisionary strategy that submits the primal act of speech to the same interpretative process we earlier saw applied to his primal childhood experiences. Just as the author of *The Prelude* creates his identity by remembering and forgetting parts of his personal past, so the poet *writes* poetry by remembering and forgetting parts of the originary speech act. He remembers its generative emotion but forgets its accompanying "painful" feelings, by first "adopting" and then modifying the real language of men (*Prose,* I, 148–51). The result is that the distinction of kind between speech and writing collapses into a distinction of degree; the writer need no longer fear the sound of his own voice.

Again, this is not a matter of problem and solution, for the sense of difference that had occasioned that fear has not been figured out; it has been reconfigured as an opportunity for development. It is an opportunity that the author demands the audience take, for development makes sense of change as normal only if everyone changes in the same basic ways. To make sure that they do, the demand itself is naturalized as a seduction. Wordsworth's "experiments" with the "language of conversation" must produce the proper amount and kind of "pleasure," if the writer who aspires to speech is to have an imminent, active audience with which to converse. The necessity of producing such seductive pleasure, Wordsworth is careful to point out in the Preface, is not

> a degradation of the poet's art . . . it is a homage paid to the native and naked dignity of man, to the grand elementary principle of pleasure, by which he knows, and feels, and lives, and moves. We have no sympathy but what is propagated by pleasure. (*Prose*, I, 140)

The reader enticed by pleasure can thus respond with sympathy, the act of identification being the only means of making "conversation" poems make sense: "the voice which is the voice of my poetry," insists Wordsworth, "without Imagination cannot be heard."[21] This myth of imaginative community is, as we have seen, yet another manifestation of the collapsing of distinctions of kind into distinctions of degree: speech and writing, poetry and prose, poets and "other men," writer and reader, all close quarters in the Preface. The language of "kind" and "degree" clearly allows Wordsworth to idealize the results of the reworking of change into development as the end of elitist hierarchy. Once we historicize development itself as a strategy, we see that its rhetoric naturalizes a shift in the procedure that does the work: revision's function is no longer additive but interpretative. And, just as that mode of interpretation always seeks a final clarification of meaning, so the wished-for end of development *and* of Romantic revision is a Unity that transcends difference.

To speak of the Romantic lyric in terms of subordinating form to expressive unity is, as I pointed out in chapter 2, to be trapped within the discourse of that desire. Romantic revision has done its work so well, that the *sense* of "natural" spontaneity and creative unity it produces blinds us to the ways in which the specific uses of revision configure the "truths" of development. I want now to pursue those formal configurations by relating the variety of Wordsworth's revisionary strategies to the models of developmental order he attempted to produce. Doing so will allow us to engage the form of the Romantic lyric (and Romanticism as an age of lyric) generically instead of thematically, as a matter of historically characteristic features and procedures rather than as an ultimately ephemeral restraint on the Poet's creativity. The revisionary labor at issue includes not only the actual rewriting of texts, but also the initial composing, prefacing, and classifying of them. In each case, revision manifests itself Romantically in the mutually interpretative relationship between parts and wholes, on a small scale accounting for the characteristic "organic" form of the individual Romantic lyric, and on a large scale describing the shape of the whole oeuvre of which each lyric is but a part.

"Tintern Abbey" has served as our example of what I shall now call intratextual, as opposed to extratextual, revision. By the latter, I mean the use of prefaces and classificatory schemes to change not the text itself, but how it is read; the former, on the other hand, refers to a similarly interpretative principle at work in the composing process, such that even "unrevised" texts exhibit revisionary behavior. If we are to believe the Duke of Argyle's account, "Tintern Abbey" was written in four days and, according to the Fenwick note, "not a line of it was altered."[22] However, we have seen that its abrupt and negative transitions place its parts (verse paragraphs) in revisionary relationships that effect spontaneity and suggest transcendence.

Rather than reifying the effect and the suggestion as absolute aesthetic criteria for all "creative" verse, and thus completing critically the canonizing work of Literature, we can historize the individual work and the work it demands by identifying genre and function. "I have not ventured," wrote Wordsworth, "to call this Poem an Ode; but it was written with a hope that in the transitions, and the impassioned music of the versification, would be found the principal requisites of that species of composition."[23] In defining the ode in terms of its transitions and passions, Wordsworth is following the conventional eighteenth-century line: Joseph Trapp, for example, in his 1713 lecture of "Of Lyric Poetry," identifies the lyric with the ode and concludes that it is chiefly notable for "that Energy of Expression; that Quickness of Transition, and Liberty of Excursion; that lively Ardour."[24] The historical continuity lies in the association of that type of transition with the ode; the discontinuity is in how its function changes as the ode comes to perform different tasks. Within an ode directed to a personification of an abstract idea (e.g., "Ode to Fear"), the "quick" turns signal the spatial and temporal movements that confirm the universality of the idea (Fear is also present and is the same in ancient Greece). But within an ode in which the "I" is the active agent, those turns function reflexively to suggest a self that, being of constantly differing parts, is a whole that can—in fact, always does—revise itself: this "I" develops.

The kind of text that writes that deep self is generically and historically specific not only in its transitions, but also in such other areas as closure. Thus Shelley's "Mont Blanc" also features an "I" reflexively turned upon its "own separate phantasy" of "mind" (ll.36–37) by an odelike division into abruptly distinct parts and an abundance of qualifiers and negatives:

> The Wilderness has a mysterious tongue
> Which teaches awful doubt, *or* faith so mild,
> So solemn, so serene, that man may be
> *But* for such faith with nature reconciled;
> Thou hast a voice, great Mountain, to repeal
> Large Codes of fraud and woe; *not* understood
> By all, *but* which the wise, and great, and good
> Interpret, *or* make felt, *or* deeply feel.
>
> (emphasis mine; ll. 76–83)

To end such twists and turns without ending the sense of transcendence they occasion, Shelley concludes the poem with a question— "And what were thou, and earth, and stars, and sea, / If to the human mind's imaginings / Silence and solitude were vacancy?"—that, in addressing the mountain as "thou" (l. 142), effectively turns momentum over to the reader.

The implications of that transfer are particularly evident in "Tintern Abbey," which also cannot end on a note of revisionary transcendence and unlimited depth unless Wordsworth presents it as a fragment or only temporarily curbs the production of new parts. He performs the latter feat not with a question, but by introducing his sister as a mirror of himself and as a surrogate for the reader: poet and reader thus achieve their desired consummation in Dorothy. This allows Wordsworth to transfer the task of the poem to her, thereby making the private public, but to do so requires that he eliminate himself from the poem. Thus he imagines his own death: "If I should be where I no more can hear / Thy voice" (ll. 147–48). In other words, what Roland Barthes presented as a major critical insight in 1968 is a narrative feature of the Romantic lyric: the interpretative search for transcendent meaning can end only with the "birth of the reader . . . at the cost of the death of the Author." "The reign of the Author," as Barthes indicates, "has also been that of the Critic,"[25] because, as an understanding of Romantic revision makes clear, the interpretative work of Literature belies any absolute distinction between the "creative" artist and the "analytic" critic.

The sheer volume of the extratextual manifestations of that work, from Blake's prospectuses to Byron's footnotes to Shelley's *Defence,* is startling, but it is particularly so in regard to Wordsworth. *Lyrical Ballads* in its various editions, for example, felt the weight of an advertisement, a preface, revisions of that preface, an appendix, and a note. After the supposed Great Decade we find the same kind and amount of activity: at least seven different prefatory pieces in various combinations burdened the poor *White Doe of Rylestone* in its various appearances. It was first published in 1815 prefixed by an advertisement, a dedicatory poem, the sonnet "Weak is the will of man," and a passage from Bacon's essay "Of Atheism." A prose preface, now lost, and twelve lines from Daniel's *Musophilus* had been considered and rejected. New material was added and the old reshuffled over the next five editions, culminating in the standard 1849–50 version which featured the advertisement, dedication, thirteen lines of Wordsworth's poetry (six from *The Borderers* and the rest original), and the quotation from Bacon.[26]

This revisionary activity is intended to work not by altering what we read, but how we read it: the enemy, Wordsworth is telling us, is not a faulty text but our "pre-established codes of decision" (*Prose,* I 116). Our bad *habits* are a sign of developmental failure that invites a literary cure. Thus, in the selection of materials prefixed to *The White Doe,* Wordsworth tries to establish a model of proper sympathetic identification; he attempts to constitute a communicative community for his poem by molding the reader's habitual expectations to match his own. The dedicatory verse addressed to Mary relating incidents from the poet's private life, for example, functions similarly to the letter to Wordsworth's friend, Robert Jones, heading *Descriptive Sketches,* to prepare the reader for sympathetic exertions by engaging his interest on a personal level. In the poem that follows, beginning "Action is transitory—a step, a blow," Wordsworth assumes a more public role to inform the reader of the seriousness of his subject and the philosophical position (faith in a "fountainhead of peace divine") from which he is speaking and at which he expects the reader to arrive.

Because Wordsworth was both eager to have his readers "arrive" and convinced that, if they did not, it was their fault, he often accompanied his prefatory efforts with disclaimers indicative of an ambivalence that was never resolved and that was at times almost humorous. In 1845 he wrote Moxon:

> Having long wished that an Edition of my Poems should be published without the Prefaces and supplement, I submit to your consideration whether that would not be well, (printing, however, the prose now attached to the Volumes as a portion of the Prose Volumes which you meditate). The Prefaces, etc contain many important observations upon Poetry—but they were written solely to gratify Coleridge; and, for my own part, being quite against anything of the kind, and having always been of opinion that Poetry should stand upon its own merits, I would not even attach to the Poems any explanation of the grounds of their arrangement. I should however by all means wish that the Vol. of prose should be printed uniform with the Poems.[27]

Even as he disowns the prefaces by blaming them on Coleridge, Wordsworth is doubly careful to insist that the poetry not appear without them. The issue here, however, is not Wordsworth's ego, for what appears to be solely personal ambivalence is in fact a behavior explicable in terms of the revisionary relationship between parts and wholes that we are examining. On this historical basis, such ambivalence can be grouped with the poet's comments on his sonnet sequences, his gothic church image, his system for classifying his poems, and *The Prelude*. All four connect within Wordsworth's career-long concern[28] with the interrelationships between individual poems and larger organizational schemes or generic groupings, and they all offer two answers to the question of whether a poem "should stand upon its own merits": yes *and* no.

With such a dual response Wordsworth defended his *Sonnets Dedicated to Liberty* in a May 1807 letter to Lady Beaumont:

> there is one thing which must strike you at once if you will only read these poems,—[they], at least, have a connection with, or a bearing upon, each other, and therefore, if individually they want weight, perhaps, as a Body, they may not be so deficient, at least this ought to induce you to suspend your judgement, and qualify it so far as to allow that the writer aims at least at comprehensiveness. But dropping this, I

> would boldly say at once, that these Sonnets, while they each fix the attention upon some important sentiment separately considered, do at the same time collectively make a Poem on the subject of civil Liberty and national independence, which, either for simplicity of style or grandeur of moral sentiment, is alas! likely to have few parallels in the Poetry of the present day. (*Middle Letters*, I, 147)

Since each sonnet is both a poem *and* a piece of a Poem, the mutually interpretative relationship between parts and wholes that we observed in "Tintern Abbey" is operative here as well. In fact, Wordsworth himself suggested an analogy between sonnets and verse paragraphs, when he noted that in his *Ecclesiastical Sketches* "the pictures are often so closely connected as to have jointly the effect of passages of a poem in a form of stanza" (*Poems*, III, 557). Even the kinds of transitions used to connect these sonnets/stanzas resemble those found in "Tintern Abbey": "When I have a large amount of Sonnets in a series," he wrote to Taylor, "I have not been unwilling to start sometimes with a logical connection of a 'Yet' or a 'But'" (*Later Letters*, III, 1097).

The need to make such connections is everywhere in Wordsworth, because it is a manifestation of the demand within Romantic revision's developmental framework for absolutely continuous growth. No matter how large the work, there is always a "connection" to a larger one. Thus his response to Patty Smith's accusation that *The Excursion* lacked "passion," was to remind the audacious *"Woman"* that his poem was

> *part* of a work . . . and that if I had introduced stories exciting curiosity, and filled with violent conflicts of passion and a rapid interchange of striking incidents, these things could never have harmonized with the rest of the work and all further discourse, comment, or reflections must have been put a stop to.[29]

The work, of course, is *The Recluse,* and what we have here is a "gothic church" defense which allows Wordsworth to justify all his poems by citing their "connections" (*Prose*, III, 5–6) to a whole that is itself actually a fragment. Wordsworth's defensiveness arises from the desire to deny that fragmentation[30] by submitting meaning to revision through larger and larger wholes so that it cannot finally be circumscribed. The end of revision is the poet's oeuvre: the transcendent signified for each of the parts.

The organization of that oeuvre is thus of absolute importance to Wordsworth; part of the work of Literature that he performs throughout his career is to perfect the two structures that he hopes will give it order: *The Prelude* and the system for classifying his poems. Since the order of Romantic revision is always developmental, one posits origin in the poet's mind and the other tendency in the completed work. Their co-relativity lies in their extra-Textuality, the text they both comment on being the Poem that is Wordsworth's completed oeuvre. Both are thus variations of the same habitual behavior identified earlier: *The Prelude* is yet another preface, and the "guiding wish" behind the classification system, Wordsworth informs us, is an "arrangement" of psychologically, formally, and thematically defined parts within a developmentally framed whole that "has long presented itself habitually to my mind" (*Prose,* III, 28). As with the other extratextual devices, the more Wordsworth works on them, the greater his defensiveness: *The Prelude* is not the product of "self-conceit" but "real humility" (*Early Letters,* 586–87), and his classification system is preferable to printing the poems in the order of their composition, for the latter would clearly be an act of unconscionable "egotism" (*Prose,* III, 127).

Until recently, almost all the critics who have addressed the classification system have indicated a preference for such authorial egotism, which is not surprising considering Barthes's connection between "the reign of the Author" and "that of the Critic." James Heffernan has even suggested that the Wordsworth who produced the 1815 system was not really the Wordsworth we all know and love: "Wordsworth himself *was* finished in 1814." Like so many of his colleagues, Heffernan does not and cannot reconcile the author of "Tintern Abbey," a poem that proceeds through the positing of overlapping alternatives, with the author of a system that classifies a poem "*either* generically *or* thematically *or* psychologically." All critics who slice Wordsworth's career in this way carry a similar switchblade up their sleeves; its cutting edge is an absolute distinction between the creative and the critical: the post-1814 pseudo-Wordsworth "can no longer create; he can only analyze, classify, and thus marmorealize what he has created." For Heffernan, then, the model for the behavior of *truly* Wordsworthian discourse is the 1798–1805 *Prelude:* "a growing chronology of the growth of a poet's mind, a vital and self-animating story of consciousness that vacillatingly and yet inexorably moves towards its visionary destination."[31]

This way of describing the behavior of Wordsworthian (and Romantic) discourse is as misleading as it is familiar, for it is grounded in the very distinctions that our analysis of interpretative revision has called into question. Because he assumes that criticism and creativity are mutually exclusive opposites, Heffernan must see the classified *Poems* of 1815 as an "attempt to displace" the "poem that gives . . . the unclassified process of a life that is *being* lived even as the poem is being written" (111). But *The Prelude* provides no such service and thus never suffered under such a threat. Experiences, autobiographical or otherwise, are textual parts for the poet and he manipulates them between 1798 and 1805 in fundamentally the same manner as he does between 1805 and 1850: he classifies and reclassifies them to meet and shape the demands of a constantly changing whole. Just as the oeuvre/Poem is the transcendent signified for the poet's "minor Pieces," so the notion of a Poetic Identity provides revisionary meaning for the pieces of the poet's life as that life is literally lyricized into poetry. To write the wholes is to read the parts and the Romantic poet as critic is critic as pluralist: one who celebrates diversity with a higher unity always in mind.

Wordsworth thus rejects a simple compositional chronology as a means of arranging his poems, and a straightforward experiential chronology as a basis for organizing his autobiography. Like the former, the latter becomes a highly complex classificatory scheme with overlapping rationales for placing each experience so as "to direct the Reader's attention by its position to its *primary* interest" (*Middle Letters,* I, 336). That interest can be psychological (Book XI: Imagination, How Impaired and Restored), or thematic (Book VIII: Retrospect: Love of Nature Leading to Love of Mankind), or chronological (Book I: Introduction: Childhood and School-time), or even generic (Book V: Books [experiences as written texts]). The fact that these headings, like those found in the arrangement, are ambiguous (is "Love of Nature" thematic or psychological?) is but additional proof that *The Prelude* is vulnerable to the same charge Heffernan levels at the 1815 arrangement: the more we study it, "the more labyrinthine it becomes" (109). The autobiographical labyrinth is no more and no less "organic" than the classificatory one, for the formal basis of Romantic Organic Unity is the mutually interpretative part/whole relationship enacted in Romantic revision.

The sense of continuous development, or growth, that we identify with the Romantic lyric is thus an *effect* of such revisionary behavior. To explore further how those effects are produced, I want to turn now to an example of revision in its familiar guise as rewriting; I will

follow the fate of the "Drowned Man" episode in the *Prelude* versions
of 1799 (I.258–87), 1805 (V.450–81), and 1850 (V.436–59). Following the advice of Gene Ruoff, Judith Herman, and Donald Ross, Jr.,
to take seriously the relationship between Wordsworth's classificatory scheme and his shorter poems, and having identified *The Prelude*
as one of those schemes, we can regard the "Drowned Man" as a
short lyrical piece classified within a much longer one.[32]

The formal core of the 1799 version is readily identifiable:

> The succeeding day
> There came a company and in their boat
> Sounded with iron hooks and with long poles.
> At length the dead man, 'mid that beauteous scene
> Of trees and hills and water, bolt upright
> Rose with his ghastly face. I might advert
> To numerous accidents in flood or field,
> Quarry or moor, or 'mid the winter snows,
> Distresses and disasters, tragic facts
> Of rural history, that impressed my mind
> With images to which in following years
> Far other feelings were attached—with forms
> That yet exist with independent life,
> And, like their archetypes, know no decay.
>
> (ll.274–87)

The structure and style of these fourteen lines is not a matter of
"natural" flow; rather, they form a coherent unit consisting of a sestet
bound to an octet by a clearly marked turn: "I might *advert.*" In other
words, this is an embedded sonnet. To thus deconstruct a long poem
into its *formal* parts is not to use the critical present to violate the
creative past, but actually to follow in Wordsworth's own footsteps.
Crabb Robinson recorded how the poet extracted fourteen lines from
Paradise Lost "which he says are a perfect sonnet without rhyme."[33]
Such extractions confirm the "habitual" connection I have been suggesting between the poet's view of his sonnet sequences and his conception of *The Prelude.* Both need to be analyzed in terms of a
characteristic relationship between parts and wholes.

The sequence of parts in this 1799 version indicates why Wordsworth avoided a relationship based on straightforward chronological
schemes. Of the three different *Prelude*(s) under discussion, this one
is most constrained by such a chronology: "Each of the two parts,"
observes J. R. MacGillivray, "has its own limits in time: the first

being of childhood and to the age of about ten, the second until the
end of school days when the narrator was seventeen."[34] Because of
these limits, the poet cannot radically disturb temporal contiguity. If
"position" is to indicate "primary interest" in such a chronology, he
has only two organizational options other than wholesale deletion:
either too many experiences demonstrating the same interest or too
many interests to be coherently ordered. Wordsworth faces up to the
latter fate:

> It were a song
> Venial, and such as—if I rightly judge—
> I might protract unblamed, but I perceive
> That much is overlooked, and we should ill
> Attain our object if, from delicate fears
> Of breaking in upon the unity
> Of this my argument, I should omit
> To speak of such effects as cannot here
> Be regularly classed, yet tend no less
> To the same point, the growth of mental power
> And love of Nature's works.
>
> (ll.248–58)

The "Drowned Man" follows, and thus is explicitly presented as a
classificatory problem. At stake once again is the principle of co-
relativity. To make "tend[ency]" co-relative with origin, the discovery of which is the "object" Wordsworth wants to "attain," the incidents must be properly placed. Those immediately preceding this
crisis of arrangement can be "regularly classed" as examples of a
ministry that

> Impressed upon all forms the characters
> Of danger or desire, and thus did make
> The surface of the universal earth
> With meanings of delight, of hope and fear,
> Work like a sea.
>
> (ll.194–98)

But those incidents that follow the crisis and the "Drowned Man" can
be even more succinctly labeled: "There are in our existence spots of
time" (l.288).

Thus "bolt upright" between an earlier "ministry" and later
"spots of time" rises a corpse that Wordsworth has trouble reembed-

ding in his narrative. He attempts an autopsy, but the results announced in the octet quoted above (ll.279–87) are not definitive: we learn only what "might" have been the case. The editors of the Norton edition I am quoting from indicate that the theory of the same "form" and other "feelings" that is conditionally presented "has no counterpart in later versions of *The Prelude*" (8), which is of course true, if they mean only that this particular passage is deleted and replaced by a substantially different one. However, I would argue that it is deleted precisely because it *does* have counterparts in all three *Prelude*(s) as well as elsewhere in Wordsworth. The poet, as we have seen, repeatedly describes his development in terms of *revising* the past through remembering *and* forgetting: "lineaments" are retained, original feelings are lost, and new ones substituted.[35] Thus for Wordsworth such an autopsy is not irregular; his "might" raises the issue of whether, in this case, it is an accurate and comprehensive indication of the episode's primary interest.

To highlight its singularities and yet prevent it from totally disrupting the narrative, the experience must be reclassified within an elaborated classificatory scheme. *The Prelude* "grows" between 1798 and 1805 only in the sense that Wordsworth's system for arranging his poems "grows" between *Lyrical Ballads* (1798) and *Poems in Two Volumes* (1807).[36] The episode changes in that it is re-placed. Appropriately enough for a text that Wordsworth has found difficult to read, it is included within a section on the value of reading texts, a shift that results not in two mutually exclusive versions, but in two mutually interpretative ones. The allusion to *Othello* in the 1799 text—

> I might advert
> To numerous accidents in flood or field
> (ll.279–80)

> Wherein I spake of most disastrous chances,
> Of moving accidents by flood and field
> (*Othello,* I.iii.134–35)

—suggests a correlation between literal experience and literary experience that becomes the informing idea of the 1805 revision. When the "ghastly face" appeared, writes Wordsworth in the new version,

> . . . no vulgar fear
> Young as I was, a child not nine years old,

> Possessed me, for my inner eye had seen
> Such sights before among the shining streams
> Of fairyland, the forests of romance—
>
> (1805, V.473–77)

Conversely, the introduction of new feelings in 1805 illuminates and substantiates the "remembering and forgetting" argument of 1799.

In arranging for the resurfacing of the corpse in 1805, Wordsworth seems concerned with smoothing out the transitions occasioned by its earlier appearance. In all matters of classification, Wordsworth wrote to Crabb Robinson, "one poem should shade off happily into another . . . and the contrasts where they occur be clear of all harshness and abruptness . . . if this be not attended to [by] classification by subject, or by mould or form . . . nothing can compensate for the neglect of it."[37] "Books" is a class that embraces both subject and form, in that it calls our attention both to experiences about books and to the revisionary ways in which books "write" experiences and experiences themselves are books to be "read." The latter phenomenon becomes the "primary interest" of the "Drowned Man" episode in its new position; together with its surrounding texts, it raises an important issue of Romantic textual economics: how the mutually interpretative maneuvers of revision produce lyrical value.

Immediately preceding the "Drowned Man," Wordsworth describes the "race of young ones" with whom he "herded," indicating that, although they "might have fed upon a fatter soil / Of Arts and Letters," they are still to be celebrated above all others as "a race of real children." The hope he expresses in the passage's concluding lines—

> May books and nature be their early joy,
> And knowledge, rightly honored with that name—
> Knowledge not purchased with the loss of power!
>
> (1805, V.447–49)

—is the epistemological equivalent of the poetical aspiration expressed in the Preface to *Lyrical Ballads:* to write experiences into poetry without losing the supposedly natural power of the original (speech) acts. For the author of *The Prelude,* writing experiences into poetry is the forming of identity, and thus he too must face the same question: can the dead word "purchase," that is, have the same value as, the living experience? The "Drowned Man" can answer in the

affirmative merely by making a now timely appearance, for he represents an experience of death whose only worth is that supplied by the
living word of the child's favorite authors. This 1805 revision thus
suggests how a mutually interpretative relationship between the "life"
of speech and written composition approaches what might be called a
revisionary equivalence: as experiences become texts, texts become
experiences. The end of Romantic revision, as I stressed earlier, is
always transcendence of differences. Thus the episode closes with the
following intimation of immortality for man made text:

> Thence came a spirit hallowing what I saw
> With decoration and ideal grace,
> A dignity, a smoothness, like the words
> Of Grecian art and purest poesy.
>   (1805, V.478–81)

But once a child—and, of course, the man he fathers—has a taste
of such transcendence, he wants more, as Wordsworth indicates in
the very next verse paragraph:

> I had a precious treasure at that time,
> A little yellow canvass-covered book,
> A slender abstract of the *Arabian Tales;*
> And when I learned, as now I first did learn
> From my companions in this new abode,
> That this dear prize of mine was but a block
> Hewn from a mighty quarry—in a word,
> That there were four large volumes, laden all
> With kindred matter—'twas in truth to me
> A promise scarcely earthly.
>   (1805, V.482–91)

To obtain this quarry, Wordsworth makes "a covenant with a friend"
to "hoard up" their "monies," but despite months of "religiously"
resisting "temptation," they never became "masters" of their "wish."
Their additive approach to transcendence, in which the sum of limited
parts is somehow supposed to equal an unlimited whole, inevitaby
leaves a gap analagous to Young's and Thomson's—one that no
seeker, however zealous, can overcome. That gap mocks their efforts
just as the "pauses of deep silence" mock the skillful hootings of the
Boy of Winander, in a passage positioned with the "Knowledge/
Power" lines just prior to the "Drowned Man" (ll. 385–422).

Romantic narratives, as I have been emphasizing, do not "close" the gap, for the interchangeability of parts and wholes effects turns that obviate the need for such closure. The turn in which the Boy is "taken from his mates" becomes an epitaphic occasion for asserting the co-relativity of origin and tendency; his silences, when placed before the speaker's ("I have stood / Mute," ll.421–22), suggest not a gap, but something evermore about to be. The "hoarding" episode is also capped by an epitaphic turn into a new verse paragraph. This one, however, is not toward heaven but toward its earthly equivalent:

> And afterwards, when, to my *father's house*
> *Returning* at the holidays, I found
> That golden store of books which I had left
> Open to my enjoyment once again,
> What heart was mine!
> (emphasis mine; 1805, V.501–5)

Just as the "yellow" book was but a part of a whole quarry, so that quarry, in turn, is but a part of the whole "golden store of books." Narratives that proceed through these interpretative turns make up the same end. The formal *effect* is what Heffernan naturalizes as "growth": a "self-animating story" that "moves toward" the animation of the self by re-moving deadly gaps. As the parts reform, they valorize the changing whole as a whole that is valuable because it changes: "What heart was mine!"

The labor of revision thus lays the "Drowned Man" to rest in Book V. The narrative problem he posed is seemingly resolved by the connections of "primary interest" suggested above, and by such scrambled imagistic links as the "fields . . . shaped like ears" (l.457) listening in silence, though not for owls but the garment's "tale" (l.467), and the boy watching over a grave made not of dirt but water (l.462). The classified corpse is no more a disturbance to the reader who has just read "There was a boy" than the actual drowned man was to the young Wordsworth who had read "Jack the Giant-killer" (1805, V.366). Major displacement is therefore not needed after 1805, though a few significant revisions are yet to come. All relate to the replacement of the 1805 line "Went there a company, and in their boat" (l.468) with the three lines italicized below:

> The succeeding day,
> Those unclaimed garments telling a plain tale

Drew to the spot an anxious crowd; some looked
In passive expectation from the shore,
While from a boat others hung o'er the deep,
Sounding with grappling irons and long poles,
At last, the dead man, 'mid that beauteous scene
Of trees and hills and water, bolt upright
Rose, with his ghastly face, a spectre shape
Of terror; yet no soul-debasing fear,
Young as I was, a child not nine years old,
Possessed me, for my inner eye had seen
Such sights before, among the shining streams
Of faery land, the forests of romance.
                                        (1850, V.442–55)

The Norton editors, from their exclusively thematic perspective, observe that the new lines "place the solitary experience recorded in
1799 and *1805* in an untypically social context" (177). Their exact
meaning is unclear, for the social context had already been established in the earlier versions by the presence of the "company." Is
this, then, only a matter of emphasis?

I think not, for a close look back at the passage just quoted and
at our discussion of "Tintern Abbey" can demonstrate its formal and
narrative significance. The revision actually adds two lines to the
quoted passage, bringing the total to fourteen, including one six-line
and one eight-line sentence. In other words, the embedded sonnet
from 1799 has reappeared in revised form. But this is not the only
such reappearance occasioned by the 1805–50 revision. Evidence
from MS. Z of April–May 1805 suggests that Book X of 1805 was
originally conceived as two separate books, bringing the total for *The
Prelude* to fourteen.[38] This division, of course, was reinstated for the
1850 version. As a result of both these actions, we have a sonnet
embedded in a Sonnet, a point I raise here primarily to remind us
that, even as Wordsworth is working to integrate parts into wholes,
he is also working to preserve the wholeness of each part. The sense
of transcendence depends upon every text being seen as both a perfected whole *and* a perfected part.

"Tintern Abbey," as noted earlier, could attain the closure necessary for wholeness only by introducing a reader surrogate to displace
the author, thereby allowing a transference of meaning from the
private to the public sphere. The public is precisely what gets greater
play in the inserted lines of the 1850 "Drowned Man"; the range of
emotions exhibited by the crowd, from anxiety to "passive expecta-

tion," mirrors the possibilities of spectator/reader response. And as in "Tintern Abbey," the greater the readerly emphasis, the less the authorial: the phrases "I saw" (l.460) and "I supposed" (l.461) are dropped from the description preceding the sonnet. With the rising of the corpse, however, all trace of mortality must vanish so that immortality can be asserted. Thus, just as Dorothy is effaced by natural objects ("thy mind / Shall be a mansion for all lovely forms" (ll.139–40) as a poem on nature is "perfected," so the "crowd" is effaced by texts in this revised poem on books. In the four-line coda following the sonnet, we are presented with "pure" text:

> Their spirit hallowed the sad spectacle
> With decoration of ideal grace;
> A dignity, a smoothness, like the works
> Of Grecian art, and purest poesy.
> (1850, V.456–59)

Even the "I saw" of the 1805 version is gone, leaving the "spirit" of the childhood texts, unencumbered by the mortality of author or reader, to go about its work of "hallow[ing]"—of making holy—of laboring to make wholes.[39]

Within Romantic discourse, such labor is represented as the natural process—development—of a natural faculty: Imagination. The product, whether it be a text or a character within a text or a "real" person, is valorized for embodying the signs of continuing growth; incompleteness and struggle, as I emphasized in chapter 2, become evidence of an ongoing state of transcendence. Criticism keeps the sense of that state going when it takes such new material as the Cornell Wordsworth to be evidence of the same kind. As in the letter to Moxon, the valorizing then proceeds interpretatively, the poem being praised both as a whole that can stand on its own *and* as a part that must be supplemented by criticism. That is how criticism justifies itself within Romantic discourse: the greater the absolute value placed on the creative as whole, the more important the criticism that makes absolute sense of it as a part.

To historicize that part/whole relationship is thus to enact and produce alternative functions for criticism. I have sought to describe literary change, as well as suggest the role of Literature in prescribing the real, by identifying the signs of developmental growth as effects of particular formal features, ones that are deployed within historically specific strategies of revision. What happens to the ode in "Tintern Abbey," the epic in *The Prelude,* and Poetry in general through extratextual activity, is not a matter of transcendence but of trans*for*mation. As part of our own present participation in generic change, we can now recognize these past generic differences and begin to assess the politics of the resulting *work* of Literature—as a labor that naturally demands more labor, as the text that is the object of that labor, and as the subject that is the very product of the texts it labors to produce.

6

Natural Results

> . . . though he admitted that her novels were an admirable copy of
> life, he could not be interested in productions of that kind; unless
> the truth of nature were presented to him clarified, as it were, by
> the pervading light of imagination, it had scarce any attractions in
> his eyes.
>
> SARA COLERIDGE, SPEAKING OF WORDSWORTH[1]

What was achieved through the revisionary writing of development
was a new "truth of nature" that Wordsworth, laboring within Romantic discourse, could simply refer to as "life." Since he took that sense
of the natural to be absolute, the fact that Jane Austen shared it did
not significantly affect his judgment of her. Instead, the evaluation
followed what we now recognize to be a characteristic procedure: a
distinction of "kind" became a distinction of degrees of imagination.
The consequences of this maneuver are still with us in entrenched
literary critical assumptions regarding Romanticism's "poetic" nature, the separate "rise" of the novel, the aesthetics of character,
Austen's artistic and feminine "limits," and our own public and private understandings of what it means to be "human."

It is the power of those assumptions that has transformed the
ongoing debate over whether Austen is a Romantic into a test case
for contemporary literary historians. From the special issue of *The
Wordsworth Circle* devoted to that topic to the divergent strategies of
Susan Morgan and Marilyn Butler to Jerome McGann's ideological
argument, it has become clear that how we place Austen has *always*
to do with how we place ourselves in relation to the past. I want now
to take the opportunity to consolidate a position outside Romantic
discourse[2] by locating Wordsworth's lyric turn toward Imagination
within it: the turn empowers the discourse by insisting on an exclusivity that denies the historicity of its own criteria for admission. Clarify-

ing Austen's status, therefore, requires that we attend to what such a turn took, and still takes, for granted: she and Wordsworth shared a sense of the natural not because of its absolute validity, but because they both participated in the literary work of making that particular reality real. The writing of development, in other words, was an intergeneric phenomenon.

A literary history of Romanticism that engages that phenomenon is "new" not only in avoiding the "six-poet" syndrome, but also in taking development to be its subject rather than its shape. It does not tell a tale of (poetry's) pre-Romantic origins or (the novel's) organic growth, for it recognizes development to be not a truth grounded in human psychology, but a formal strategy for naturalizing social and literary change: it functions to make change appear to make sense. This chapter thus concludes the section on the historicity of development by establishing the historicity of an author whose texts helped to redefine character as naturally "round," that is, capable of the ongoing transcendence of developmental change. The self made continuously deeper by interpretative revision became the psychologized subject. To see that redefinition as a formal activity shared by apparently diverse texts and writers is to reassess Austen's relationships to her predecessors in the novel, to contemporaries such as Wordsworth, to later nineteenth-century writers such as Marx and Darwin, and also to those twentieth-century critics who have found her such an attractive, but elusive, subject.

Although the language of desire easily insinuates itself into critical discourse, it is at first somewhat surprising to find it so pronounced in the criticism of one of our most "proper" authors. Walter Scott, for example, was but the first admirer to argue that her innovation was her mode of "excitation."[3] For Ian Watt her efforts, "representative" of "the increasingly important part" women were "playing . . . in the literary scene," bring about the "climax" of a rising genre (*Rise of the Novel*, 298). Such language suggests the intensity both of the desire to know Jane Austen and of the resulting frustration so memorably expressed by Virginia Woolf: "of all the great writers," she is "the most difficult to catch in the act."[4]

Woolf's confession, of course, tells us more about the critic-as-voyeur than about Austen-as-artist. Peeking into another person's room is an inevitable posture of criticism that subordinates history to "greatness" and mystifies analysis as pursuit.[5] To pursue past greatness only exacerbates the great difficulties in knowing the past. In

Austen's case, the obstacles are particularly treacherous not because she is inherently mysterious in her achievements or in her limits, but because the very distinctions (i.e., centuries, periods) that are the enabling acts of historical knowledge have only succeeded in obscuring our view and therefore heightening our interest. Jane Austen, in other words, is an object of such intense critical desire largely because our understanding of what she wrote is so radically triangulated by our confusion as to *when* she wrote it; as in her novels, attachment is finally a product of circumstance.[6]

The issue of Austen's revisions casts the question of "when" into very literal terms: are *Sense and Sensibility, Pride and Prejudice,* and *Northanger Abbey,* begun in 1795, 1796, and 1798 respectively, and published in 1811, 1813, and 1818, eighteenth- or nineteenth-century novels? Even if we shy away from the literal and grant more leeway between the critical categories and the actual digital shift, there is the temptation to dismiss the eighteenth/nineteenth-century distinction as the overzealous hindsight of contemporary scholars. A turn back to Scott, however, can allay such suspicions. His chronology of change leaves little leeway. Writing in 1815, he argues that Austen's works exemplify a new "style of novel" that "has arisen within the last fifteen or twenty years."[7] Thus Ian Watt's claim of climax in *The Rise of the Novel* is but another entry in a debate over Austen's turn-of-the-century role that originated while she was still alive and to which Wordsworth contributed in his comments to Sara Coleridge.

Watt's is a particularly important entry, however, because the notion of an eighteenth-century "rise of the novel" is still an entrenched part of our critical vocabulary. But the question of what it was that rose problematizes that developmental history. If Watt is referring to a rise in esteem within the generic hierarchy, he is not accounting for the following: (1) the novel is a low form throughout the eighteenth century; (2) it is not until the 1820s that we find the following kind of statement: "The times *seem* to be past when an apology was requisite from reviewers for condescending to notice a novel" (emphasis mine)[8]; (3) the novel does not approach the top of the hierarchy until the end of the nineteenth and beginning of the twentieth centuries. The "success" of Richardson and Fielding is misleading unless we realize that, although both were imitated, their works were generally regarded as sui generis masterpieces. Professional critics of the 1770s, for example, were not concerned, as J. M. S. Tompkins points out, with defining the novel as a distinct—let alone distinctive—form (Tompkins, 329).

If "rise" refers in some way to popularity in terms of the number of novels published, then Watt must be referring not just to the fifty years that are the major focus of his book, but to the entire century, since the annual production figure he cites is minute until 1740: seven a year. The subsequent "rise," however, poses yet another problem. It "was not in any way matched," says Watt, "by an increase in quality. With only a few exceptions the fiction of the last half of the eighteenth century . . . had little intrinsic merit" (290). Does this mean that, for Watt, the more the novel rises (numerically), the worse it gets? It would, if his "sociological" description of generic change did not turn out to be so heavily dependent on the notion of individual genius, the "exceptions."[9] His history's elision of a half-century of writing[10] thus necessarily increases the critical need for Jane Austen. She *must* be inserted at the end of the argument—that is to say, of the eighteenth century—to climax a rising form or, to put it more accurately, to revive a sagging one.

If different literary historical assumptions engender the desire for a more maternal Austen, a switch in centuries can produce the mother of the nineteenth-century novel. Some critics, especially those who assume change is necessarily continuous, prefer a Janus-headed Austen whose work bridges the centuries.[11] Others, such as T. B. Tomlinson, emphasize discontinuity: "Jane Austen's realisation of what living in society can mean is more like a literary revolution than a step in developing the novel."[12] As with her heroines, choice is inevitably the fate of Austen's critics.[13] Even those who disdain historical intentions, as Emma does matrimonial ones ("it is not my way or my nature"[14]), inevitably find themselves committed to the most "appropriate" embodiments of their desires. Thus what have often been presented and/or perceived as the two essentially autonomous endeavors of Austen criticism—the social, ranging from the ideological to the contextual, and the formal, including the appreciative and the stylistic—are both rooted in the debate over her role in literary change initiated by Scott.

The recent surge of interest in defining a Romantic Jane Austen[15] should therefore be seen as anything but a peripheral undertaking of renegade Austen scholars and imperialistic Romanticists. Rather, the turning of it into what I have called a "test case" is not at all antithetical to the essentially historical nature of all Austen criticism. It allows us to refocus our attention on the problems of the conventional periodization of Romanticism that I raised in the introduction. First, as traditionally dated from 1798 to 1832, Romanticism complicates rather than clarifies the eighteenth/nineteenth century distinction: on the one hand, it is usually depicted as a reaction to or rejection of the former; on the other, the tag "nineteenth-century literature," particularly in regard to the novel, conventionally refers to post-1830 productions. A traditionally Romantic Jane Austen would thus belong to neither century, her isolation begging the essential questions of change and continuity. She would also, in a period that purports to be historically but is in fact generically defined, suffer a second type of isolation: how can an age of lyric poetry accommodate and account for a novelist?

These problems are most evident in the most determined efforts to place Austen in the company of her contemporaries. Joseph Kestner, for example, in trying to define "the tradition of the English Romantic Novel" with Austen as its "exemplar," arrives at dates (1800–32) that match the conventional ones, but only at the price of forgoing any meaningful connection between poetic and novelistic activity. He dismisses all questions of interaction or influence as "coincidence."[16] Susan Morgan does estabish a link to the poetry in the shared "concern" with "perception," but her price is to turn her back on precisely what Kestner thinks he has gained: "I do not claim that Austen is a Romantic, primarily because readers as yet have no shared definition of a romantic tradition in fiction." Morgan's theoretical dilemma is dramatically evident, when, a few pages later, she writes: "And there is no forgetting Charlotte Lucas as she tells Elizabeth Bennet that 'I am not romantic, you know, I never was.' But Austen is. She always was."[17]

Marilyn Butler includes Austen in a book entitled *Romantics, Rebels and Reactionaries,* but then calls into question the validity of "Romanticism" as a historical label and dubs much of what is conventionally considered Romantic with the art-historical designation "Neoclassical."[18] Thus, in challenging Romanticism, Butler does not deny the need for making historical distinctions; in fact, it is the proliferation of those distinctions, both in terms of a severe fragmentation of temporal divisions and a profusion of labels for them, that indicates the generic limitations of an "empirical" history of "ideas" in which art is an "outlet" of social "controversy" (186—87). The five-year period from 1814 to 1819, for example, is divided by Butler into "three more or less chronological *phases*" (emphasis mine; 138). That kind of division is invoked again, along with a host of others, when Butler tries to sum up in the final chapter:

> Social pressures are complex, and the literary movements which reflect them may not succeed each other, but continue to coexist. In an effort

> to summarize the cultural crosscurrents of the revolutionary period one
> might point to some sort of division into successive phases, but these
> would be rough and the dates unreliable. It would seem that from
> about 1760 to the mid- or late 1790s a style prevailed which modern art
> critics have designated Neoclassicism. (180)

Butler slips with startling ease from "movements" to "crosscurrents"
to "periods" to "phases" to "styles," because her concern with change
is not clarified by a hierarchy of change. What, in other words, distinguishes a phase from a period? A developmental step from a revolution? An innovation from a variation?

Any barometer Butler might construct to measure what she calls
"the pressure of ideas upon the entire social fabric" (186) would
fluctuate unreliably and ahistorically, because the kind of history she
writes idealizes ideas by granting them an autonomous existence outside the forms in which they are produced and received. Since, at any
given historical moment, as I emphasized in regard to the footnote
analyzed in chapter 3, those forms interrelate in a manner that determines the functions of their constituent parts, a history of idealized
ideas cannot benefit from diachronic comparisons of those functions.
When, for example, Butler argues that

> Wordsworth's experiments with subjects from among the lower orders
> of society, in metres appropriately taken from popular poetry, follow
> thirty years of public interest in this matter and this manner, and are
> thus characteristic of the culture of the Enlightenment (58)

the "thus" begs the question of change. Butler can and does consider
how shifting political and social conditions affect the reception of such
usages, but her kind of analysis cannot engage the crucial literary
historical question of whether those thematic and metrical features
function differently in Wordsworth's texts than they did in earlier ones.
The same difficulty troubles her treatment of anti-jacobin story lines
(100) and explains why Austen is treated at length in chapter 4 and the
"Romantic Novel" separately three chapters later: delaying consideration of the contemporary sense of a "revolution . . . in fiction" until
the latter chapter, well after the extended discussions of Austen's
novels, effectively limits analysis of her role in generic change to a brief
generalization concerning the conservative tendencies of realism.

To expand that analysis requires avoiding both the pitfalls of the
conventional periodization of Romanticism as well as the temptation

to discard that label without an adequate conceptual replacement. A first step, as I pointed out in chapter 1, is to think of Romanticism as a norm rather than a period, so that the emphasis falls less on exact chronological margins than on generically configured discourses that are normative (or in transition) for a length of time; a distinction can thereby be made between change understood as variation within the normal set of generic interrelations and an innovative shift in the overall hierarchy that signals norm change. Austen's novelistic efforts are in that sense innovative, for they participated in an alteration of interrelations in which "old" and "new" parts perform different functions within a whole that is thus conceptually different from its predecessors.

The generic part that I am arguing is of particular importance to an analysis of Austen—development—has not previously been treated as such, for, as we have seen in the last two chapters, the culture has so heavily invested it with truth value. How dear a commitment that has continued to be, in criticism of the novel as well as of poetry, is evident in A. Walton Litz's response to a generous quotation he provides concerning the structuralist critique of "psychological coherence":

> If we leave aside this modern assault upon the very notions of identity and the "self," I think we can say that Jane Austen at her best managed to create characters which satisfy the broadest range of critical expectations: they are both mimetic and autonomous, matching our sense of external reality and our sense of structural completeness. . . . A combination of absolute naturalness and absolute self-consciousness has been the foundation of Jane Austen's enduring reputation.[19]

What we cannot "leave aside" is the fact that we are now experiencing a kind of change that has not occurred since Austen's own time. The same shift in generic interrelations that is allowing for a new literary history is also providing us with an often unsettling perspective on our Romantic/nineteenth-century origins. That perspective suggests not that we must choose a "best" sense of character, but that we can recognize the historicity of all versions by calling into question such concepts as "absolute naturalness."

Having done so in the first two chapters of this section, I can turn to the novel without treating development thematically, in the manner of almost all Austen criticism,[20] as an attribute of "rounded" characters representing a truth of human psychology. Instead, I will analyze it as a formal strategy, originating in late eighteenth- and early nineteenth-century discourse, for naturalizing the changing in-

terrelations of social and literary forms. Its intergeneric presence in
Romanticism indicates that we are seeing in Austen the beginning of
the lyricization of the novel, a process culminating in the late nineteenth and early twentieth centuries and descriptive of the actual
hierarchical generic rise of the modern novel. In analyzing the kind of
change formalized in development we see how Wordsworth and Austen, poetry and the novel, do much more than just, in Stuart Tave's
word, "touch." They cannot be known in isolation from each other.

Both forms, as I indicated in chapter 4, performed conduct book
functions at the turn into the nineteenth century, redefining "real"
behavior as the material conditions of English society were being
transformed by an economic "takeoff." Debate over the form of the
novel, for example, quiescent during the 1770s, accelerated in pursuit
of a principle of stabilizing unity (Tompkins, 331) in a language prescriptive of behavior intended to conserve that unity. Wordsworth's
Preface to *Lyrical Ballads,* as well as the reactions it inspired, were
similarly permeated with claims as to the truly "natural" and with the
word "real" in all its grammatical forms.[21] In other words, what appeared as aesthetic arguments over the principle of verisimilitude in
the novel, and over linguistic propriety in poetry, was a highly
charged debate over the modes of *conformity* appropriate to a "new"
society.

Our earlier turn to the novels of Sensibility gave us some sense of
the shape of this debate in its novelistic incarnation. I now want to
place it within a broader historical field by briefly examining the
midcentury positions of Fielding and Richardson, as evidenced in
their extratextual defenses of *Joseph Andrews* and *Clarissa.* What is
especially noteworthy about those defenses is that they are consistently two-pronged; that is, defense of form is always mutually re-
inforced by defense of behavior. In his Preface, for example, Fielding
offers his theory of the novel as well as a justification of the morality
and behavior of his characters, particularly Parson Adams. The key
word informing both endeavors is "nature," for the "comic" is distinguished from the "burlesque" by its adherence to the natural, with
the former supposedly featuring "characters" who are so "real" that
Fielding must disavow any resemblance to actual people. The latter,
however, "exhibits monsters, not men": "what *Caricatura* is in painting, Burlesque is in writing."[22]

By calling his "comic romance" a "comic epic-poem in prose"
predicated on a "lost" Homeric model, Fielding is, as noted by Watt

and others, attempting to put a disreputable genre "into the highest possible literary context" (Watt, 258). The historicity of "highest," and the accompanying idea of interrelations, however, have not been sufficiently stressed. Fielding chose epic because he and other writers at that time took it and dramatic tragedy to be dominant forms.[23] They assumed that incorporating features from those forms into their own would raise their productions within a hierarchy that they took to be absolute. As the products of such an interrelation, the epic features are supposed to serve the purpose in Fielding's comic "modern" romance of suggesting the eighteenth-century ideal of order in variety.[24] The epic's "exten[sion]," "comprehensiveness," "large[ness]," and "variety," expanded comically to include "inferior" persons, are turned by the circular pattern of romance to satiric affirmations of natural rank. The story of form in the Preface thus parallels the form of the story. Both the novel and Joseph must recover "lost" parents to lay claim to higher status.

Clarissa, like *Joseph Andrews,* is described on its title page as a "History," but, as with Fielding, Richardson's formal ambitions are extratextually evident. The Preface to volume one, split cleanly between discussions of the epistolary form and the characters' behaviors, implicitly suggests his strategy by emphasizing the "dramatic" strength of the novel.[25] It is not until the Postscript to the entire work, however, that it is explicitly clarified:

> The author of the history (or rather dramatic narrative) of Clarissa, is therefore well justified by the Christian system, in deferring to extricate suffering virtue to the time in which it will meet with the completion of its reward.
>
> But not absolutely to shelter the conduct observed in it under the sanction of religion (an authority perhaps not of the greatest weight with some of our modern critics) it must be observed, that the author is justified in its catastrophe by the greatest master of reason, and best judge of composition, that ever lived. The learned reader knows we must mean ARISTOTLE. (IV, 554)

Not only has the "history" become a "dramatic narrative," but a dramatic narrative of a "high" kind: the discussion of Aristotle, of course, concerns his definition of tragedy. Again, the interrelations tell the story. Clarissa's behavior is justified and her fate patterned by the providential conventions of Christian romance: the author "hast endeavoured to draw that [the death] of the good in such an amiable manner, that the very Balaams of the world should not forbear to wish that their latter end might be like that of the heroine" (IV, 554). Lovelace's behavior, however, requires a different formal explanation: his failure to reform is defended in terms of the incorporation of tragic features. They function providentially to enforce the "doctrine of future rewards" by setting Lovelace's death, as the "tragic poets" were wont to do, in the "shocking lights" of absolute despair.

As with Fielding, who observes that his heightened writing has not "hitherto [been] attempted in our language" (7), Richardson claims that he has done "something that never yet had been done" (IV, 553). But eighteenth-century innovation is always posited as imitation, suggesting the recovery and reinforcement of traditional hierarchy rather than the breaking of boundaries. In Fielding, the act of imitation mystifies authority through absence: the loss of the Homeric model. Richardson accomplishes the same task by invoking Presence: the "poetical justice" of his providential tragedy is but a reenactment of what "God, by revelation, teaches us."

Thus, in terms of hierarchical interrelations, these arguments for incorporating the epic and tragic in the novel represent efforts to produce a generic "rise" of the novel in the first half of the eighteenth century. Efforts to do the same in the second half point not to sagging quality or to a lack of able imitators or new genius, but to the same kinds of generic impasse we noted in Young's prose and Collins's poetry. *The Castle of Otranto,* the first of the Gothic novels that dominate prose fiction in the latter part of the century, is another example of an effort to bring into an established set of interrelations ways of behaving that no longer seem to fit. Walpole moves from an initial posture of embarrassment—he disavows authorship in the first edition, claiming to have found the manuscript—to presenting arguments in prefaces that, like his predecessors', fuse formal and behavioral issues; he justifies his novel's action and his characters' actions in terms of the same "high" precedents. Like Richardson, Walpole appeals to the drama; Shakespeare as tragedian is his particular authority for a fiction that is superior because it is theatrical. The literary historical results of this venture, however, were mixed. Although the concept of romantic realism, Fancy and Nature combined, drew many imitators, *Otranto* itself, as a *formal* model for accomplishing that feat, proved to be problematic: in fact, it was the particular "tragic" features singled out for praise by Walpole, strict adherence to the unities and the necessity of exaggerated comic contrast, that were selected out of Gothic fiction as the century drew to a close.[26]

Evidence of generic difficulties can also be found in contemporary critical writing. In 1775, for example, Henry Mackenzie described the "degradation into which" the novel "has fallen" by invoking the still nominally accepted high forms, but not, significantly, in
terms of shared strengths:

> Considered in the abstract, as containing an interesting relation of
> events, illustrative of the manners and characters of mankind, it surely
> merits a higher station in the world of letters than is generally assigned
> it. If it has not the dignity, it has at least most of the difficulties, of the
> Epic or the Drama.

Mackenzie attributes the novel's failure to live up to its "abstract"
potential to a lack of judgmental and compositional criteria; the available normative models, in other words, are somehow inadequate. The
resulting "debasement" is behavioral as well as formal: a "perversion
from a moral or instructive purpose to one directly the reverse."[27]

Any literary historian recounting these types of statements faces
the temptation to abstract them from their conceptual context and
posit them as *inherent* difficulties in the "development" of *the* novel.
Jane Austen, as we have seen, can then be conveniently introduced as
the solution: a writer who, for a start, appears to be neither morally
perverse nor problematically committed to a single insufficient model
of the novel. The most common scenario has Austen combining Fielding's "outer" view and Richardson's "inner" view into a more complete
whole.[28] But to posit that kind of connection is to replace an analysis of
change with a deterministic narrative in which the possibility of radical
difference is submerged in assumptions of continuity. The contours of
the resulting literary history are all too familiar: the eighteenth century, particularly its latter half, pays the price of such assumptions by
being implicitly or explicitly subordinated to Romanticism. The price
the literary historian pays is the inability to gauge his or her own
historicity: the extent to which key aesthetic judgments and critical
interpretations are but repetitions of Romantic formulations supposedly "discovered" in the texts. To assume unself-consciously, for example, that a merging of the inner and outer constitutes a solution to any
literary historical problem is itself a literary historical problem.

Austen's own sense of her relationship to the past is clearly
falsified by the insistent continuity of the causal perspective. She does
not, for example, answer Mackenzie's complaint regarding the morality of the novel. In fact, in a gesture indicative of conceptual disconti-

nuity, she refuses to even accept it as a valid issue for a novelist to address: "I leave it to be settled by whomsoever it may concern," says the authorial voice at the end of *Northanger Abbey,* "whether the tendency of this work be altogether to recommend parental tyranny, or reward filial disobedience."[29] This disavowal does not, of course, mean that Austen is unconcerned with morality or the pedagogical function of the novel. It does indicate that questions under the pressure of historical change do not engender answers but are reclassified into a new set of questions. Austen recasts the behavioral issue in terms that were meant to be, and still often are, taken as morally neutral. Her apparently modest intention is just to describe how people really act in everyday situations. This is Wordsworth's language in the Preface to *Lyrical Ballads,* and as we saw in regard to the notion of "habitual" perception in chapter 5, such descriptions of "reality" are never morally neutral.

Neither can they be informal, by which I do not mean "casual" or "disordered," but "unrelated to a characteristic set of formal interrelations." Like Richardson and Fielding, Austen offers a story of form in her extratextual comments, but its historical significance has been overlooked through a combination of authorial modesty and critical misdirection. Austen's apparently self-deprecatory references both to her "bit[s] . . . of Ivory," as opposed to "strong, manly, spirited Sketches, full of Variety and Glow," and to her supposed inability to write "serious romance" or "epic poe[try],"[30] have been swept up by critics into the Limitations Debate: an effort, perhaps inspired by her supposedly elusive greatness, to catch her, this time, in the act of weakness. Only Donald Greene, among the many participants in this debate, has argued forcefully for the importance of organizing it along formal lines. But Greene's purpose is, finally, to vindicate Austen, and his game plan requires that he substitute "Tradition" for diachronicity: he formally divides his novelistic all-stars into two opposing teams—the Epic, featuring Fielding-Scott-Dickens, and the Dramatic, featuring Richardson-Austen-James—and awards the game to the latter, where "the true genius of the novel lies."[31]

When genres are essentialistically transformed into traditions, the result is not just, as Greene admits, "oversimplification," but fundamental confusion. Thus in opposing Fielding to Richardson as the respective Fathers of the Epic Novel and of the Novel as "drama, in particular the comic drama," he fails to acknowledge that for those midcentury novelists the epic model, as we saw in *Joseph Andrews,* is comic, and the dramatic model, as in *Clarissa,* is tragic. As a result, if we were to describe the latter work using Greene's distinctions, it would be a novel that does *not* have "tendencies" to "sprawl" or "to describe things in black and white, exaggerating the goodness of the hero and the badness of the villains." It *would,* however, be "neat" and "compact" with "ordinary, easily recognizable characters," and a "preference for saying to the reader, in effect, 'That's how it was; make up your own mind about it'" (165–66). This last characteristic provides particularly vivid proof that the continuity of tradition is no more reliable than the continuity of cause and effect. The specific dramatic features Richardson introduces into *Clarissa* are interrelated not to displace moral judgment onto the reader but to heighten the novel's overt didacticism: a didacticism characteristic of the discourse of his time but, as I argued in chapter 4, an embarrassment in ours. The displacement is not, as Greene would have it, a historical characteristic of an ongoing tradition, but a generic feature subject to historical change. Its striking appearance in the concluding sentence of *Northanger Abbey* is linked, as we have seen, to a discontinuous conceptual shift.

The Limitations Debate has functioned critically as but a blind to the manner in which Austen's statements about form confirm not an individual preference or fault but the scope of that shift. They indicate, with remarkable precision, that she rejects, not as wrong but for her inconceivable, the earlier strategies for raising the novel through the incorporation of epic "variety" or tragic "seriousness." But the apparent modesty of the maker of "bits of Ivory" is once again deceptive; Austen by no means abandons the task of bettering the novel. Her efforts transpire, however, within an altered set of interrelations in which "old" and "new" features perform different functions within a form that is thus conceptually different from the productions of Richardson and Fielding. To understand that difference we need to turn first to the description of it by Austen and her contemporaries.

Mary Brunton's *Self-Control,* according to Austen, was "an excellently-meant, elegantly-written Work, without anything of Nature or Probability" (*Letters,* 344). The modern reader may be tempted to assume a significant degree of synonymity between the latter two terms, but in the early nineteenth century it was the difference that was significant—so significant, in fact, that it bore the weight of a major historical distinction. Both Scott, in describing Austen as a "new" novelist, and Richard Whately, who five years later quotes at length from Scott and elaborates the argument, posit generic change in terms of the degree of conformity to what is natural, within the realm of possibility, *and* what is probable, that is, likely. Whately explains that

> a fiction is unnatural when there is some assignable reason against the events taking place as described,—when men are represented as acting contrary to the character assigned them, or to human nature in general; as when a young lady of seventeen, brought up in ease, luxury and retirement, with no companions but the narrow-minded and illiterate, displays (as a heroine usually does) under the most trying circumstances, such wisdom, fortitude, and knowledge of the world, as the best instructors and the best examples can rarely produce without the aid of more mature age and longer experience.—On the other hand, a fiction is still *improbable,* though *not unnatural,* when there is no reason to be assigned why things should not take place as represented, except that the *overbalance of chances is* against it; the hero meets, in his utmost distress, most opportunely, with the very person to whom he had formerly done a signal service, and who happens to communicate to him a piece of intelligence which sets all to rights. Why should he not meet him as well as any one else? All that can be said is, that there is no reason why he should. (Southam, 89–90)

According to both critics, the eighteenth-century novel was distinguished from the "ancient romance" by an adherence to the natural but not the probable. Its author, explained Scott, was "expected to tread pretty much in the limits between the concentric circles of probability and possibility; and as he was not permitted to transgress the latter, his narrative, to make amends, almost always went beyond the bounds of the former" (Southam, 61). Whately argues that this is a form of duplicity, for the author who "professes to describe what may actually take place . . . [in] human affairs," but then presents us "with a series of events quite unlike any which ever do take place," gives us "reason to complain that he has not made good his profession." This improbability, concludes Whately, is an inadequacy that is at least partially responsible for the formerly low generic rank of the novel beneath "plays" and "verse." The achievement of Austen as a "new" novelist is to adhere to the probable as well as the natural, thereby "elevating" the form "in some respects at least, into a much higher class" (Southam, 91–92).

    At issue, of course, keeping in mind the relationship between form and behavior, is not only literary class but social class as well; for defining probability is a matter of setting standards of behavior, and adhering to it indicates the skillful conformity that assures social security. However, insecurity of social rank, as I noted earlier, is precisely what accelerates in the latter half of the eighteenth century, thus inflating the value of the probable. To ascertain how that value comes to be represented in the novel, we need only compare representative texts: *Joseph Andrews* and *Pride and Prejudice*. Both Scott and Whately cite Fielding for a combination of naturalness and improbability. The central improbability of *Joseph Andrews* is the main character's relationship to his own origin; he does not know it because he was kidnapped as a babe by gypsies. For him to assume his proper rank and thus smooth the social fabric ruffled by his marital intentions, he requires, to use two of Whately's synonyms for the improbable, "lucky accidents" and "singular coincidences." Elizabeth Bennet, on the other hand, knows who her parents are and, following Darcy's lead, decides they are inadequate. How, then, can the social gap be bridged and the marriage occur? In lieu of gypsies and luck, Austen posits what by the early part of the nineteenth century is understood as a "real" behavior; she psychologizes her characters' differences and posits a probable solution: development. They come to love each other as origins are reexamined and newly understood not as absolutely restrictive, but preparatory. By midcentury, autobiography is understood as prelude.

Our continuing commitment to those concepts as truths has prevented us from gauging the historicity of development as both a probable behavior and an innovative formal strategy. It is, in fact, no more inherently probable than coincidence, and, in our sense of the word, it would have been as foreign to Homer or Shakespeare or Pope as gypsies are to us. Thus, unless we assume that Austen was the first author to notice that people develop, or that development is a biological trait that first enters the gene pool in the late eighteenth century, we must account for it in terms of a reclassification of the changing forms of social and literary experience: it recasts the "natural" relationships between parts and wholes, individuals and communities.

Socioeconomic historians such as Harold Perkin and Dorothy Marshall have exploited a spatial metaphor from the nineteenth century to help clarify this change. "At some point," argues Perkin, "between the French Revolution and the Great Reform Act, the vertical antagonisms and horizontal solidarities of class emerged on a national scale and overlay the vertical bonds and horizontal rivalries of connection and interest" (*Origins*, 177). The concept of "Interests" applied to the eighteenth century, Marshall emphasizes, must not be taken to imply actual nationwide "organization," for that "would have been beyond the administrative capacity of the age."[32] What it does describe is a historical form of social experience in which the individual's place is within a particular "community of advantage," whether it be Landed, Commercial, Financial, or Industrial, that embraces the entire range of social and economic ranks. The embrace is won and held by using the patriarchal language of patronage to naturalize those hierarchical distinctions as distinctions of kin/kind. But the price of vertical familiarity was horizontal estrangement. Individuals, observes Perkin, "were acutely aware of their exact relation to those above and below them, but only vaguely conscious except at the very top of their connections with those on their own level." Such consciousness, concludes Perkin, is possible "only in large scale communities, where the individual can unite with others of his kind to defeat the ubiquitous pressures of personal dependency" (24, 37).

That type of community was, of course, a major product of Britain's acceleration into a growth economy in the last two decades of the eighteenth century. "Growth" here refers not only to economic statistics, but also to population and the makeup of that population. As total industrial production doubled between 1780 and 1800 (Perkin, 2), Britain was experiencing a sharp rise in population that Marilyn Butler, among others, speculates was "perhaps the most significant agent of change in the second half of the eighteenth century" (12). "Not only," notes Dorothy Marshall, did "the most rapid rise in the birth rate between 1780 and 1820" increase "the population materially," but it also "altered the composition of the age groups within it. Though the death rate was heavy . . . it seems to have dropped below its eighteenth-century peak. The result was a greater proportion of children, teenagers, and young adults in the population" (4).

The vertical and horizontal changes described by Perkin thus occurred within a society in which a growing economy was altering the lives of a growing population increasingly concerned with the phenomenon of growing up.[33] The hierarchical distinctions of kind, most suited to small-scale communities, thus came to be experienced as restrictive by those whose sheer numbers prevented them from being accommodated within the old bonds of patronage and personal dependency. Families in Austen, usually represented by the patriarch, are experienced as inescapably present, perhaps well-meaning, but always inadequate.[34] Sir Walter Elliot reads his family history over and over again because it is never enough, and when he tries to supplement it by adding the name of an heir presumptive, inadequacy manifests itself as humiliation. Supplementation in terms of the projection of kinship ties on social interactions outside the "exceedingly fluctuating" (*Sense and Sensibility*, 373) immediate family—Knightly is Emma's "Uncle" and Miss Taylor is her "Sister"—is also understood as impermanent and therefore potentially treacherous. The vocabulary of relationship in Austen is therefore strikingly violent, filled with "stabbings," "cruelty," "pain," "agony," "terror," and "betrayal." People, to use one of Austen's favorite verbs, cannot help but "impose" upon other people and upon themselves, their impositions being a product of the increasing insecurity of hierarchical position.

As vertical estrangement increased, so did horizontal familiarity. But to become "conscious" of "connections" with others on one's "own level," one first must know how to identify that level. Such knowledge, which had been seen solely as a variable of external familial fact, was now, given the inadequacy of kind, thought to be at least partially the result of a reflexive turn inward: the degree of self-knowledge. "To understand," says the narrator of *Emma,* "thoroughly understand her own heart, was the *first* endeavour" (emphasis mine; 412). As the product of an act of mind—"understanding"—social position was effectively psychologized into a state of mind. And the strategy for naturalizing a hierarchy of such states manifests itself as a behavioral truth cast in the language of economic growth: development. It makes probable a reality that accommodates the experience of instability as a prelude to a more mature order. Thus, after Harriet's revelation, Emma "realizes" that she has not been in her right state of mind; instability understood as "madness" (408) had led her to violate social position by toying with Harriet and insulting Miss Bates. Getting "acquainted" with her true self reestablishes propriety in psychosocial terms both through the discovery of horizontal connection, with Knightly, and through the heightening of vertical paranoia, toward Harriet. "Such a development of self, such a burst of threatening evil" (409) is the form of fate faced by all of Austen's heroines: just as Elizabeth's union with Darcy entails a defensive distancing from Lydia and Wickham, so Fanny's love of Mansfield Park is keyed to her dislike of Portsmouth.

The innovative significance of these developmental texts is in no way diminished by Austen's domesticity or by her politics. Far from signaling limitation or detachment from the sweeping social changes I have described, her domesticity is itself a product of the gap between home and the workplace opened by those changes. Since that distinction is a historical rather than biological phenomenon,[35] development, as a contemporary strategy, can work its magic in both realms. Domesticated within "feminine" discourse, it produces what many even admiring readers take to be relatively innocuous novels of courtship and marriage: the horizontal connections extend only to a husband and a "small band of true friends" (*Emma*, 484), and the vertical antagonisms are directed primarily at familial dead weight and former rivals. How far from innocuous these spatial maneuvers are becomes unavoidably clear when we observe the results in "masculine" discourse. There, the psychologizing of social position through self-conscious horizontal solidarity and vertical difference shows itself to be the strategy by which the early nineteenth century reordered its understanding of social relationships. As opposed to the concept of "Interest," notes Diana Spearman, "an essential element in the idea of class is that it is somehow an ineradicable part of the psychological make-up of its individual members, and also something shared with others."[36] Development, in other words, is the in*form*ing strategy of class consciousness. Whether employed by Austen, or a few decades later by Engels and Marx, it presents hierarchical change wrought by growth as natural by linking economic activity and behavioral probability.

In *The Condition of the Working-Class in England*, for example, Engels describes "class" in terms of a "way of thinking and acting" and claims his "premises" are based on "undeniable facts, partly of historical development, partly facts inherent in human nature."[37] For him, for Austen, and for others who share such a combination of "natural" assumptions, the resulting narratives of "reality" emerging out of everyday experience posit causality as materialistic and circumstantial, and closure as a return from illusion rewarded by (horizontal) union. Engels and Marx's proletarian protagonists are, like Marianne Dashwood, "born to an extraordinary fate" (*Sense and Sensibility*, 378): to experience change as inevitable, threatening, but ultimately accommodating to class-ified desire.

To suggest this strategic connection with radical discourse is not to argue for what David Monaghan calls the "subversive" Austen. He is right in asserting that the "case made out by Duckworth and Butler" for Austen's conservatism is "essentially indestructible" (*Austen in Social Context*, 6). Development's function is not necessarily to undermine hierarchy but, as I have tried to show, to naturalize its instability as a sign of maturation. That sign may point to a rejustified gentry or a galvanized proletariat, but it always does so in order to make change make sense.

How culturally pervasive a goal that becomes after Austen can be seen by turning from literary and philosophical discourse to the scientific. Darwin's "natural" nineteenth-century concern with nature was to naturalize biological *change* by classifying his data into a developmental narrative. This effort was, of course, no more ideologically innocent that Austen's or Marx's. We cannot, however, grasp its historical and cultural significance if we do not have the critical vocabulary to acknowledge radical/conservative distinctions as important but different in kind from the conceptual changes that accompany new sets of normative interrelations and strategies. Romanticism is thus a very valuable label when used to describe the shared formal activity of apparently diverse authors. In regard to Austen, it clarifies the innovative status of her novels and provides a sound theoretical basis for intergeneric comparison.

Austen's rejection of epic and tragic models for the novel in favor of a turn to the probable confirms that the sense of the hierarchy of literary forms, like the social hierarchy, was undergoing significant change. To analyze how the novel is reclassified, we need to decode that turn, since, as we have seen, the probable was not a given but the product of a formal strategy. Marianne's "extraordinary fate" is, through the ironic magic of probability, to be ordinary, because that is precisely what development does to the experience of change: it makes it fit in with everyday life. The "ordinary extraordinary," that problematic Romantic relationship between what we experience and how we experience it,[38] was a central concern of Austen in her novels as it was for Wordsworth in his poetry, for her texts, like his, played major roles in reforming and replacing their respective genres in a reordered hierarchy: a hierarchy that authorized development through the revisionary activity of features (e.g., Trapp's odal turns and the apostrophe to the reader) that came to be associated with lyric subjectivity.

To note these interrelations of kind in texts such as *The Prelude* and *Northanger Abbey,* two early, much revised, and posthumously published works, is to exhibit the explanatory power of a history in which genre is not essentialistically defined and historical classifications are not unigenerically constrained. *The Prelude,* for example, begins with what is usually discussed as a "personal" crisis: an initial lyrical outburst quickly collapses into thematic confusion and authorial self-doubt. However, the issue here is the same impersonal one that informed Austen's supposedly self-imposed limits. Neither writer finds it possible at the turn of the century to use the traditionally normative models. Wordsworth recites an entire catalogue of inherited possibilities, including epic and tragedy, but finds them all inadequate: "either still I find / Some imperfection in the chosen theme, / Or see of absolute accomplishment / Much wanting" (I.261–64).[39] That want is then internalized as a want "in myself," a gesture of inadequacy that paradoxically justifies the author's "creative" authority. In the lyric turn that I have shown to be normative for nineteenth- and much of twentieth-century literature *and* criticism, Wordsworth modestly retreats from "work / Of ampler or more varied argument" to "a theme / Single and of determined bounds" (I.641–44). Like Austen, who insists "I must keep to my own style and my own way," a bounded way in which "3 or 4 Families in a Country Village is the very thing to work on" (*Letters*, 453, 401), Wordsworth argues that he *must* do what he can do best. What they both do best, of course, are studies in characterological development, for the turn to development allows them to naturalize the destabilizing experience of social and literary change.

Wordsworth's repeated justifications of this turn, in Book I and throughout *The Prelude,* are revisionary both in the attempt to change how the reader reads (he begs Coleridge, the reader surrogate, for tolerance and sympathy), and in their interpretative relationship to each other (the repetition suggests an ongoing struggle in which something—himself—is evermore about to be). To take egotism as the central issue raised by Wordsworth's decision to write about himself at a length "unprecedented in Literary history" (*Early Letters*, 586–87), is thus to miss the point: without a developmental strategy in which ongoing revisions of the types detailed in the last chapter extend the text, the most egotistical person in the world would not—in fact, could not—write that much about himself. Egotism is also not the issue in Austen's famous defense of the novel in chapter 5 of *Northanger Abbey.* This is no plucky young thing spontaneously defending all novels, but an innovative writer carefully defending her type of new novel against "improbable" and "unnatural" writing (38).

Austen's narratives connect probability to change in much the same way Wordsworth's efforts do: the central character becomes deep by embodying problematic forms of behavior only to return to the probable and the rewards of horizontal union.[40] The Poet cannot begin *The Prelude,* for example, without rejecting inherited forms and seeking communion with Coleridge, and he cannot end it, as I emphasized in chapter 4, until he rejects the false behaviors attributed to the French Revolution and Godwin and "marries" into a new/old family: Coleridge as the father/brother, Dorothy as the mother/sister, Mary as the wife, and Raisley Calvert, given significantly strong billing as the rich uncle who dies to ensure that the stability is economic as well as spiritual. In *Northanger Abbey,* Catherine Morland's "probable" fate is similarly to reject the Gothic forms of behavior she has internalized, thanks to a developmental revelation ("how altered a being did she return," 237) that is characteristically accompanied by a clarification of everyone's real socioeconomic status. Since development psychologizes that status as the proper state of mind, it is appropriate that the rejection of old behaviors involves guilt-ridden reactions to breaches of propriety that are also violations of private property. The young Poet steals a boat, only to find that a "huge peak" overlooking the lake "Towered up" and "like a living thing, / Strode after me" (I.378–85). Catherine, who had earlier violated an old chest only to find "a white cotton counterpane," steals a look at a pile of papers whose secret turns out to be not romantic but economic: it is a collection of bills. Her guilt at having "*imposed* on herself" (emphasis mine) is imaged in strikingly Wordsworthian fashion: "She felt humbled to the dust. Could not the adventure of the chest have taught her wisdom? A corner of it catching her eye as she lay, seemed to rise up in judgment against her" (173).

Wordsworth calls these episodes spots of time, for development plots temporal change spatially so that it can always be represented as a return to one's proper economic/psychological place.[41] The journeys may be more (*Mansfield Park*) or less (*Pride and Prejudice*) spatialized, but the temporal dimension always fades into a "natural" mystery, for what is found has been there as the most probable alternative all along: the real self. In developmental analysis, says Wordsworth, each particular "Hath no beginning" (II.232). Edmund, we are told at the end of *Mansfield Park,* fell in love with Fanny "when it was quite *natural* that it should be so" (emphasis mine; 470). This decision to "purposely abstain from dates" is also Darcy's tactic in answering Elizabeth's dangerously loaded question concerning the "beginning" of their love: "I cannot fix on the hour, or the spot, or the look, or the words, which laid the foundation. It is too long ago. I was in the middle before I knew that I *had* begun" (380). Critics who ask whether Darcy or any of Austen's other char-

acters "really change" only trip over the historicity of their own
adverb, for development defines the real in a manner that finesses
the whole issue: difference, in Austen's and Wordsworth's developmental reality, collapses imperceptibly into continuity.

The lyrical model in both cases is the sonnet, in which the radical
discontinuity of the turn is always rounded off by the radical continuity of the fourteen-line whole. Longer narratives depicting that continuity, in the words of a midnineteenth-century reviewer, consist not
of a "labyrinthine *nexus* of events" but the "skillful evolution of . . .
processes." Echoing the spirit of Scott's 1815 judgment that "*Emma*
has *even less* story than either of the preceding novels" (emphasis
mine; Southam, 65), the reviewer concludes of Austen that of "plot
she has little or none."[42] The novels are, of course, not really void of
events; rather, developmental strategy has dictated that they be
psychologized so that the instability they threaten can be naturalized
by a proper turn of mind. Just as in *The Prelude* the Poet's journeys to
the Alps and France are depicted as mental detours, so Catherine's
psychological and physical return to the safety of her English home is
preceded by imagined stops among the "vices" and "horrors" of "the
Alps and Pyrenees . . . Italy , Switzerland, and the South of France"
(200). That such threats can be transformed into what Wordsworth
calls that "calm existence that is mine when I / Am worthy of myself"
(I.49–50), is a matter of developmental faith: "strange things may be
generally accounted for if their cause be fairly searched out"
(*Northanger Abbey,* 16).

The narrator's immediate reference is the heroine's empty love
life, but the language unmistakably echoes a description of Catherine
herself offered a few paragraphs earlier: "What a strange, unaccount-
able character!" (14). To simplify the accounting process, Austen
posits character as a problem of unity: how, for example, to reconcile
Catherine's "profligacy" with her good heart, or why Emma only
"*seemed* to unite some of the best blessings of existence" (emphasis
mine; 5). As I suggested at the end of chapter 4, when characterological unity informs textual unity, form is effectively psychologized, producing developmental models that become normative for Romanticism. Within those models, authors and readers have distinctive roles
to play. Since the experience of reading, for example, is now the
experience of knowing a character, authors must make their characters, in G. H. Lewes's words, "equal to actual experience." To make
them "accurately real"[43] is the new mode of "excitation" Scott attributed to Austen.

How this is accomplished, and the reader's appropriate response, have been the subjects of an unintentional but, I would argue, not surprising intergeneric critical consensus. Both Robert Langbaum, in analyzing the nineteenth-century poetry of experience initiated by Wordsworth, and Wayne Booth, in discussing Austen's innovative techniques, speak of the author's activity as an inside/outside movement and the reader's response as a combination that, by this point in our argument, is most familiar: sympathy and judgment.[44] Far from being coincidental, this critical match confirms the presence of a strategy shared by both poet and novelist. Once we acknowledge it, the rationale behind the prescribed behaviors is clarified. Reading and writing, like all forms of experience, must be naturalized through the spatial maneuvers I described earlier: the value of the literary is psychologized by engaging it through both horizontal union (inside sympathy) *and* vertical distancing (outside judgment). This is why "accurately real" literature becomes in the nineteenth century a really "exciting" part of growing up, an index to development: witness Coleridge's *Biographia Literaria* and Mill's description of Wordsworth's effect on his life. It is a phenomenon that is central to both *The Prelude,* with its Book on Books, and *Northanger Abbey,* in which what one reads so clearly affects how one matures.

If Austen had this much in common with Wordsworth and other nineteenth-century writers, why did he, Charlotte Bronte, and others later in the century dismiss her?[45] The answer is simply that, for them, development came to be the "truth of nature"—a given—and thus a no more valid basis of comparison than death or taxes to us. Judgment thus depended upon the turn to psychological degree that Wordsworth mystified as a "clarifi[cation]" of nature "by the pervading light of imagination." He disregarded Austen because *her* mystification of the newly "natural"—what one critic has labeled the "improvement of the estate"[46]—varied from his. Bronte was similarly affronted, as have been all those critics who, even in supposed admiration, have embraced the "limited" Austen. But the Austen they get reflects the historicity of their desires, and Bronte's generic fate was not to innovate upon Austen's model, but to more *overtly* lyricize it. By attending to such interrelations, a generic history can distinguish variation from innovation and thus clarify the relationship of the present to the past. When we place ourselves outside Romantic discourse we see Austen's novels, as well as Wordsworth's poems, within it.

III

Desire and Discipline:
The Politics of Mind

7

High Wages
and High Arguments

> This is not to suggest, of course, that the *desire* to consume
> was an eighteenth-century novelty. It was the *ability* to do so
> which was new.
>
> To speak of a birth indicates the organic nature of the whole
> development, the need for a long preceding period of growth, and
> the necessity for many further stages before the maturity of "a
> society of high mass consumption" would be reached; and yet also
> indicates the importance, the excitement, the novel sense of a
> dramatic event which is what I want to convey.
>
> *The Birth of a Consumer Society*[1]

To historicize Romantic discourse is to identify the self that produces
it, and is produced by it, as something that *must* grow. In the previous
section we saw how development became such a "natural" imperative, its sense of ongoing transcendence configured by the lyric turns
that always revise parts into wholes and wholes into parts. By connecting, within this shared sense of the natural, a novel that rounds character into "a development of self" (*Emma,* 409) to a "faithful picture"
that makes history into a "mighty development" (Engels, 9, 332), I
have called into question the literary historical utility of conventional
notions of political difference. But I have done so only to invite
political inquiry of another kind—one that recognizes the relationship
between the politics being analyzed and the form of the analysis.

That relationship is illustrated in the two quotations that head
this chapter. The longer paragraph provides yet additional evidence
of our being in an era of generic transition, for Neil McKendrick
spends this paragraph, and close to three more pages, defending the

use of a metaphor that he himself admits has been an accepted commonplace of nineteenth- and twentieth-century historical writing. In his justification for organizing his argument around the "vital metaphor" of birth and development, McKendrick exhibits an acute awareness, which is itself historical, of some of the conceptual difficulties regarding continuity and discontinuity that it raises. The equally perceptive tale that he and his coauthors tell is, as a result of such consideration, a particularly useful description of change.

The formal consequence that it does not engage, however, is that even a modified developmental narrative produces a sense of progressive transcendence fraught with *political* implications. Commercialization becomes a wish come true for those who, according to the first of the above quotations, had the "desire" but not the "ability" to consume. The description of what and who "helped to release and to satisfy" the "consumer boom" (2), posits the repression of "more" (marriage, love, family) and "less" (the need to be fashionable) "basic human drives" by "social, cultural and economic restraints": those "historical forces" that were a "buttress against change" (36). The birth metaphor, in other words, may make development more abrupt and dramatic, but it also carries with it the developmental sense of a liberating progress. With desire as absolute and ability as what was "new," the shift in the workings of power that accompanied commercialization is cast politically in terms of increasing freedom: the extension of the privilege of realizing that desire from the few to the many.

But if, as I have been arguing, the self was itself reconstructed at that time, then the desire as well as the ability was "new"; in that case, any political analysis must engage the ways in which this reclassifying of the basically "human" into that which develops, by altering the agent and object of power, changed power itself. My purpose in this final section, then, is to raise the polemical ante in my argument for the value of a new literary history by briefly exploring the politics of developmental desire in regard to three highly visible and supposedly familiar concerns: money, sex, and drugs. Following up on my earlier analyses of the kind/degree and sympathy/judgment maneuvers of Romantic discourse, I will argue that such desire is inherently disciplinary. When literacy became the means and measure of social power (see chapter 4), the relationship between that power and the knowledge made, accessed, and valorized by that literacy shifted. Power came to be exerted not through the repression, but through the professional production and circulation, of that knowledge. Since its newly constructed depths are the objects that are being *made* known, the developing self is subject to this professional power. Such a self, I argue, is self-disciplinary: by requiring and expecting unlimited development, it always opens deeper depths to surveillance and invites more and more specialized intervention. The "new" desire functions as a new form of control.

In this first chapter, I examine the late eighteenth-and early nineteenth-century rewriting of economic behavior that accompanied the commercialization of England described by McKendrick. My method is to compare the generic experimentation with "imaginative" mixed forms that proliferated at that time to the contemporaneous arguments about man's "nature" that came to dominate the ongoing debate over high wages for laborers. Such a combination allows me to clarify the role of what appears to be *only* a literary concern in the writing and naturalizing of apparently nonliterary behaviors. It also places within a larger cultural context the literary historical issue we first engaged in chapter 3: the function of the Romantic critical procedure of fetishizing the past into parts with various inherent values. I begin and end with one of the forms—the prospectus—in which such valorization first took place.

Readers who find it strange that I have chosen to link a specific kind of generic change—the use of "imaginative" mixed forms—to the contemporaneous debate over high wages for laborers, should not chalk that reaction up, and probably out, to a pluralistic difference of critical approach. For that strangeness was, in fact, *made* by some of the very historical changes I intend to address, and in that sense *it* is my subject. By the early nineteenth century, the work of the artist was reclassified within Romantic discourse as essentially psychological and was thus conceptually estranged from the materiality of worldly labor. In the light of that distinction, a poet such as William Blake appears in most literary histories as a powerful but eccentric visionary. Largely ignored[2] has been the pragmatic technician whose 1793 prospectus for works of a special kind at a "fair Price" can show my concern with the economics of mixed form to be less strange than it may at first appear:

> The Labours of the Artist, the Poet, the Musician, have been proverbially attended by poverty and obscurity; this was never the fault of the Public, but was owing to a neglect of means to propagate such works as have wholly absorbed the Man of Genius. Even Milton and Shakespeare could not publish their own works.

> This difficulty has been obviated by the Author of the following
> productions now presented to the Public; who has invented a method
> of Printing both Letter-press and Engraving in a style more ornamen-
> tal, uniform, and grand, than any before discovered, while it produces
> works at less than one fourth of the expense.
>
> If a method of printing which combines the Painter and the Poet is
> a phenomenon worthy of public attention, provided that it exceeds in
> elegance all former methods, the Author is sure of his reward.[3]

Blake's advertising strategy for his mix of poetry and painting is
to tout the value of the product by stressing the efficiency of the
method of production. Although he does not call into question the
Romantic conception of the mixing of forms as a visionary effect of a
synthesizing Imagination, Blake emphasizes that it is also a material
matter of reproducing combinations of text, design, and color. The
artist-as-laborer suffers from a lack not of inspiration but of the
means, fiscal and technological, of propagation. Here and throughout
his career, Blake denied the assumption that the artist's "proverbial"
poverty was a necessary condition of his productivity. In fact, as he
asserted in his description of "A Vision of the Last Judgment," "the
Argument is better for Affluence than Poverty & tho he [the painter
of "A Vision"] would not have been a greater Artist yet he would
have *produced* Greater works of Art in proportion to his means"
(emphasis mine; 551).

In making this argument, Blake was participating in a national
debate over the relationship between wages and productivity that was
fought throughout the eighteenth century, increasing in frequency
and intensity during the final decades as inflation widened the gap
between customary wages and wartime prices.[4] By sorting out the
ways in which this issue is posed and the kinds of answers proposed,
we can identify a shift in the latter half of the century in such key
concepts within the debate as property, value, and desire. To see the
desire as "new," as I have been emphasizing, is to recognize that the
re-solving of the debate entailed the rewriting of the human—its
transformation into the developmental self of Romantic discourse.
As new forms of socioeconomic behavior became innate characteristics of that self, the society's hierarchical structures were rationalized
and their inevitable inequities were justified.

Literature's role in this naturalizing process was particularly evident in generic experimentation with imaginative mixed forms. Generic mixing, of course, was not new in the late eighteenth century; as

I have been stressing throughout this book, all forms are always synchronically interrelated within a hierarchy with all other forms. But what is distinctive about the variety of mixing in, for example, Blake's *Poetical Sketches*—the blending of poetry and painting suggested by the title, and the combinations in the contents of poetry, prose, and drama, and within the poems, of hymn, ballad, and sonnet—is that the act is being self-consciously employed as a *procedure* that is an end in itself. Whereas a fantasy of purity of genre— Milton's epic sublimity, Shakespeare's tragic perfection—was used by writers such as Collins and Gray to construct tales of poetic inadequacy that subordinate the present to a Golden past, Blake, Wordsworth (*Lyrical Ballads*), and others at the turn of the century invest mixing with the power of transcendence: present over past, the mental powers of the expressive artist over what came to be seen as the historical restrictions of genre.

The issue here, let me stress again, is not progress, but the ways in which this generic behavior both generates and exemplifies a recasting of what late eighteenth-century English culture takes to be human. Within Romantic discourse, mixing is the activity by which the self always transcends itself—it is how that self develops. As such, it is the type of activity that I described in the previous section of the book as revisionary: parts and wholes, past and present, mix in a mutually interpretative process that reformulates desire as "something evermore about to be." The self that mixes becomes a complex mix that is deeply in need of ongoing interpretation.

Prior to 1750, and thus in the absence of those depths and that imperative, most of those writers who addressed the issue of wages based their advocacy of keeping them low on two truisms: one derived from "common sense" mathematics and one from human "nature." The former was simply the assertion that higher wages translated into higher prices and the loss of a competitive edge for manufactured exports. The latter was the "fact" of the incorrigible idleness of the laborers, who were "industrious only in the degree they [were] necessitous."[5] In both cases the logic connecting truism and conclusion was simple and direct cause and effect: high wages result in high prices and indolent workers. Although the second point does engage the seemingly more complicated issue of behavior, it is asserted in a manner no less cut-and-dry than the mathematical one, for it is not a psychological argument but a theological and moral one: man's laziness was considered to be a "fact" of his sinful nature. To identify change in the wage debate, we thus need to be aware not only of different positions, but of shifts in the combinations of the kinds of arguments being offered for them.

Inattention to such shifting interrelations is precisely what has troubled the scholarly debate over changing attitudes toward labor during the eighteeenth century. What A. W. Coats describes as a post-1750 turn to a newly typical position advocating high wages, Richard Wiles brands as but a "consolidation" of earlier views.[6] Since they refer to essentially the same works, Coats attributes much of their disagreement to the subtleties of textual exegesis.[7] But the subtlety of particular importance to identifying change—recognizing the interrelations of kind in the written texts—is ignored by both authors. Coats, for example, thematizes the psychological *features* of his post-1750 texts as ideas spread by direct or indirect contact of individual authors. Idealized in this fashion, they leave history and enter the romance of influence, as the debate over change into which they are marshaled becomes an unending controversy over original presence. What happened to the writings on wages in the late eighteenth century can thus be best described as neither the birth of new views nor the consolidation of old ones, but as the foregrounding of psychological arguments within the economic and philosophic texts in which the debate transpires. The resulting transformation in the kinds and modes of assertion constitutes evidence for an argument for change.

In a 1793 essay competition on "the best means of providing employment for the people," the winning entry, penned by a Samuel Crumpe, begins: "There is no branch of philosophy, which has been cultivated with less success, than that which professes to analyze and explain the different tendencies and operations of the human mind."[8] "Mind" needs to be understood here not as a transcendent idea, but as a historical feature of a discourse that is increasingly psychological; it functions to frame naturalistically a problem whose complexities, in a time of accelerated social and economic change, could no longer be accommodated by earlier formulations. Not only had the simple cause-and-effect relationship between high wages and high prices been disrupted by increasing evidence of a distinction between the productivity and the money cost of labor (Coats, 87), but the direct connection between necessity and industry was undermined by redefinitions of need occasioned by rising domestic consumption. Crumpe's first insight into what he calls the "movements of mind" is, in fact, a distinction between the kinds of needs that raise naturally indolent man into activity: the animal necessities, on the one hand, and the civilized ones on the other (10–13). This strategy of retaining the assumption of idleness while emphasizing luxury as a powerful motive to industry allows for favoring high wages without presenting them as deserved: productivity is encouraged, an aura of sympathy is maintained, and inequities of income and power are left unchallenged.

For Crumpe to posit what he calls "the different tendencies" of mind as potentially conflicting and yet part of a coherent whole, one whose needs were ever increasing, the linearity of cause-and-effect explanations of moral behavior had to give way to a multidimensional model of the psychological mix. Mind, in the late eighteenth century, was spatialized as a location in which multiplicities of desire and their inevitable contradictions could be mixed into unity of self under the banner of personal development. The rapidly growing study of chemistry had been instrumental in promoting this model of transformation through mixing; Joseph Priestley's multifaceted career was but one manifestation of its spreading importance. To describe the "father of modern chemistry" as a Renaissance man because he had a very "versatile mind," is to miss the historical point.[9] The index to the scope and influence of his ventures into philosophy, politics, history, education, and theology is the increasing conformity of late eighteenth-century discourse to the model he and his colleagues had described. That shift indicated why, at midcentury, while the Scottish chemist Joseph Black was learning how to make carbonic acid gas, David Hume extolled the faculty of mind called imagination as the "unlimited power of mixing."[10]

Hume's writings are of particular importance to understanding the wage debate because of the manner in which psychological concepts such as the imaginative mix formed his philosophical and economic arguments.[11] His famous assault on cause and effect is the most obvious and pertinent example, the skeptical key to inherited certainty being a focus on the activity of the mind. The explanatory power that such descriptions of the mind's behavior as "custom" came to have in the latter half of the century was extended by Hume into the economic realm to assess the relative importance of necessity and incentive to the industriousness of the laborer. Identifying the latter as the more effectual was an indirect argument for the higher wages needed to purchase such incentives and an explicit elevation of mental over physical need, of the mind's desire over the body's demands. By 1771, the anonymous author of *Considerations on the Policy, Commerce, and Circumstances of the Kingdom* could confidently echo as a given the Humean notion that it is "more a turn of mind than multiplied necessities that induces men to become industrious, which will be better excited by encouragement than compulsion."[12]

Our tendency to assume that a "turn of mind" is a *natural* explanation of behavior is itself a measure of our own historicity. For the "mind" at issue is not an ahistorical source of truth but, as I have been arguing, a *construct* that accounts naturalistically for particular kinds of behaviors and prescribes preferred ones. Any turn that it might take has meaning only in relationship to the norm that it helps to define, and that norm is precisely what is changing in the late eighteenth century. In other words, like the mind described as taking it, the turn to the kind of luxury consumption increasingly favored in the wage debate was being made, learned, and justified in the texts produced at that time.

At stake in this rewriting of consumption was not only the logic of incentives—high wages induce greater productivity; more important to the English economy as it accelerated toward its takeoff phase in the last decades of the century was the recognition that by far the most crucial factor in sustaining growth was increasing domestic consumption. Despite the time and attention paid then, and still paid now in our histories of that time, to British colonialism and foreign trade, domestic "taxes on malt and beer alone produced more revenue" at the turn of the century "than all shipping and foreign commerce put together; the value of the trade to America was actually less than that of the porter consumed in the City of Westminster."[13] "Consumer demand," according to historian Harold Perkin, "was the ultimate economic key to the Industrial Revolution."[14]

So astonished were late eighteenth-century visitors to England by the amount of money changing hands, that they sought frantically for explanations of such mobile wealth. Invariably, these rationales were grounded in usually negative assertions about national character, particularly the susceptibility of the English to "frequent changes of fashion." In 1791, for example, Frederick Wendeborn attributed this predilection to the "listlessness" of the English that "made them tire of everything after a few months."[15] By comparison, Perkin's twentieth-century analysis of socioeconomic conditions provides what at first appears to be a very different kind of explanation. Citing England's lack of peasantry, deep penetration of the money economy, and social mobility, he concludes that "social emulation was the key to consumer demand": "nearly everyone . . . received a money income, and nearly everyone was prepared to spend a large part of it in 'keeping up with the Joneses'" (91–92, 96–97). Although clearly a more involved analysis than Wendeborn's, this answer turns out, if Perkin's language is carefully examined, to perpetuate that observer's fundamental assumption: some behaviors, whether of an individual or of a nation, are just natural. Why was everyone "prepared to spend"? How did they spend? What led them to posit the social relationship with the Joneses as one of competitive identification? To say that these are, given certain conditions, natural manifestations of man's inherent acquisitiveness and envy is finally to invite further historical inquiry; if, in every culture at any historical moment, there is a *form* of acquisitiveness and of envy, then we need to identify the particular forms they assume in the late eighteenth century.

Perkin's pursuit of that inquiry slackens because his method focuses on writings about social behaviors rather than on the ways such behaviors are written. We can read a poem or a conduct book or we can read the marketing strategy for Wedgwood china to see how a variety of "texts" formally inscribe a culture with naturalness. The latter exercise, for example, reveals how the emulative spending that translates high wages into consumer demand was cultivated by a recasting of value through manipulative mass production. To convince people to dispose of their perfectly good earthenware and buy his creamware, Wedgwood artifically juxtaposed high quality, defined by exclusivity, and low, actually lowered, price. In the early days of a new line, sales were limited to the nobility at inflated prices even as cheaper imitations were stockpiled in warehouses, to be released only when exclusivity and curiosity merged as desire.[16] Although John Clarke is correct in emphasizing the newness of that desire—"The promotion of a product by its associations rather than by its intrinsic merits is the most striking feature of modern salesmanship" (97)—he does not point to the strategy's more profound innovation. Of central importance to naturalizing the spending described by Perkin is the change in the object of desire as value is transferred from the product, *whatever* its associations, to the act of possession. The realization of desire thus lies in the perpetuation of that action, turning spending into a behavior so natural that it swallows up its immediate material end—the possessed product becomes valueless—as it redefines its long-term goal, an upper class identified by conspicuous consumption rather than blood.

Keeping up with the Joneses is, therefore, neither a British vice nor an ahistorical compulsion, but a mystification of a particular set of socioeconomic relationships. It simultaneously reinforces hierarchy, since we must always aim upward, and idealizes the economic activity within it as a search for transcendent equality: the parity we seek is at a level that is, to borrow the phrase yet again, "something evermore about to be." This formulation posits transcendence as a matter of mind, and mind as that location in which competitively mixed desires lead to the endless self-revision of development.

The dialectic of object and subject that is so central to this conception of mind assumes the economic guise of a dialectic between property and possession. In his commentary upon the former, Sir William Blackstone argues:

> Necessity begat property: and, in order to insure that property, recourse was had to civil society, which brought along with it a long train of inseparable concomitants; states, government, laws, punishments, and the public exercise of religious duties. Thus connected together, it was found that a part only of society was sufficient to provide, by their manual labour, for the necessary subsistence of all; and leisure was given to others to cultivate the human mind, to invent useful arts, and to lay the foundations of science.[17]

The myth of property, in other words, is the inevitability of hierarchy. The myth of possession, on the other hand, is, as we have just seen, developmental transcendence through "natural" emulative spending. Together, these myths bring the eighteenth-century tale of wages to a conservative close. The laborer was given the higher wages denied him at the beginning of the century, but only as a means of ensuring the domestic demand that helped to entrench the new industrial state and his position within it. That hierarchy was thus established and sustained in an era of turbulent change both by the profits that concentrated power at the top, and by the idealization of the resulting gap as an occasion for fostering individual growth.

What enacts the dialectic of property and possession in the latter half of the century is a reformulation of ownership along private/public lines. If value lies in the act of possession, exclusivity guarantees not permanence of ownership but the convertibility necessary for economic transcendence. Thus we find the systematizing of exclusivity in the country in the astonishing rise in enclosures, and in the city in such acts as the numbering of individual houses, first undertaken in London in 1764. In both cases, property is privatized so that it can be more easily possessed.

This complex of behaviors is written and rewritten, until it becomes natural, in literary texts as well as in the wage debate, legal commentaries, and marketing strategies. Blake's writings of the 1780s and 1790s, for example, psychologize the value of his labor in terms of the model of the mind as an elusive unity of contentious parts. The competition among those parts is valorized as a necessary opposition, a "true friendship," between the two "portion[s] of being": the "Prolific" and the "Devouring" (*Blake*, 39). When the supply of one and the demand of the other are absolutely matched, the result is transcendence of self: "The desire of Man being Infinite the possession is Infinite & himself Infinite." Transformed by every consumer's dream, the perfect purchase, we become the Joneses and the Joneses become us: "God becomes as we are," within the kind/degree economics of Blake's psychologized religion, "that we may be as he is" (*Blake*, 2; see my chapter 3). In other words, as consumption is mystified as imaginative desire, hierarchical relationship is idealized as identity. Thus the social emulation Perkin finds so central to economic change becomes in literature, by the turn of the century, the normative model of communicative activity: successful reading requires, as we have seen, the identification of reader and author.

In doing this, of course, the author does not actually surrender any of his hierarchical authority. In fact, to convert the property at issue, in Blake's case the poem, into an exchangeable commodity, he privatizes it as the unique imaginative expression of his own individual creative genius. To possess the poem, according to the logic of this myth, the reader who becomes the poet must himself become imaginative; thus by the early nineteenth century J. S. Mill was able to "discover" that art's function was to heal the wounded imagination. The healing possessions were often presented as fragments or parts of larger wholes, such as Wordsworth's gothic church, because, as we have seen, if value lies not in permanence but in transcendence, a fully possessed object is valueless. In Blake's words:

> He who binds to himself a joy
> Does the winged life destroy
> But he who kisses the joy as it flies
> Lives in eternity's sun rise
>
>   (*Blake*, 461)

What did need to be fully and permanently possessed, so that its value could be transferred to the present, was the past—and the vehicle for this transfer was genre. In poets such as Collins and Gray we see particular forms initially privatized as the property of individual authors: Milton wears the girdle of pure epic, and pure tragedy is Shakespeare's domain. The poetic present is then represented as inadequate by depicting the poet-reader as unable to identify with the past masters and thus helpless to claim their generic possessions as his own.

This argument for impoverishment became an argument for excess through the kind of transformation that we saw in the low-to-high shift in the wage debate. Both Milton the poet and Miltonic epic are psychologized upon the model of a competitive mix. The former was engaged as the Miltonic *mind,* which Blake could possess as his own precisely because, as a mix of contentious desires, it was never fully in possession of itself: being of the devil's party, for example, and not knowing it (*Blake,* 35). The latter was then seen as being not inviolably pure, but most valuable only in parts, which Blake can then more efficiently combine with other parts to produce the mixed forms that supposedly evidence his creative superiority (and which then can be resold within evaluative criticism). Asserting, in the name of mixed forms, the imaginative present over the not-as-natural past became a characteristic literary gesture by the turn of the century: witness Wordsworth's condemnation of past practice in the preface to poems described as lyrical ballads.

Let me conclude this chapter in kindly fashion by returning to the form with which I began: the prospectus. In offering a plan for *The Recluse* in 1814, Wordsworth, like Blake, possesses Milton's value for his own enterprise by arguing from the "mind of Man." He presents this mind as an absolute truth discovered in his time, turning history into a tale of transcendent psychological development that, four years later, Keats imaged as "a large Mansion of Many Apartments":

> Now if we live, and go on thinking, we too shall explore them. he is a Genius and superior [to] us, in so far as he can, more than we, make discoveries, and shed a light in them—Here I must think Wordsworth is deeper than Milton—though I think it has depended more upon the general and gregarious advance of intellect, than individual greatness of Mind . . . He did not think into the human heart, as Wordsworth has done—Yet Milton as a Philosopher, had sure as great powers as Wordsworth—What is then to be inferr'd? O many things—It proves there is really a grand march of intellect. (Keats, *Letters,* 95–96)

When we recognize the Romantic "mind" (and, in criticism, the equally Romantic "human form"), as well as the developmental tales told of it, as constructs, however, their functions as features within diachronically shifting hierarchies of social and literary forms illuminate the late eighteenth-century conceptual change we have been tracing.

In that light, Wordsworth's Prospectus to *The Recluse* appears as yet another text that helps to write off the change as inevitably natural. Like all prospectuses, particularly those for real estate, it does so by offering the reader an apparently irresistible bill of goods:

> Paradise, and groves
> Elysian, Fortunate Fields—like those of old
> Sought in the Atlantic Main—why should they be
> A history only of departed things,
> Or a mere fiction of what never was?
> For the discerning intellect of Man,
> When wedded to this goodly universe
> In love and holy passion, shall find these
> A simple produce of the common day.
>
> (ll.47–55)

This man is trying to sell you something, but the historical nature of his pitch has been obscured in the work both of those who have resold it as their own critical property, and of those who, toiling for the cause of a "history" of heroes and villains, condemn Wordsworth as a traitorous conservative while celebrating Blake as a radical labor theorist.[18] By steering clear of these dated alternatives of sympathy and judgment, I hope I have shown that these authors' texts participate in a common enterprise: the naturalizing of a new complex of human behaviors.

Wordsworth thus proceeds generically and thematically as Blake did, justifying the importance of his work, the philosophic poem, by explicitly describing it as a mixed form, combining Miltonic epic with descriptive verse with autobiography. Stressing efficiency of production ("A simple produce of the common day"), he casts its "high argument" in the same mold as the argument for high wages: a harmonious mix of supply and demand, objects and desirous subjects, will produce a transformation of self into developed self that rationalizes growth, both personal and, naturally, economic, as beneficial to all. *The Recluse,* of course, remained a fragment, making it yet another possession from its time that, until recently, has strangely possessed us.

8

Great Sex and Great Decades

It is a truth, which history I am afraid makes too clear, that some men of the highest mental powers, have been addicted not only to a moderate, but even to an immoderate indulgence in the pleasures of sensual love. But allowing, as I should be inclined to do, notwithstanding numerous instances to the contrary, that great intellectual exertions tend to diminish the empire of this passsion over man ; it is evident that the mass of mankind must be improved more highly than the brightest ornaments of the species at present, before any difference can take place sufficient sensibly to affect population. I would by no means suppose that the mass of mankind has reached its term of improvement ; but the principal argument of this essay tends to place in a strong point of view, the improbability, that the lower classes of people in any country, should ever be sufficiently free from want and labour, to attain any high degree of intellectual improvement.

THOMAS MALTHUS, 1798[1]

By putting sex into a discourse that is both informed by the concept of addiction and concerned with the relationship between development and labor, Malthus helped to produce the kinds of knowledge whose power is my subject in these last three chapters. *An Essay on Population* altered the wage debate not by turning back to earlier assumptions regarding the laziness of labor, but by rewriting supply and demand in terms of the new psychological truth of development. The writing took Malthus in directions that at that time were not yet clearly distinguished, but that we now take for granted as the proper disciplines of knowledge: a philosophical introduction frames an economic analysis that takes a scientific turn to statistics as a means of offering a sociological description of historical change rationalized by a psychological understanding of behavior that relegates morality to the status of a concerned afterthought.

Struck by this new comprehensiveness, Malthus's admirers thought him capable of confirming matters "in the most *absolute* manner" (emphasis mine),[2] while his detractors were often as infuriated by the breadth of his argument as by what they took to be its inaccuracies. Hazlitt, for example, was driven to write a reply to the essay that became, in an attempt to match what Hazlitt calls his opponent's "systematic ardour,"[3] as long as its object. It is because that object helped to write and empower our current disciplinary distinctions that it can help us to understand the significance of the disciplinary tales of sexuality and addiction I am about to analyze. The validity of the "principle of population" is not important here, particularly given the recent work of E. A. Wrigley. He has shown that two key correlations that had held steady for close to two centuries—those between England's compound annual growth rates of population and changes both in the price of consumables and in real wages—altered "with astonishing rapidity" right at the time Malthus was making his predictions: "Previous experience . . . was a fallible guide to future behavior" (Turner, *Malthus,* 8–11). My focus thus lies not on Malthus's predicted "facts," but on the literary historical "fact" that both the *Essay* and the tales can be shown to have been configured by the politics of developmental desire.

Like Austen and Wordsworth in the 1790s, Malthus was part of a society in which, as I pointed out in chapter 6, a growing economy was altering the lives of a growing population increasingly concerned with the phenomenon of growing up. His particular focus was on how the macro growth issue of population influenced the micro issue of each individual's chance of growing up. But he also linked growth, as the full title of the *Essay* makes clear, to the matter of "Improvement" that he identified with Godwin and Condorcet. Since he argued against their notions of perfectibility, it is tempting to think of him as denying the possibility of growth and improvement occurring together—the notion that individuals can, or even want, to develop. But in fact, it is his assumption that all men naturally possess this desire, at least in moderation, that poses the competitive situation that population growth would always, according to the logic of the *Essay,* magnify into crisis. Malthus summarized this position in a letter to Godwin written only a few months after the appearance of the *Essay:*

I cannot look forward to a period when such a portion of command over the produce of land and labour as cannot be within the reach of all will cease to be an object of desire. Moderate cloathing, moderate houses, the power of receiving friends, the power of purchasing books, and particularly the power of supporting a family, will always remain objects of rational desire among the majority of mankind. If this be allowed, how is it possible to prevent a competition for these advantages? . . . The consequence of this desire in the proprietor to realise a sufficiency to maintain and provide for a family, together with the desire in the labourer to obtain the advantages of property, would be that the labourer would work 6, 8, or 10 hours in the day for less than would support 3, 4, 5 persons, working two hours a day. Consequently the equal division of the necessary labour would not take place. The labourers that were employed would not possess much leisure, and the labourers that were not employed would perish from want, to make room for the increase of the families of proprietors, who, as soon as they were increased beyond the power of their property to support, must become labourers to others, who, either from prudence or accident, had no families. (Malthus, v–vi)

The self that suffers in this system is the self that has already been described in this book. It is a self that desires to develop and that measures development according to such conditions and needs as literacy.

When the "power of purchasing books" is ranked alongside "moderate cloathing" in a description of natural human desire, we should not be surprised to find that description closing with a rationalization of all of man's and God's actions in terms of what Malthus himself, in the Preface to the *Essay,* called a "theory of mind" (iv). "Evil exists in the world," argues Malthus, in what is certainly an understatement after nineteen chapters that describe misery as necessary and in detail, "not to create despair, but activity" (395). The purpose of that activity, he claims, is to "improve and exalt" man's "mind" and thus "fulfill the will of his Creator" (396). Although the creator is certainly a presence in the final chapters, Malthus deliberately steers his argument from the theological to the philosophical and psychological. Asserting that "life is, generally speaking, a blessing independent of a future state," he turns from the absolute truths of divinity to "the striking necessity of general laws for the formation of intellect" (391).

In that arena, sin is not the issue and evil is not a test. Malthus uses a metaphor of human development to clarify what is at stake:

> A state of trial seems to imply a previously formed existence, that does not agree with the appearance of man in infancy, and indicates something like suspicion and want of foreknowledge, inconsistent with those ideas which we wish to cherish of the Supreme Being. I should be inclined, therefore, . . . to consider the world, and this life, as the mighty process of God, not for the trial, but for the creation and formation of mind. (353)

This distinction, between a mind that is made by developing in the world versus a soul that can only be tested by it, was also central to an argument made by Keats two decades later: the world that is a world of misery, claimed the poet, is a "School" for "the proper action of *Mind and Heart* on each other" for the purpose of development (*Letters*, 250). And just as Keats posits that development on a larger scale as a "grand march of intellect" (see the previous chapter), so Malthus speculates that without such schooling "it is probable that man might never have emerged from the savage state" (364).

For Malthus, the "wants of the body" (356) occasion the primary schooling from which only some minds have the opportunity and the ability to graduate. The description of their fate shares a language of "torpor," "stimulation," and "excitement" with Wordsworth's almost contemporaneous Preface. Both texts project the mind as further "awaken[ing] into activity" through "intellectual wants" of its own, particularly the "desire of knowledge" (359, 377). The self makes itself by producing knowledge engendered by its own making; the subject is increasingly its own, and only, object of inquiry. Development thus proceeds in revisionary part/whole fashion, desires producing minds which produce desires.

Malthus switches the blame for the misery that is an integral part of this process from Godwin's target, "human institutions," to the individual. Each person, he argues, is capable of the prudence necessary—hard work and limiting procreation—to avoid adding to the master problem of overpopulation, and this "very admission of the necessity of prudence . . . removes the blame from public institutions to the conduct of individuals" (vii–viii). Those who come to know themselves through development best realize that individual responsibility is necessary, if misery is to be kept within limits and development is to continue. Proper conduct is thus connected, in this version of the *Essay,* to proper development.

In the second version, that connection is strengthened and explicitly moralized: its preface suggests that a "strict examination" must be made of "modes" of keeping population down and of "consequences" (xv). As Gertrude Himmelfarb points out, the modes discussed in 1798

> were "positive" and "preventive." The positive checks—starvation, sickness, war, infanticide—reduced the population after it came into existence (that is, reduced longevity); the preventive ones—delay of marriage, restraint of sexual passion, forms of sexual intercourse which did not result in procreation—inhibited the increase of population before it occurred (reduced fecundity). The effect of both was "misery and vice," misery being an "absolutely necessary consequence" and vice a "highly probable one."[4]

The stricter examination a few years later, however, expanded the litany to a "trinity, moral restraint, misery, and vice." The new term suggested that reduced fecundity must be more than a matter of population prudence: "'moral restraint' was a delay in marriage," as Himmelfarb observes, "not accompanied by 'irregular gratifications,' and therefore not 'resolvable' into misery and vice" (115). With this higher resolution, the second edition offered a principle of population that worked more "selectively, punishing the improvident and rewarding the provident. 'He who performs his duty faithfully will reap the full fruits of it, whatever may be the number of others who fail'" (118).

Revision thus occasioned for Malthus a shift between 1798 and 1803 that parallels the one usually attributed to Wordsworth for almost exactly the same time period: "Tintern Abbey" to the "Ode to Duty" and "Elegiac Stanzas." In neither situation, however, can the change be described as what M. H. Abrams calls a "departure" (*Norton Anthology,* II, 214); what happens is less a personal matter, involving individual biography, than a formal one of making more explicit the *inherently* disciplinary plot of developmental desire. In Malthus's case, the theory of mind that informs the original essay presents population pressure as an occasion for intellectual development. If the population were checked by those methods that did not further but even hindered that development—such as "irregular gratifications"—the logic of the essay would collapse.

Thus, what configures Malthus's work is not the difference between arithmetical and geometrical ratios; that aspect is as much a blind to the literary historical and political significance of his texts as the differences between kinds of imagination and fancy have been to the efforts of Wordsworth and, as we shall see in the next chapter, of Coleridge. Texts from all three tell powerful tales of development and the ways in which it functions politically,[5] for both liberal and conservative alike, to rationalize hierarchies of suffering and to enact self-discipline. Just as Malthus was not, as Hazlitt impotently emphasized and Malthus himself admitted, the *first* to address population as a problem, so, as we saw Marilyn Butler point out (chapter 6), the authors of *Lyrical Ballads* were not the first poets to write up "the lower orders." The power of their texts does not have to do with (Romantic) conceptions of absolute originality; it has to do, instead, with the ways they interrelate those topics with the features and procedures that became normal for Romantic discourse.

Malthus's model of disciplinary development is particularly relevant to understanding the interrelations of Romanticism and sexuality, since his concern with population growth directs his attention, as in the quotation that prefaces this chapter, to sexual activity. There he presents sex as an addiction, which raises two basic historical issues: the historicity of the concept of addiction, which I address in the next chapter, and the addiction of our culture to the putting of sex into discourse—a phenomenon that Foucault dates as beginning in the eighteenth century and to which I will now turn. To clarify the historicity of that addiction, we need to examine the role of gender distinctions in the empowering of development.

　　Malthus's positioning of the sexes is crucial: women are, in a biological sense, centered, in that they are the immediate agents of population growth; but they are centered only as a problem to be resolved by the actions of men. The development of the latter is threatened, in the immediate sense, by personal addiction to sex at the expense of intellectual activity, and in the long term, by the overcrowding hastened by their lack of prudence. Women's bodies become a liability that distracts them and men from the dutiful work of development. Thus, with the increasing emphasis on male "moral restraint" in the second edition, come increasingly detailed plans for decentering the female biological center. A section on "old maids" asks women to do it to themselves: "The matron who has reared a family of ten or twelve children . . . has therefore rather substracted from, than added to, the happiness of the other part of society. The old maid, on the contrary, has exalted others by depressing herself."[6] That self-depression, argues Malthus, deserves our "approbation."[7]

　　Historicizing this particular form of centering/decentering is essential to understanding the gender politics of developmental desire. Those politics are not desribed by critics who today retell developmental tales of repression and struggle—tales that inevitably constitute the Romantic self as the psychologized stuff of history. Neither are they illuminated by merely opening the canonical door, as is dramatically evident in this *Norton Anthology* headnote to Dorothy Osborne's six-page debut in the fifth edition (1986):

> And in describing the great fight with her brother, how ready and *natural* is her access to the emotions! Neither Henry Osborne nor any other man of his day could have written such an acount of a family quarrel.
>
> (emphasis mine; I. 1747)

The editor can center attention on Osborne only by *naturally* decentering her skills both as foreign to those possessed by almost all the other writers the anthology celebrates (males), and as in need of the break in scholarly decorum signaled by the exclamation point.

Rather than repeating such Romantic gestures, I want to show both that the developmental tales which occasion them are still, as we saw in Malthus, inherently disciplinary, centering and negating women while negating but then valorizing men, and that the historical construct of sexuality, with its emphasis on repression, makes that disciplinary mechanism "naturally" effective. The institutional politics of our profession in the 1980s clarify how effective it still is. In 1985, for example, almost all the Modern Language Association Convention's major meetings in the late eighteenth and early nineteenth centuries (the Late Eighteenth-Century and Romantic Divisions as well as the Wordsworth/Coleridge Association and the Byron Society) focused on gender. That uniformity confirmed that to speak sexuality and to speak Romanticism, and particularly to speak them together, is to participate in power—the professional power to prescribe present cures by pathologizing the past.

We misread that phenomenon if we assume power to be essentially negative, a matter of prohibition and exclusion. Then, the inter-relations of Romanticism and sexuality describe acts of repression that define a period around the creative work of six male poets, leaving little room for women. The only solution to that scenario of discrimination is to discover as creative, and salvage, *individual* women to compete with *individual* men. Left intact are categories taken to be timeless—Male versus Female, Individual versus Society,

Creative versus Critical—and the "naturally" competitive mode of their interaction. Present analysis, in other words, perpetuates the past by misconstruing its power.

That is precisely why, as I have been emphasizing throughout this book, almost all our literary histories of the late eighteenth and early nineteenth centuries are themselves Romantic. Like the texts they propose to interpret, they tell tales of lyrical development. To classify within that category of development our obsessions with "Great Sex" and "Great Decades" is to detail the workings of modern power—a power for which repression is not a method but a diversion. An undiverted analysis of the lack within the canon of Romantic women writers reveals not a marginalized but a centered femininity; not the masculine valorized to the exclusion of its supposed opposite, but the culture-specific *difference* between them functioning to make Romantic development inherently disciplinary.

That difference naturalized the later eighteenth-century split between work and home by making it appear not historically and economically circumstantial, but bio-logical for women to preside emotively over the domestic realm, and for men to dominate the workings of the "real" world external to it. As Philippe Ariès has pointed out, one's "craft" and one's "private life" had been closely linked before the latter fell within the exclusive circle of the family.[8] As space was enclosed physically and conceptually throughout the culture, producing private property, society was reorganized into parts that made such change make sense. The rewriting of sexual difference, in other words, naturalized the advent of middle-class culture. "Sensible" women of that class thus accepted their isolation within the home as the price of their dominion over it. The more complete their claim to being the emotional, life-giving center of the household, the more the house held them, delimiting their power as it was being constituted.

This paradox of centering also informed another contemporaneous act of enclosure: the claim by Wordsworth and other writers we now call Romantic to the cultural center. In fact, the language with which Wordsworth stakes his claim, in the Preface to *Lyrical Ballads,* is the familial language of what he himself calls the "household." As the "inmate" most versed in "passion," the Poet, in this Romantic tale, like the Woman in the tale of sexuality, "sympathizes" and "binds together," serving as "the rock . . . ; an upholder and preserver, carrying every where with him relationship and love" (*Prose,* I, 141). As texts like this one wrote the centering functions of the Poet as "a man speaking to men," those functions were simultaneously being written as female. This feminization of the writer was most accelerated and obvious in what were still, until well into the nineteenth century, low forms, such as the journal and the novel, the latter being increasingly dominated in the late eighteenth century by women writers and men who, following Richardson, wrote as women. Thus as the novel rose as a feminine form, the feminine was domesticated, and the result was, as we saw in chapter 6, a kind of writing articulating, and articulated by, the new norms of "natural" behavior: the domestic novels of writers such as Jane Austen.[9]

Its domestic values are precisely what highlights *The Prelude*'s final description of the Poet made "Perfect" as "full" of "female softness." Far from being minor additions to a male repertoire, these qualities correspond to the major poetic innovations that criticism has attributed to Wordsworth and Romanticism: the turn toward "humble" concerns and a "humbler" articulation of them; the focus on the "heart" and the idealizing of the "feeling intellect"; the emphasis on the poet's salutary function as "nurse" and "mother" to those it engages through "sympathy." Without these female qualities, Wordsworth argues, the Imagination "cannot stand." From *The Prelude* to the notorious feminine pronouns of the "Poems of Imagination" such as "A Slumber Did My Spirit Steal," to the prose of the prefaces, the language of sexual difference permeates the writing of Romanticism.

Why? And why is the *center* of that which is written feminized? At issue is the way in which the norm change we have been discussing valorized what could be called a "horm" change, making it essential to the conception of human identity as something that, as we saw in Malthus and Keats, had to be made. Ariès points out that before the advent of development and age consciousness, human life was understood to be divided into two stages: youth and adult. "People had no idea, " he observes, "of what we call adolescence" (29). Once the self was rewritten as I have described, however, with consciousness and time newly interrelated within the work of endless self-revision, the making of identity proceeded, as in the "Immortality Ode," through the identification of stages: parts multiplied as wholes became "something evermore about to be." As adolescence thus became the crucial passage between childhood and adulthood, the hormonal metamorphosis of the body was psychologized as the act of maturing, and sexuality became an essential condition of the maturity of individual identity.

In Wordsworth's Preface, the self as mind is "built up" and then "exists" *only* in "pleasure," a concept which is itself rewritten by sexual differentiation as "depend[ent]" upon a principle that is "the great spring of the activity of our minds." That "spring" (similitude in dissimilitude) is not only invested with the power to valorize the metrical language of Poetry by explaining how it can "raise the Reader to a height of desirable excitement," but it is also presented by Wordsworth as the principle from which "the direction of the sexual appetite, and all the passions connected with it, take their origin" (*Prose,* I, 148). The repetition with variation of meter leads us to prefer poetry to prose, and the sameness with difference of our bodies inspires our mating preferences. Both our linguistic and our physical desires, in other words, have the same psychological origin. What is important here is not the "scientific" validity of Wordsworth's theory, but the linkage between the Romantic glorification of art and sexual classification.

Casting the lyrical ballads as "experiments" in producing "pleasure" clarifies these interrelations: as that psychologized pleasure became the code of poetic knowledge, sex became the code of all pleasure. The discursive apparatus that arose from this innovative literary encodation, Romanticism, wrote and was written by the apparatus of sexuality that emerged from the new encodation of sex. Just as we believe, as Foucault has argued, that we are "liberating" ourselves when we decode all pleasure in terms of a sex at long last exposed (*Power/Knowledge,* 191), so we believe that we are "humanizing" ourselves when we decode the "cultural" knowledge of poetry in terms of pleasurable psychologized truths discovered under textual surfaces. When, as professional critics, we speak sexuality *and* Romanticism, finding incestuous desire or absent parents at the heart of Literature, we feel doubly powerful: power analyzed as repression produces truth understood as transcendent.

The deceptive nature of that transcendence, whether found in early nineteenth-century "creative" texts or twentieth-century "critical" ones, is evident when we reconceptualize the function of limitation by engaging the centering of the female. Within the repressive model, to gain power is to overcome limits. But we have seen that the woman centered in the home delimits her power in the very act of constituting it; the power of the Romantic artist (and critic) similarly sexed and placed is similarly self-constrained, its impact upon the supposedly "real" world surrounding the cultural center being simultaneously understood as *both* essential and minimal. In other words, limitation and control in the nineteenth and twentieth centuries are self-imposed; that is, the very conception of self as developmentally self-centered is, as Malthus's model makes very clear, inherently disciplinary.

It is the cultural myth of sexual difference cast in terms of that development that makes this disciplinary mechanism so naturally effective. When, for example, the Romantic artist "full" of "female softness" is physiologically female, her activities and production are developmentally judged to be invariably limited and ultimately arrested. The trope that figured so centrally in the writing of the modern subject—the self synecdochically made mind—is itself similarly troped so that women are taken to be but parts of that part made whole. The bodies, and bodies of work, of such writers as Dorothy Wordsworth, Jane Austen, Mary Wollstonecraft, and Mary Shelley have been so inscribed. Dorothy Wordsworth, for example, became her brother's "eye," her gaze both credited and devalued "creatively" as a means of softly but thoroughly imposing discipline on harshly productive men. Whenever the developmental model is employed, even for purposes of praise (Austen's greatness *lies* in her limited sexual and social scope) or understanding (Mary Shelley wrote *Frankenstein because* her infant died), the centered softness of the female body is written and read, following Malthus's description of the matron, as a pathological sign of limitation.

The effect of this pathologizing is repressive, but—an absolutely important distinction—that does not mean repression is its cause. It can more profitably be historicized as a feature of the Romantic discourse of development. For any self to be condemned to the abnorm of limited development, the conception of self as inherently developmental must first be normalized. Health is thus written as continuous and unending growth even in texts written by those fated to fall ill.

Dorothy Wordsworth, for example, innovated upon the genre of the journal by recasting it as a lyricized medical chart. Epiphanic observations of a healthy Nature punctuate a precisely dated and timed history of progress and setbacks. The effects on mental and physical health of external environment—the weather—as well as prescribed treatments—the precisely detailed meals—are carefully monitored:

> [November] 23rd, Monday. A beautiful frosty morning. Mary was
> making William's woollen waistcoat. Wm. unwell, and did not walk.
> Mary and I sate in our cloaks upon the Bench in the Orchard. After

dinner I went to bed unwell. Mary had a headach at night. We all went
to bed soon.

> [November] 24th, Tuesday. A rainy morning. We all were well
except that my head ached a little, and I took my Breakfast in bed. I
read a little of Chaucer, prepared the goose for dinner, and then we all
walked out. I was obliged to return for my fur tippet and Spenser, it
was so cold.[10]

These nursing narratives help to write the role of the middle-class
female as domestic supervisor: "a woman who, unlike the poor
woman," as Nancy Armstrong has put it, "never labors, but who,
unlike the rich, is never idle."[11] Her "natural" busi-ness, is, quite
simply, to ease development. As a result, she has been easily dismissed as the disembodied gaze of her brother.

Mary Wollstonecraft, writing development as a gloriously natural "unfolding," totally disembodies herself: because female physical
inferiority is a "law of nature," vindication is a matter of pure mind.
And, as we have repeatedly seen, the politics of mind always collapses distinctions of kind into distinctions of degree:

> Let it not be concluded that I wish to invert the order of things; I have
already granted, that, from the constitution of their bodies, men seem
to be designed by Providence to attain a greater degree of virtue. I
speak collectively of the whole sex; but I see not the shadow of a reason
to conclude that their virtues should differ in respect to their nature. In
fact, how can they, if virtue has only one eternal standard?[12]

Differences in degree are tied, as in Dorothy Wordsworth, to matters
of "health," and health is identified with uninterrupted growth:
women are "not in a healthy state" because the "state" they are in is
"perpetual childhood." The metaphors of "flowers" and "blooming,"
as well as the repeated references to "education" as an ongoing process of unlimited improvement, confirm that the politics of the *Vindication* are the middle-class politics of development. Wollstonecraft,
in fact, explicitly argues that the "middle class" is the "most natural
state." Her text, then, helps to naturalize the disciplinary imperatives
of self-improvement: the ongoing need to pull one's self up by one's
own bootstraps. The woman who gains her "rights" is free to develop
like a man.

But how do men develop? Is the phrase "free to develop"

oxymoronic? If, for example, female softness and its steady surveillance is centered for the entire culture, then where do we find tales of
pathologically interrupted male development? Everywhere—from
Wordsworth's Great Decade to, as we shall see, Coleridge's drug
addiction to Keats's health to Blake's eccentricity to Byron's self-
destructive sexuality. To assume that the promise of development—
of continuous and transcendent psychological change—is *ever* innocent of disciplinary power is to miss the entire historical point. That
has been easy to do not because we have not noticed these interruptions, but because conceptions of "male" creativity have valorized
them as evidence of the truly imaginative activity that was, and as
confirmation of the developmental achievements that could have
been. Those conceptions strategically surface in Wordsworth's Preface, for example, right after he codes pleasure as sex in the "similitude" passage; the next paragraph begins with his famous description
of poetry as "the spontaneous overflow of powerful feelings." There
and elsewhere in the Preface, and throughout Romantic writing, the
male creativity that female softness disciplines by decentering is cast
epiphanically as a sudden coming. Quality, intensity, and brevity are
interrelated in what becomes a psychological truism that writes texts
(Romantic fragments), careers (Great Decade), and periods (1798–
1832 Romanticism) as lyricized developments: sweet because short.

In other words, when the artist does not conveniently cooperate
by dying young, we valorize him anyway by writing him off. Career
after career is cut short, but the promise of development is not threatened as long as accidental biographical reasons (the drowning of
Wordsworth's brother) and ahistorical aesthetic judgments (Arnold
was "right" about Wordsworth) are supplied. When we do the supplying, whether we are Great Decade-ing William or conventionally
canonizing Dorothy, we are engaged in a *political* activity that implicates us in the workings of disciplinary power. Only when we shut off
that supply can we see that Wordsworth's turn to "Duty" was not
"caused" by personal grief or by a reaction to Revolutionary excess,
but rather was already written by the same inherently disciplinary
model of development that we traced in Malthus and that both writers' texts helped to articulate.

Romantic development is idealized so that it can *always* be pathologically interrupted. Those interruptions, after all, are opportunities
for professional intervention and surveillance—the ongoing prescribing, that we shall pursue in the next chapter, of disciplinary cures
(Coleridge's doctor saving the poetic self from the addictive self, or

Wordsworth's critic cutting the later writer off from the earlier one)—cures that are essential to the social and economic well-being of modern society. Sexuality writes Romantic development as a natural ideal by spinning a tale of repression that convinces us to desire what we are denied. For women, that denial is cast as an inevitably "natural" limitation that socially and canonically negates them, but *appears* not to trouble men. This developmental negation of the centered female is one of the primary strategies by which modern disciplinary power disguises its own operations. Sexed as feminine nurturing, disciplinary surveillance subordinates itself naturally to the much more familiar "masculine" mode of power—the sovereign authority to exclude, block, censure, and repress that has turned almost all our histories, from Left and Right alike, into Romantic subject/object tales of conspiratorial oppression and heroic resistance. But modern power can configure and conserve hierarchical relations in large populations because it does *not* work in that negative way. It cultivates rather than represses desire and, in doing so, makes the acting out of desire an occasion not for the prevention but for the production of knowledge—professional knowledge of the psychologized subject.

That imperative clarifies the politics of sexual difference in Romantic development. As the disciplinary center, the female must be negated so that the disciplinary nature of that power remains disguised. But to opt for an apparently valorized "male" development, as the solution to limitation explained away as repression, is *not* to be positively affirmed; it is to leave the communal center for the epiphanic and alienated, where development will inevitably, but of course "accidentally," fall victim to death, drugs, or depleted desire. Nobody gets it, everybody wants it, and we need experts to console us and to tell us why.

In our expert tellings as critics, we can continue to psychologize rather than historicize, and thus further afflict Romantic women by doing to them what we have been doing to Romantic men: make them long so that we can cut them short and then be there to bandage the wounds. To argue for or to accept a developmental Romanticism of Great Decades is to argue for or to accept the disciplinary gender distinctions of Great Sex; the resulting fate, for both men and women, is canonical subjectivity. To say this is certainly not to make claims for equal suffering; I am, in fact, insisting that the negation of women is not only different in degree but in kind from what was done to men. Nor am I precluding other analyses of the workings of power, particularly since I understand the historicizing of the canonical Romantic texts to be a means of facilitating future work—in which I intend to participate—that addresses writings and writers that the power of that discourse has negated. My purpose is not to let anyone or anything off the hook, but to suggest that we participate as little as possible in further hooking. Once we detail how Romanticism and sexuality write each other, our own writing can be powerful without being blind to power.

9

Conclusion:
Romantic Addictions

> . . . these stimulants could not be withdrawn from the mass of mankind, without producing a general and fatal torpor, destructive of all the germs of future improvement.
>
> MALTHUS[1]

> I want to grow up to be an ex-junkie.
>
> UNIDENTIFIED INNER-CITY YOUTH

> FORMER DRUG ADDICT NOW GETS HIS KICKS BY EARNING COLLEGE DEGREES
>
> HEADLINE FROM THE *Detroit Free Press*

> In trying to cope with this [inability "to progress"], I had to shift. . . . This shift, which is typical of my generation, is of more interest in its results than in its causes.
>
> PAUL DE MAN[2]

To understand the historicity of Romantic discourse is to be able to hear within it the discourse of addiction. As at the start of chapter 2, my interest here is in causes—not in the sense of assigning absolute origins, but in terms of identifying interrelations among texts. It is more than coincidence that most of one chapter and sections of others in the first edition of Malthus's *Essay* provide a theory of stimulants to supplement his theory of the development of mind. Although he is not talking directly about drugs, but about the physical and mental stimulations occasioned by the pressure of population, his notions touch many of the bases of what comes to be the medical model of addiction. Stimulation is necessary to improvement, but the dosage becomes problematic since it cannot "be repeated often with the same effect, as it would by repetition lose that property which gives it its strength" (222). Increasing the dosage, however, poses another problem, for if stimulants of greater strength "be continually applied, instead of tending to immortalize, they would tend very rapidly to destroy the human frame." This lesson of development is thus the same one we saw in regard to sex: the self-disciplinary ability to be "temperate" (230) maximizes development.

A similar turn marks another historical "coincidence": in 1793, the very year in which he penned his prize-winning essay on wages and employment and their relationship to "mind" (see chapter 7), Samuel Crumpe published another, apparently unrelated, treatise: *An Inquiry into the Nature and Properties of Opium.*[3] While it is true that low incomes led laborers from gin to the less dear alternative of opium eating, this fact does not figure in Crumpe's choice of topics. In his analyses, money and drugs tell tales of each other only when we attend to the historicity of their conversation: how, in the late eighteenth century, do economic and pharmacological texts interrelate? What links the logic of productivity sought in the wage debate to what Crumpe calls the "truths" of intoxication pursued by "medical reasoning" (5, vi)? To show, as the example of Malthus suggests, that these questions point to the historical importance of the politics of development, I will pursue the making of that "reasoning" within medicine and literature, using Coleridge as my focus. In writing up the history of addiction, I also hope to clarify the way it still configures many of our contemporary critical behaviors, resulting in what appears to be an ongoing addiction to the Romantic discourse of addiction itself.

When Molly Lefebure cast her 1974 biography as "an attempt to present Samuel Taylor Coleridge as it seems that he really was—a junkie,"[4] she effectively placed her work within the mainstream of Coleridge criticism. Despite the street terminology, we recognized yet another study that could approach Coleridge only by positing pathology. Whether taken as a sign of defective character, insufficient Imagination, or physiological weakness, drug use has figured in the construction of all our images of Coleridgean genius. I do not intend to explain the "real" nature either of the "flaw" or of the "genius," but to establish the historicity of their relationship in our anatomies of Romantic art. To show, in other words, why we need to engage the autopsies of the 150 years since his death not in terms of their descriptive accuracy, but of our interpretative procedures. In doing so, we discover how the past and the present, as well as the

medical and the literary, have written each other, allowing Coleridge's and Romanticism's supposed deviations to be the very means
by which we most pressingly feel his and its presence.

The central importance of opium to our portraits of the artist lies
not in the degree to which they directly engage Coleridge's drug habits.
I shall show that all our critical accounts have been unavoidably dependent upon a discourse of addiction that has inscribed the canonical
history of the early nineteenth century with a catalog of characteristic
Romantic behaviors: to explore mind, to undergo epiphany, to alter
vision, to dream dreams, to intensify imagination, to heighten depres-
sion, to suffer ecstasy, to fragment experience, to burn out—to flower
lyrically and then wither. In comparing sleep to poetry, for example,
Keats set up the latter as a restorative flight of fancy that we must
repeatedly retake even though the effect is temporary:

> The visions all are fled—the car is fled
> Into the light of heaven, and in their stead
> A sense of real things comes doubly strong,
> And, like a muddy stream, would bear along
> My soul to nothingness: but I will strive
> Against all doubtings, and will keep alive
> The thought of that same chariot, and the strange
> Journey it went.
>   ("Sleep and Poetry," ll. 155–62)

We must retake that lyric turn because, like the song of the nightingale, it helps us, to use Paul de Man's word from this chapter's
epigraph, "cope." The "Ode to a Nightingale" makes the connection
to intoxicants explicit[5]: the beauty of poetic imagination is a more
sophisticated but still temporary high that we take over and over
again to lift us from the lows of "The weariness, the fever, and the
fret" (l. 23). The endless self-revision of life as development entails
the repetition, in what Keats called "a finer tone" (*Letters,* 37), of the
up-and-down behaviors I have catalogued above.

Every portrait of Coleridge, from genius to plagiarist to poet to
philosopher to friend to addict, has been in large part assembled from
that catalog, as two very powerful cultural myths came to write each
other in the late eighteenth and early nineteenth centuries. Developmental reconceptions of drug use as addiction and of literary production as imaginative creativity helped to naturalize the above behaviors, empowering them to "describe" texts, careers, and periods

along the lines of lyric epiphany and despair so darkly drawn in the
many portraits of Coleridge as flawed genius. Actual drug use is thus
not an essential issue in such descriptions; within the kind of literary
history that frames them, as we saw in regard to the strategies of
sexuality in the last chapter, the drowning of a dear brother or, even
more conveniently, early death, may function as surely as withdrawal
pangs to signify the end of a "naturally" brief high.

Adonais's resurrection, for example, is an elegiac convention,
but that convention functions Romantically by turning not upon a
theological concept of immortality, but upon the (nineteenth century)
psychological truism interrelating quality, intensity, and brevity; the
value of the poetical figures that mourn their maker's short life lies,
like the worth of that life, in their and its evanescence:

> And one with trembling hands clasps his cold head,
> And fans him with her moonlight wings, and cries,
> "Our love, our hope, our sorrow, is not dead;
> See, on the silken fringe of his faint eyes,
> Like dew upon a sleeping flower, there lies
> A tear some Dream has loosened from his brain."
> Lost Angel of a ruined Paradise!
> She knew not 'twas her own; as with no stain
> She faded, like a cloud which had outwept its rain.
>   (*Adonais*, ll.82–90)

Shelley can accept Keats's career as a model for his own only by
insisting that such an early death is not really early but naturally right:

> Why linger, why turn back, why shrink, my Heart?
> Thy hopes are gone before; from all things here
> They have departed; thou shouldst now depart!
> A light is past from the revolving year,
> And man, and woman; and what still is dear
> Attracts to crush, repels to make thee wither.
> The soft sky smiles,—the low wind whispers near:
> 'Tis Adonais calls! oh, hasten thither,
> No more let Life divide what Death can join together.
>   (ll. 469–77)

The equivalent in criticism of this affirmation of early death is the
idea of a Great Decade, which, as I have been emphasizing, can
purport to be an ahistorical aesthetic judgment only as long as the

possibility of a Great Half Century remains Romantically oxymoronic. It has remained that way for so long because two disciplines, medicine and literature, representing what we take to be two different kinds of knowledge, the scientific and the humanistic, have grounded their claims to professional status in a tale of lyrical development—one that, at the turn into the nineteenth century, transformed the drug user into a patient requiring a doctor, and the writer into a genius requiring a critic. To study that transformation, we need to attend not only to the substances consumed by one of the major characters to undergo it, Coleridge, but also to our own dependence upon the (Romantic) literary historical assumptions that allow us to tell it.

It is no coincidence that one of those who has most brilliantly fed that habit began his career with a book on opium usage. *The Milk of Paradise* was no mere youthful diversion for M. H. Abrams; its eighty pages helped to appropriate for modern literary criticism a relationship between conceptions of opiate addiction and of writing literature that validate the Romantic views of art, mind, and nature underlying *The Mirror and the Lamp* and *Natural Supernaturalism*. Abrams's strategy, shared by many literary professionals after the rise of the medical profession during the nineteenth century, is to transfer analogically the scientific credibility we grant statements regarding pharmaceutical effect to assertions of Imaginative power. The greater the certainty, for example, with which he can state that opium's chemical "gift" was "access to a new world as different from this as Mars may be," the more authoritative his celebration of the *natural* power of the "poet's selective spirit" to "creatively" unify "fragments" of that (supernatural) world and the "everyday." To heighten the value of those creations, Abrams derives from the supposed "facts" of addiction a *moral* economy of the imagination: the poems "are to be the more dearly cherished because of the fearful toll exacted for beauty stolen from another world."[6]

The historical irony of using the medical to validate the literary lies in the fact that such a strategy merely completes a circle, for until recently the supposedly authoritative medical accounts of drug use were themselves largely, and often directly, drawn from literary sources: the writings, in particular, of Coleridge and De Quincey. The latter's *Confessions,* for example, was taken by the *Eclectic Review* in 1822 to be primarily a medical treatise; although today's physicians certainly would not accept that classification, it remains in many cases the chief authority behind even their knowledge of opium's effects.[7] Its

early status as both a literary and a medical text confirms Paul-Gabriel
Boucé's observation that, at the turn into the nineteenth century, "the
borderline between 'science' and 'literature' was not as sharply defined
as now."[8] In Julian Drachman's words: "It would be harder to isolate a
body of scientific literature from other writing before 1800 than
since."[9] That isolation resulted not from a lack of engagement between
medicine and literature, but from a pattern of mutual reinforcement:
by writing and rewriting each other for the past 200 years, they drew
the disciplinary boundary line that has by now constituted them as two
very separate realms of knowledge.

Thus when Wordsworth redrew the contract between the poet
and the reader in the Preface to *Lyrical Ballads* by insisting, as we
saw in chapter 4, that the reader be in a "healthful state of association," his use of the language of the new medicine both naturalized
his differences with potential critics (they must not be just wrong or
uneducated, but "sick"), and helped to establish the norms of disease
and deviance essential to a medicalized society. The two professions
were similarly served in 1823 by Dr. Andrew Jacob's *An Essay on the
Influence of the Imagination and Passions in the Production and Cure
of Diseases*. That use of a concept of Imagination recently invigorated
and *psychologized* by the literary texts of Wordsworth, Coleridge,
and others, helped solidify for the "creative" arts the public's belief in
the Imagination as an actual and essential faculty of mind, as it as-
sisted medicine in extending the physician's powers to monitor mental as well as physical health.[10]

Coleridge's life is a text inscribed by these relations of power: the
Poet/Patient who is both the lyrically brilliant practitioner and theore-
tician of the Imagination and, to the best of our knowledge, the first
Englishman to commit himself to the full-time and long-term care of a
surgeon for treatment of drug abuse. The text thus functions as one of
the earliest and most striking embodiments of how the discourse of
addiction enabled the literary and the medical to secure each other's
professional status. To ignore the historicity of that discourse is to
transform the life, Romantically, into a timeless morality tale. Linking "the" opium high and the creative mind in a metaphor of a flame
lyrically exhausting its fuel, Abrams closes *The Milk of Paradise* with
a most familiar portrait: "For fleeting moments of relief and revelation, Coleridge *paid* with a loss of creative power, even of moral
sense, and with a lifetime of physical and mental torture" (emphasis
mine; 49).

This view of Coleridge neither originated with Abrams nor

ended once critics such as Elisabeth Schneider effectively undermined his Martian view of opium. For Schneider, opium "was the
instrument more than the cause" of Coleridge's behavior. Although
she disposes of opium as the inspiration for "Kubla Khan," she does
not step outside the discourse of creative addition. In fact, by relocat-
ing blame from the drug to a type of personality ("his 'lies' [not highs]
were almost always doomed to sink him into a deeper morass than
before"), she inadvertently demonstrates, even more clearly than
Abrams, how thoroughly that discourse penetrated Romantic concepts of the mind, the unconscious, and the individual subject (*Coleridge,* 108–9).

   Alethea Hayter's pluralistic effort to mediate between Abrams's
Coleridge and Schneider's thus proceeds from fundamentally false
assumptions of difference—both between her predecessors and the
two elements of her title: *Opium and the Romantic Imagination.* Because both sets of supposed opposites are generated from the same
discourse, analysis of opium usage becomes, for *all* these critics, an
occasion for asserting the prior and independent existence of an actual faculty of mind called Imagination.[11] Hayter, for example, asserts that opium gives the poet a "chance of observing" the "hiding
places" of his mind "under a stronger light . . . but he can only do this
if he already has a creative imagination."[12] To argue that opium does
or does not have an effect upon *the* Imagination, in other words, is to
authenticate the concept of Imagination. And, as in "primary" Romantic texts such as *The Prelude,* the interpretative descriptions of
the poet that emerge from this critical procedure become, inevitably,
developmental narratives of that Imagination—an Imagination, of
course, addictively conceived: both the "primary" and "secondary"
versions are stories of highs and lows, health and sickness, that invariably entail medical intervention—whether in the form of Nature's
nurselike ministry, a sister's solicitude, a fellow patient's generosity, a
doctor's care, or a critic's posthumous reappraisal.

   The critical intervention may be under the guise of helping the
poet out of an interpretative low, as when Lefebure urges "that un-
scrupulous plagiarism should not be confused with an advanced case
of morphine reliance" (15), but it always ends up preserving the
"flawed genius" model and the necessity of ongoing medi-critical
supervision. Lefebure's purpose in her Coleridge biography, for example, like Matthew Arnold's in regard to Wordsworth, is to save the
patient from himself. Both try to isolate the flaw from the genius by
constructing developmental case histories that distance the lows from

the lyrical highs: Arnold surgically removes, with supposedly timeless taste, a great decade from sixty years of writing, while Lefebure distinguishes, as a matter of what she takes to be ahistorical medical truth, the poet from the junkie. The very fact that the matter is medical, however, attests to it being culture-specific—a concept tied to the new norms of health and sickness essential to the professionalization of early nineteenth-century English society.[13] Within those norms, the highs and lows, the Poet and the Junkie, call each other forth so that they may be, time after time, expertly separated.

In our calling, this separation is executed through what I have been terming the lyric turn. The discourse of addiction, in other words, inscribes the critic as well as the poet, the doctor as well as the patient. In performing the revisionary work of Literature (see chapter 5), the literary professional has addictively returned to the turn. That behavior has been particularly evident in much of the most prominent scholarship on the Romantics over the past decade: those efforts that, as I pointed out in chapter 1, sought to demystify the notions of the Visionary Imagination popularized during the 1950s and 1960s. They did so by modifying the adjective and replacing the noun, so that *Language* rather than the Mind was seen as the source of an absolute *Re*visionary activity.

In Harold Bloom's case, it would be more accurate to say that the sources conflated, since he identified linguistic tropes as psychological strategies. The result was a series of ahistorical "revisionary ratios" that turned *all* reading into misreading and *all* writing into revision. For the younger Yale scholars, the literary problem was not the Father's overwhelming Presence but His devastating Absence; in a poststructuralist twist on Abrams's secularization scenario,[14] the Romantic poets were seen to face the Abyss with revisionary Words rather than with Imagination as their consolatory weapon. Yet their actions, particularly for Leslie Brisman, were no less heroic: "Poets," he proclaimed at the end of *Romantic Origins,* "restore the romance of both theories of origin ['God' and 'Bare earth']. Secular heralds of a second coming, they challenge our complacency about what is first in importance or first in time." Notice that the "Poets" to whom Brisman referred were not just the Romantics but *all* poets, from the authors of Genesis through Wallace Stevens. The lower case *r* in the sentence "Christian myth was similarly romantic in countering original sin with a pre-Genesis account of Satan and Son"[15] confirms a Bloomian elision of historical differences. Perhaps we should say a Wordsworthian elision, since this strategy is most familiar to us as enacted in the "Immortality Ode": the poet becomes philosophic hero, as change felt as loss is transformed by re-vision into intimations of the unchanging. Whether performed by Wordsworth, Bloom, or Brisman, the apotheosis of the "Poets"[16] entails the displacement of history by transcendent continuities.

The demystification of the Imagination has thus yielded yet another mystification, this time of Revision. The discourse of addiction, after all, valorizes both the high *and* the compulsive effort always to get higher—even the cures, of course, as evidenced in the late 1980s by the *prestige* attending admission (and readmission) to the Betty Ford Hospital, are but a special kind of high. An alternative to further mystification, then, is to historicize that discourse. We can do so by returning to opium and examining its transformation into an addictive drug.

In the eighteenth century, opium use was common and as casual an act as taking aspirin today. It functioned as a cure-all, as a poor man's gin, and, as evidenced by widespread infant doping, as a form of social control. However, since the way in which a society lives on terms with a drug determines how the drug's effects are experienced,[17] there was no need for a coherent concept of addiction. When, at the beginning of the century, for example, Dr. John Jones published *The Mysteries of Opium Reveal'd,* he explained essentially the same paradoxical workings of opium with which we are familiar, as well as "The Effects of the going off (or declination) of the Operation of Opium,"[18] without recourse to the addictive model of disease, character flaw, and social problem. Finding in opium a "pleasing Delight" (254) and "the strangest Catalog of Riddles, that ever was seen" (33)—a drug that excites and quiets, maddens yet composes— Jones praises its charms, insisting, despite his awareness that sudden abstention leads to "Great and even intolerable Distress" (32), that "Opium *does not* diminish *or disable the Spirits* by *any* means whatsoever" (81). Its opposing effects merely allow it to perform two different functions: it is both a "stupifying *Medicament*" deadening pain and an irritant that "causes *Erections,* & c." (25) The overall effect is "a permanent gentle *Degree* of that Pleasure, which Modesty forbids the naming of" (20). It "particularly" effects "the Stomach and Venereal Parts, as being more exquisitely disposed for sensation for the Preservation of the Individuum and Species" (191).

Occasional ill effects and the distress of abstention are also easily explained as matters of "accident," impurities, or overindulgence: "There is nothing so good, whereof an *intemperate use* is not *mischie-*

vous, God having so ordered it to deter from, and punish *Intemperance,* and the *Abuse* of his *Creatures*" (193–94, 245). This Providential logic both dovetails nicely with the "preservation of species" argument—withdrawal pains as natural birth control—and, in embracing all "things," clearly precludes the distinction between addictive and nonaddictive substances so essential to the modern medical model. In addition, the characteristic eighteenth-century emphasis on moderation (not, significantly, abstention) is presented as a generalized observation applicable to everyone without reference to concepts of disease or individual susceptibility. Jones's conclusions, as a result, lack the hysterical tone and signs of moral condemnation and alarm typical of nineteenth-century treatises.[19] For him, the drug is naturalized sexually, rationalized procreatively, and moralized theologically. For us, it is naturalized psychologically, rationalized professionally, and moralized characterologically.

The emergence of the latter version early in the nineteenth century was thus not simply a matter, as the doctors would have it, of dispelling ignorance, for this shift entails conceptual changes that alter the relationships between knowledge and power. Psychologizing the drug's effects, for example, requires that the drug taker be reconstituted as a possible patient—an individual whose depth of *mind* invites deep professional intervention. To expose hidden flaws, one must first construct a hiding place. Not until the end of the eighteenth century, in Crumpe's treatise, is opium posited as a problem for certain "constitutions."[20] "The history of addiction," points out Dr. E. W. Adams in 1937, "necessarily begins, not with the first addicts, but with the first physicians who were able to recognize addiction."[21] They were "able" to do so, of course, only when they *needed* to do so. When the individual becomes the patient, the doctor becomes the professional and the relationship between the two becomes "sacred."

Nineteenth-century medical texts focused upon that bond as they redefined the nature of disease and the role of the doctor in treating it. What are now taken to be common-sense warnings against quack remedies and quacks, were and are a part of a larger argument against the disease and cure model of medicine. In Dr. P. M. Latham's words from the midnineteenth century, we must recognize the "distinction, plain, simple, and needful as it is, between *curing* the disease and *treating* the patient."[22] It is "needed" professionally because, if the cure is found and made known, the doctor becomes essentially irrelevant, except perhaps as a technician to administer it. But in the treatment model the doctor's role is ensured and prolonged: "by knowing *what* a man is, and *how* he lives habitually," claims Latham, "a physician arrives at a . . . better treatment of his diseases" (344). Professional status lies in the authority to convert such personal knowledge into juridical prescription: "Diseases are not abstractions: they are . . . modes of acting *different* from the *ordinary* and *healthy* modes—modes of *disorganizing,* modes of suffering; and modes of dying; there must be a living, moving, sentient body for all this" (emphasis mine; 70). That "body" requires a doctor whose value to the health of the individual and the stability of society is the ability to define and then distinguish the "different" from the "ordinary" and to naturalize oppositions among modes of organization as matters of health and sickness.

The emergence of the concept of addiction thus signals the establishment of a new medical, literary, and social norm in which power is exercised through the pronouncement of knowledge. In fact, the root meaning of both "diction" and "addiction" is "to say," "to pronounce." To dictate diction is to determine *how* we say, which of course is to delimit *what* we *can* say. It is no accident, therefore, that at the same historical moment literary experts made an issue of poetical diction, defining the "real" language "really" spoken by "real" men, medical experts made a disease of opiate addiction, exposing the "reality" of drug use. The sympathetic identification of writer and reader, asked by authors, and the same relationship between doctor and patient, required by physicians, were the idealized conditions for communicating these new realities as an assertion of professional power. That power aggrandized itself through the celebration of lyric highs, which it then domesticated within developmental narratives such as the "Immortality Ode," *The Milk of Paradise,* and addiction; the latter, in Alfred Lindesmith's words, owes its "origin . . . not to a single event, but to a series of events, thus implying that [it] is established in a learning process extending over a period of time."[23] In both the literary and the medical versions, as in the economic version, development's promise of "something evermore about to be" always requires a turn to "Duty" that inculcates the values of conformity and self-help—pulling one's "low" self up "high" by one's own bootstraps.[24]

Thus at the end of the eighteenth century, as professional power was mystified in psychological terms such as the creative imagination and the dependent personality, opium was rewritten by the culture to write the rules of the new hegemony. Simultaneously celebrated on the one hand for its link to imagination, self-exploration, and expression, and condemned on the other for its destructive effect on "char-

acter," opium *became* an addictive drug. The resulting discourse of
addiction, as we have seen, inscribed upon the culture an inherently
disciplinary model of lyrical development, in which individual aspiration was idealized but at the same time placed under professional
surveillance for signs of immoral overindulgence requiring "treatment." By 1868, with the Pharmaceutical Act and Arnoldian High
Criticism, opium could be dispensed only by druggists, and "culture"
was the preserve of literary critics.

By portraying Coleridge as an addict or flawed genius we, as
doctors of literature, have succeeded in authorizing our own professional status, but we have also missed the literary historical point.
The texts by and about him under our "care" do not detail the "discovery" or "uncovering" of addiction, the mind, imagination, the unconscious, and genius, but the construction of them. Only when we recognize their historicity can we break our own critical habits and treat an
issue such as plagiarism, for instance, as a matter not simply of total
borrowings or personal motive, but of a discourse that turns upon a
moral distinction between the natural and the counterfeit, the imagination and the drug. By the middle of the last century, that discourse
of addiction had entrapped not only Coleridge, but, as we read in an
anonymous treatise of 1868, all "literary men, persons suffering from
protracted nervous disorders, women obliged by their necessities to
work beyond their strength," and "prostitutes" into the "fraternity"
of potential "opium-eaters" in need of the cure.[25] It is time, after
more than 150 years, to reconceive, within a new literary history, our
relationship to the Romantic discourse of addiction and creativity
that Coleridge helped to articulate, and that has, with our help, written all of us.

Coda: A Reconception of Kind

I conclude with a tailpiece that retells a tale that Wordsworth retold
from Milton and that Milton retold from Geoffrey of Monmouth. By
incorporating this feature of repetition, I establish continuity with the
critical discourse of addiction; I also, however, assert discontinuity by
producing a difference in kind rather than aiming for a "higher"
degree. Wordsworth's version of 1815 was also offered as an act of
kindness: in his own words, "Artegal and Elidure" was a "token of
affectionate respect for the memory of Milton."[26] By composing that
poem, Wordsworth was responding to an invitation Milton had issued

in his *History of England:* "I have determined to bestow the telling over even of these reputed tales, be it for nothing else but in favour of our English Poets and Rhetoricians, who by their art will know how to use them judiciously."

The tale that Wordsworth chose was itself chosen by Milton from Monmouth's *The History of the Kings of Britain* as a lesson in royal politics. Gorbonian, the eldest of Morindus's five sons, is presented as treating all his constituents in kind; Milton goes to the trouble of carefully ordering Monmouth's list of Gorbonian's accomplishments, so that kingly perfection can be imaged as the proper hierarchical treatment of "the gods," "men of desert," and "the commons." Having detailed proper government, Milton can explain the fate of Archigallo (Wordsworth's Artegal), the second of the brothers to become king, with terse precision: "Archigallo, the second brother, followed not his example: but depressed the ancient nobility: and, by peeling the wealthier sort, stuffed his treasury, and took the right way to be deposed." The next brother, Elidure, "a mind so noble, and so moderate, as almost is incredible to be found," proves to be both a more Gorbonian-like leader and an exceptionally compassionate brother. When Archigallo returns secretly from exile in order to regain the crown, Elidure chances to meet him, and although "but thinly accompanied, runs to him with open arms," conveys him to the city, and hides him with the purpose of restoring him to the throne. His strategy, as described by Monmouth, is to feign sickness, invite the peers one by one into his bedchamber, and threaten to cut off the head of any one of them who would not swear allegiance to Archigallo.[27]

Such violence does not suit Milton, who just says that Elidure "causes them, willing or unwilling . . . to swear allegiance," as the story for him teaches the political lesson that the crown "for which thousands of nearest blood have destroyed each other, was in respect of brotherly dearness, a contemptible thing." Brotherly dearness was clearly on Wordsworth's mind when he chose to retell the story, for he places it next to "The Brothers" in "Poems Founded on the Affections." However, in 1815 the decision to retell a tale of a despotic leader returning from exile to try to regain a throne was certainly not underdetermined. The fact that Archigallo is converted by Elidure's love and becomes a worthy ruler had the potential of resolving twenty-five tumultuous years into a fairy tale: the Fraternity of the Revolution would emerge triumphant over past misdeeds.

Since Wordsworth does not alter the basic story line, the poem can be read that way. But in the telling he does something that can help us clarify our relationship to the Romantic past. This particular kind of historical information has gone largely untapped primarily because this poem was written almost a decade after the supposed Great Decade. That myth of lyric brevity, as I have been emphasizing, has helped sustain the illusion that our aesthetic preferences are somehow natural. To pick a poem and argue about what is "really" great has not been, and is not here, my point, since that would only reinforce the illusion; I make use of material the Great Decade excludes in order to historicize the limits it imposes and thus clarify what has been at stake throughout this book: an understanding of the formal and conceptual limitations of different kinds of literary historical knowledge.

"Artegal and Elidure" assists us both thematically and formally. Wordsworth problematizes the question of what he is writing about by providing eight full stanzas before introducing Gorbonian. They interrelate the literary production of texts with the political history of Britain, starting with a gesture that recalls the dream of the Arab in Book V of *The Prelude*. What prevents the "fatal dissolution" of what man "had ever been" (ll.7–8) from becoming an end to history itself, and thus an apocalyptic theft of our identity, is a book:

> Nathless, a British record (long concealed
> In old Armorica, whose secret springs
> No Gothic conqueror ever drank) revealed
> The marvellous current of forgotten things.
>   (ll.9–12)

The retelling of those "things," and the telling of new ones, is represented as playing such an integral role in the growth of a British identity that the same metaphors are used for both the people in the records and the records themselves. Britain is "happy" because it is written about, its ancient "silence" broken by individual actions and the texts that tell of them (ll. 25–32). Imaged as a garden, it grows "weeds" that are at one point (l.30) villains, like "Guendolen," who threw her "blameless child" into the Severn, and are at another point (l. 64) poems "that, wanting not wild grace, are from all mischief free!"

This particular weed is characteristically Wordsworthian in its formal play, since, as we have seen, variations on the sonnet and on its constituent parts, the octave and the sestet, occupy a central role in his overall poetic production. Here, as with a fourteen-book *Pre-*

lude filled with embedded sonnets and sonnet parts, we have a poem of eight-line stanzas featuring an eight-stanza introduction, the volta for the whole piece marked, in the one irregular stanza, by a final couplet of rhyming alexandrines (ll. 64–65). The stanza is a unique variation within the family of stanzas that Wordsworth and the other Romantics used primarily in their narrative poems. It has the same number of lines as the ottava rima of *Don Juan,* the rhyme scheme differing by a couplet, and it shares a closing alexandrine with the Spenserian stanza of "The Eve of St. Agnes" and "Adonais."

The eight lines are divided by rhyme and meter into an initial heroic quatrain rhyming *abab* and two concluding couplets. Both of those are metrically broken, the first by a turn to trimeter, and the second by the extra foot of the alexandrine—the stanzaically repeated irregularity producing the architectonic effects of a Pindaric ode. By linking the stanza of Gray's "Elegy" to the Pindaric, Wordsworth was able to combine a turn to the English past that presents Britain as a garden naturally suited to what Coleridge called the "reflective mind" of elegy, with the formal high purpose of an ode that speaks of British kings and ends with a monumental inscription: "And, from this triumph of affection pure, / He bore the lasting name of 'pious Elidure!'" (ll. 240–41).

Such a combination is also particularly suited to the way Wordsworth tells that triumph. Because it is relatively intricate in its rhyme and in its metrical variation, this composite arrangement cannot carry a narrative line as efficiently as a simpler stanza like the ballad. But the line of actions is precisely what Wordsworth revises out of the tale. An early manuscript spends four full stanzas conveying the particulars of how Elidure convinced the peers to accept Artegal. This version not only elaborates on Milton, but even surpasses Monmouth's account of the threat to cut off their heads; it goes to the length of describing a "dread summit" from which Elidure threatened "to fling their bodies to the wind" (*Poems,* 21–22). In the published version (1820), all thirty-two of those lines were reduced to one: "The Story tells what courses were pursued" (l.218). If the reader wants a recounting of the political actions, "The Story" will tell them, but not Wordsworth. The body of his poem consists instead of talk, the twists and turns of speech being far more suited to his stanza:

> "By heavenly Powers conducted, we have met;
> —O Brother! to my knowledge lost so long,
> But neither lost to love, nor to regret,

Nor to my wishes lost;—forgive the wrong,
(Such as it may seem) if I thy crown have borne,
   Thy royal mantle worn:
I was their natural guardian; and 'tis just
That now I should restore what hath been held in trust."

                                                        (ll.130–37)

The talk is politics psychologized—thirteen stanzas of Elidure and Artegal planning the new reign by discussing how the people will behave if properly manipulated. This Romantic discourse transforms politics into an act of conversation, the conferring being a means of constituting expertise, an expertise whose object is the subject and how it develops:

"Dismiss thy followers;—let them calmly wait
   Such change in thy estate
As I already have in thought devised;
And which, with caution due, may soon be realized."

                                                        (ll. 214–17)

Wordsworth honors Milton by transforming Elidure's piety, his "brotherly dearness," into an act of sympathy and judgment—a professional intervention that straightens out Artegal's development by prescribing "caution" and discipline: "'respect / Awaits on virtuous life'" (ll. 186–87). We can, in turn, honor Wordsworth by pre-scribing another kind of professional behavior, one that transforms kindness itself, from a lyrical feature of psychological poetry that points to the affections as origin to a theoretical feature of literary history that enables an understanding of change.

I offer that understanding not as a "cure" for our Romantic addictions; addiction is itself, as I have shown, a tale of the need to be cured. What a new literary history offers instead is the ability to hear that tale within Romantic discourse and thereby recognize that discourse's ongoing power. The developing self that writes and is written by the features and procedures I have analyzed is subject to addictive desire and is thus the object of disciplinary cures. To classify that self as a construct—to put it in the past—is to obviate the need for such discipline: differences of kind need not collapse sympathetically into the psychological depths of degree, and absolute judgments of degree need not function as a blind to other ways of reading the past and of writing the present.

Notes

Chapter 1

1. Otto Friedrich, "Onion Theory," review of *Home: A Short History of an Idea,* by Witold Rybczynski, *Time,* 4 August 1986, p. 64.

2. Advertisement in the *New York Review of Books,* 29 May 1986, p. 48.

3. For a very useful effort to define what it means "to write a theory in words," see Ralph Cohen, "Literary Theory as a Genre," *Centrum* 3:1 (Spring 1975), 45–64.

4. Marilyn Butler, for example, sees parallels between past and present change in the final chapter of *Romantics, Rebels and Reactionaries* (Oxford: Oxford University Press, 1982).

5. Geoffrey Hartman, *Wordsworth's Poetry, 1787–1814* (New Haven: Yale University Press, 1971). M. H. Abrams, *Natural Supernaturalism* (New York: Norton, 1971). Idem, *The Mirror and the Lamp* (New York: Oxford University Press, 1953).

6. Thomas Weiskel, *The Romantic Sublime* (Baltimore: Johns Hopkins University Press, 1976). Frances Ferguson, *Language as Counter-Spirit* (New Haven: Yale University Press, 1977). David Simpson, *Irony and Authority in Romantic Poetry* (Totowa, N.J.: Rowman and Littlefield, 1979). See also Tilottama Rajan, *Dark Interpreter: The Discourse of Romanticism* (Ithaca: Cornell University Press, 1980), and Michael Ragussis, *The Subterfuge of Art: Language and the Romantic Tradition* (Baltimore: Johns Hopkins University Press, 1978).

7. As I discuss in detail in chapter 4, critical close reading is formally related to the Romantic procedure of description: "look[ing] steadily," as Wordsworth put it, at the "subject." See his Preface to *Lyrical Ballads* in *The Prose Works of William Wordsworth,* ed. W. J. B. Owen and Jane Worthington Smyser (Oxford: Clarendon Press, 1974), I, 132. This source is cited hereafter as *Prose.*

8. All these reviews appeared in *The Wordsworth Circle* 15:3 (Summer 1984).

9. Jerome McGann, *The Romantic Ideology: A Critical Investigation* (Chicago: University of Chicago Press, 1983). Morris Eaves and Michael Fisher, eds., *Romanticism and Contemporary Criticism* (Ithaca: Cornell University Press, 1986).

10. Mitchell both speculates about how the Romantic "stands in a number of relationships to modern and contemporary culture" and suggests "that the question of semantic determinacy has just about played itself out," leading to "certain things that are happening within literary theory." Serious analysis of those "things," however, is precluded by such supposedly "common sense" statements as this one: "This intuition is probably nothing more than the usual stock-market sense that what goes up must come down" (94–95).

11. Charles Ryzepka, *The Self as Mind: Vision and Identity in Wordsworth, Coleridge, and Keats* (Cambridge: Harvard University Press, 1986).

12. Geoffrey Hartman, *Criticism in the Wilderness: The Study of Literature Today* (New Haven: Yale University Press, 1980).

13. For a discussion of the concepts of normative innovation and variation, see Ralph Cohen, "Innovation and Variation: Literary Change and Georgic Poetry," in *Literature and History: Papers Read at a Clark Library Seminar, March 3, 1973* (Los Angeles: William Andrews Clark Memorial Library, 1974), pp. 3–42.

14. Ralph Cohen, "A Propaedeutic for Literary Change," *Critical Exchange* 13 (1983), 11–12.

15. I make extensive use of Wordsworthian texts because I find them, in Jerome McGann's words, "normative and, in every sense, exemplary" (*Romantic Ideology,* 82). The fact that he and I would offer different critical rationales for that judgment only confirms the discursive power of the texts. I would point not to particular ideological "patterns" in Great Decade works, but to the extensive temporal and generic range of the entire oeuvre—a range full of the evidence, as my book demonstrates, of a formal working through of the "problems" and "solutions" of Romantic discourse.

Chapter 2

1. Paul de Man, *Allegories of Reading* (New Haven: Yale University Press, 1979), p. ix.

2. James Engell, *The Creative Imagination: Enlightenment to Romanticism* (Cambridge: Harvard University Press, 1981), p. 266. The reviewer is Ralph Cohen in *Criticism* 24:2 (Spring 1982), 174–80.

3. Cyrus Hamlin, "The Hermeneutics of Form: Reading the Romantic Ode," *Boundary 2* 7:3 (Spring 1979), 21.

4. Robert Mayo, "The Contemporaneity of the *Lyrical Ballads,*" *PMLA* 69 (June 1954), 486–522.

5. Chaviva Hošek and Patricia Parker, eds., *Lyric Poetry: Beyond New Criticism* (Ithaca: Cornell University Press, 1985).

6. Fredric Jameson, *The Political Unconscious* (Ithaca: Cornell University Press, 1981), p. 105.

7. Ralph Cohen, "History and Genre," *New Literary History* 17:2 (Winter 1986), 204.

8. Jacques Derrida, "The Law of Genre," *Critical Inquiry* 7:1 (Autumn 1980), 65.

9. Alastair Fowler, *Kinds of Literature: An Introduction to the Theory of Genres and Modes* (Cambridge: Harvard University Press, 1982).

10. William Elford Rodgers, *The Three Genres and the Interpretation of Lyric* (Princeton: Princeton University Press, 1983), p. 30.

11. Hošek and Parker, *Lyric Poetry,* p. 225. Chase takes her Keats quote from John Keats, *Selected Poems and Letters,* ed. Douglas Bush (Boston: Houghton Mifflin, 1959), p. 292. I use John Keats, *Letters of John Keats: A New Selection,* ed. Robert Gittings (Oxford: Oxford University Press, 1970), pp. 52–55. It is the latter edition that as *Letters,* is hereafter cited in the text.

12. Dorothy Osborne's letters were admitted to *The Norton Anthology of English Literature* in the fifth edition only to be introduced by a profoundly sexist headnote I address in chapter 8. The "kindness" letter is that of 4 February 1654. See M. H. Abrams et al., eds., *The Norton Anthology of English Literature,* 5th ed., 2 vols. (New York: Norton, 1986), II, 1749–50.

13. The terms "strophe" and "antistrophe" refer in Greek to the chorus turning to move from one side of the stage to the other.

14. See Ronald Sharp, *Keats, Skepticism, and the Religion of Beauty* (Athens: University of Georgia Press, 1979), pp. 174–75.

15. M. H. Abrams, "Structure and Style in the Greater Romantic Lyric," in *From Sensibility to Romanticism,* ed. Frederick W. Hilles and Harold Bloom (New York: Oxford University Press, 1965), p. 522.

16. John Louis Rowlett, "The Generic Wordsworth," Diss., University of Virginia, 1987. Cited hereafter as Rowlett.

17. Jeffrey Baker, "Prelude and Prejudice," and Robert Young, "A Reply: To 'Prelude and Prejudice,'" in *The Wordsworth Circle* 13:2 (Spring 1982), 79–86, 87–88. Herbert Lindenberger made one of the first efforts to put the 1805/1850 debate in "historical context" in a paper delivered at the 1984 Wordsworth Conference and *Prelude* Colloquium. The finale of that event, including Lindenberger's talk, is reprinted in *The Wordsworth Circle* 17:1 (Winter 1986), 1–38.

18. Tilottama Rajan, following Frances Ferguson, argues that thematizing the problem of reading is characteristic of Romantic texts. See *Dark Interpreter,* p. 262.

19. Paul de Man, *Blindness and Insight: Essays in the Rhetoric of Contemporary Criticism,* 2nd ed. (Minneapolis: University of Minnesota Press, 1983), p. 198. "The Rhetoric of Temporality" was originally published in Charles Singleton, ed. *Interpretation* (Baltimore: Johns Hopkins University Press, 1969).

20. For a critique of de Man "asserting the essential identity of three works in three languages spanning nearly a century, one in prose, the others in radically different forms of poetry," see Karl Kroeber's bibliographic essay on Wordsworth in *The English Romantic Poets: A Review of Research and Criticism,* 4th ed., ed. Frank Jordan (New York: Modern Language Assocation of America, 1985), pp. 336–37.

21. "Through" should be "though" and "latter" should be "letter." The quotation as printed on page 206 of *Blindness and Insight* differs in these places, and in others, from Wordsworth's text. See both de Man's source, *The Poetical Works of William Wordsworth,* ed. E. de Selincourt and Helen Darbishire (Oxford: Oxford University Press, 1940–49), IV, 446, (cited hereafter as *Poems*), and *Prose,* II, 51.

22. Rowlett, p. 168. By placing the Lucy poems within a specific ballad line, Rowlett pulls the historical rug out from under the feet of the many biographical critics who have personalized and psychologized the William/Lucy relationship.

Chapter 3

1. Plato, *Ion,* in *The Dialogues of Plato,* trans. Benjamin Jowett, 4th ed. (Oxford: Clarendon Press, 1953), I, 116.

2. Thomas McFarland, *Originality & Imagination* (Baltimore: Johns Hopkins University Press, 1985), p. xiii.

3. For examples of such procedures, see the discussion of Keats's letters in chapter 2, the Hartman section of this chapter, and chapter 5.

4. Thomas McFarland, *Romanticism and the Forms of Ruin* (Princeton: Princeton University Press, 1981), p. 418.

5. Ronald Wendling, quoted in *The Wordsworth Circle* 15:3 (Summer 1984), 97.

6. See J. Robert Barth's comparisons between McFarland's books and Coleridgean form in *The Wordsworth Circle* 15:3 (Summer 1984), 96.

7. By analyzing McFarland in this manner, I am not trying to valorize Bloom.

Both critics turn from history in their shared desire to venerate a transcendent poetical "greatness." For further comments on Bloom, see chapter 9.

8. See Cohen, *Literary Theory as a Genre,* p. 57.

9. Advertisement in the *New York Review of Books,* 4 March 1982, p. 33.

10. Geoffrey Hartman, *Criticism in the Wilderness: The Study of Literature Today* (New Haven: Yale University Press, 1980), pp. 5–6, 14. Cited hereafter as *CIW.*

11. Geoffrey Hartman, "How Creative Should Literary Criticism Be?" in the *New York Times Book Review,* 5 April 1981, p. 26. Cited hereafter as *NYT.*

12. Jonathan Culler, "The Mirror Stage," in *High Romantic Argument: Essays for M. H. Abrams,* ed. Lawrence Lipking (Ithaca: Cornell University Press, 1981), pp. 150, 163.

13. "Essay, Supplementary to the Preface," in *Prose,* III, 81. See my discussion of the author-reader relationship in "Wordsworth's Gothic Endeavor: From *Esthwaite* to the Great Decade," *The Wordsworth Circle* 10:2 (Spring 1979), 161–73.

14. James Beattie, *Essays on Poetry and Music, As They Affect the Mind,* 2nd ed. (Edinburgh, 1778). James Engell, in *The Creative Imagination,* discusses how the "idea of sympathy . . . had become intimately connected with the idea of the imagination" (143) during the eighteenth century. In its celebration of the "creative imagination," Engell's book becomes yet another expresson of anxiety over the whereabouts of that "faculty."

15. Samuel Coleridge, *Biographia Literaria,* ed. J. Shawcross (Oxford: Oxford University Press, 1907), II, 5–6.

16. *The Poetry and Prose of William Blake,* ed. David V. Erdman (Garden City: Doubleday, 1970), pp 1–2. Cited hereafter as *Blake.*

17. As of the fourth edition, it has been included in *The Norton Anthology of English Literature.*

18. For interesting analyses of the imaginative economics of Romanticism, see David Aers, Jonathan Cook, and David Punter, *Romanticism and Ideology: Studies in English Writing, 1765–1830* (London: Routledge & Kegan Paul, 1981), pp. 24–26; and Kurt Heinzelman, *The Economics of the Imagination* (Amherst: University of Massachusetts Press, 1980), pp. 196–233.

19. William Godwin, *Caleb Williams,* ed. David McCracken (New York: Norton, 1970, 1977), p. 4.

20. Ferguson connects this paradox to Wordsworth's notion of immortality in *Language as Counter-Spirit* (33). See my comments on this connection in chapter 5.

21. No text, in other words, is "original" or "primary." Thus J. Hillis Miller can criticize M. H. Abrams for his "mode of citation" in *Natural Supernaturalism,* "which is to illustrate some straightforward point with a quotation which is not 'interpreted,' in the sense of being teased for multiple meanings or implications, but which is taken as the confirmation of the 'point' which has just been made." See "Tradition and Difference," *Diacritics* 2 (Winter 1972), 11.

22. Part of the Romantic sympathetic strategy is to locate the author's most overtly aggressive tactics and assertions "outside" the work of art in such extratextual forms as prefaces, essays supplementary to prefaces, and afterwords. See chapter 5.

23. Jerome McGann, *The Beauty of Inflections: Literary Investigations in Historical Method and Theory* (Oxford: Clarendon Press, 1985), p. 334.

24. In Chapter 9 I show how, beginning in the late eighteenth and early nineteenth centuries, the medical language of health and sickness reinforces the literary language of Romantic imagination.

25. Michel Foucault, *Power/Knowledge: Selected Interviews and Other Writings, 1972–1977,* ed. Colin Gordon (New York: Pantheon Books, 1980), p. 118.

26. The mystification of the Great Decade is exemplified by McGann's reference to "the notorious waning of Wordsworth's poetic powers" (110). Is notoriety a form of proof? Is poetry always the product of special powers? What kind of powers are they? Why do they mysteriously appear and disappear?

27. To borrow an image that enters the literary when this dialectic does, the vampire must first be admitted (through and into human kindness) before it can use its fangs to undo, in the name of individual desire, the inherited hierarchy of blood.

28. David Simpson raises the issue of the individual author in terms different from but compatible with mine: "The kinds of meanings of poetry discussed here are not simply to be adjudicated by reference to a biographical entity called 'Wordsworth,' helpful and important though such reference may be. They relate to 'discourse,' to something which is rather loosely under the control of the independent subject, conscious and unconscious, inevitable as it is that they are announced through and refracted by that subject. . . . meanings are to be sought as much in the interrelations of the language of poetry with the languages of contemporary argument and expression as in the corporate identity 'Wordsworth.'" See *Wordsworth and the Figurings of the Real* (London: Macmillan, 1982), p. xxvi.

29. L. J. Swingle, "On Reading Romantic Poetry," *PMLA* 86 (1971), 974.

30. Repetition is also suggested by the phrase "the human form," since McGann takes it from Hegel's "negative judgment" of Classical Art. The return to the human form is thus offered as a kind of cyclic turn from the Romantic ideology back to something resembling the older, anthropomorphic ideal.

31. In an essay written after *The Romantic Ideology,* even the ideological "displacements" are familiarized as a natural "process by which people have preserved the divine vision in a time of trouble" (*Beauty of Inflections,* 340).

Chapter 4

1. *Collected Works of Oliver Goldsmith,* ed. Arthur Friedman (Oxford: Clarendon Press, 1966), III, 53. Cited hereafter as *Goldsmith.*

2. Karsten Harries, "Metaphor and Transcendence," *Critical Inquiry* 5 (1978), 84.

3. Simpson argues that "the making of metaphor serves to bind the subject into a wished-for relation to its context, in that the conjunctions which it establishes are the wished-for features of an imaginary world which the subject can then reflect back in order to constitute itself. It is the subject which 'holds together' the terms of the comparison, and it can therefore focus itself as the origin of the perception of that comparison, which thus becomes an expression of how this subject wants to be." *Irony and Authority,* p. 153.

4. Ted Cohen, "Metaphor and Cultivation of Intimacy," *Critical Inquiry* 5 (1978), 9.

5. See Ian Watt on the "ironic posture" of the "Augustan" writer, whose sense of his audience "resulted in a continual pressure toward shaping every element of discourse, from the single word to the total work, with two opposite categories of people in mind: the 'mob' and the 'chosen few.'" The posture is "both a formal expression of the qualitative divisions in the reading public and a flattering reenforcement of the sense of superiority that animates the more sophisticated part of it." Watt, "The Ironic

Voice," in Ian Watt, ed., *The Augustan Age* (Greenwich: Fawcett Publications, 1968), pp. 12–19.

6. Harold Perkin, *The Origins of Modern English Society, 1780–1880* (London: Routledge & Kegan Paul, 1969), p. 29.

7. Raymond Williams, *The Country and the City* (New York: Oxford University Press, 1973), p. 78.

8. Oliver Goldsmith, "An Account of the Augustan Age of England," in *Goldsmith*, I, 504.

9. Martin Price, *To the Palace of Wisdom* (Carbondale: Southern Illinois University Press, 1964), p. 344.

10. "In praying," argues Philip Wheelwright, "a worshipper speaks as if to a living presence in direct address, and by speaking to it he tends to conceive it in a certain way, as a semi-personal being who can hear and respond." See *Metaphor and Reality* (Bloomington: Indiana University Press, 1968), p. 150. Martin Price's terminology makes the eighteenth-century connection explicit: "personification is achieved only by the mind at the limits of its power, exploring dim realms or even creating its own fiction. . . . If the sublime is the art of transcendence, the personification is among its characteristic works" (*To the Palace of Wisdom*, 369).

11. Steven Knapp, *Personification and the Sublime: Milton to Coleridge* (Cambridge: Harvard University Press, 1985), p. 87. Knapp's study is provocative, particularly in its concluding suggestion of a relationship between personification and the literary institution: "But in later writers these already allegorical agents were enlisted in a further allegory: with their peculiar combination of power and fictionality, they came to personify an emerging political and philosophical ideal of literary agency itself" (141).

12. "Whether or not," argues Harold Perkin, "we accept all the implications of Rostow's 'take-off into self-sustained economic growth' between 1783 and 1802, it is clear that these years spanned the central phase of a transition which was to carry the British economy from a lower to a higher plane of productiveness, and create the framework of the modern industrial system" (*Origins*, 2).

13. Richard Altick, *The English Common Reader* (Chicago: University of Chicago Press, 1957), p. 30.

14. From the *Adventurer*, 115, 11 December 1753, in *The Yale Editions of the Works of Samuel Johnson*, ed. W. J. Bate, John M. Bullitt, C. F. Powell (New Haven: Yale University Press, 1963), II, 457. Ian Watt discusses the reactions of Johnson and his contemporaries to this phenomenon in *The Rise of the Novel* (Berkeley: University of California Press, 1957), p. 58.

15. From a review of *The Beldames: a Poem* in the *Critical Review* for February 1759 (vii. 173) cited as "quite possibly by Goldsmith" in *Goldsmith*, I, 504.

16. *Goldsmith*, I, 310–11, 498–504.

17. Gene Ruoff was one of the first critics to point out the importance of sympathy for Wordsworth in "Wordsworth on Language: Toward a Radical Poetics for English Romanticism," *The Wordsworth Circle* 3:4 (Autumn 1972), 204–11. L. J. Swingle discusses the idea of a "circle of like selves" in "The Poets, the Novelists, and the English Romantic Situation," *The Wordsworth Circle* 10:2 (Spring 1979), 218–28.

18. Wordsworth spent the spring of 1794 planning to begin his literary career in earnest by starting a "monthly miscellany" on moral issues "from which some emolument might be drawn." *The Letters of William and Dorothy Wordsworth: The Early*

Years, 1787–1805, ed. Ernest de Selincourt and revised by Chester L. Shaver (Oxford: Oxford University Press, 1967), I, 118–20. Cited hereafter as *Early Letters*.

19. See *Blake*, pp. 143–44. For a discussion of Blake's idea of community, see Morris Eaves, "Romantic Expressive Theory and Blake's Idea of the Audience," *PMLA* 95 (1980), 784–801.

20. See the definition in the *OED* of a "style" as a "weapon of offence, for stabbing, etc."

21. Garry Wills, *Inventing America: Jefferson's Declaration of Independence* (New York: Vintage Books, 1978).

22. Sarah Fielding, Introduction to *The Cry: A New Dramatic Fable* (Dublin, 1754). The novel was published anonymously and may have been the product of a collaboration with Jane Collier. As with many of the more obscure novels I refer to in this chapter, it is available on microfilm as part of the eighteenth-century collection of Research Publications, Inc., Woodbridge, Conn. This first quotation is from the Introduction as reprinted in George L. Barnett, *Eighteenth-Century British Novelists on the Novel* (New York: Appleton-Century-Crofts, 1968), p. 106. Subsequent page numbers refer to Barnett.

23. *Female Friendship; or, The Innocent Sufferer. A Moral Tale* (London, 1770). Quoted in J. M. S. Tompkins, *The Popular Novel in England, 1770–1800* (Lincoln: University of Nebraska Press, 1961), p. 71. Cited hereafter as Tompkins.

24. Joseph Addison, "Essay on Virgil's *Georgics*," in A. C. Guthkelch, ed., *The Miscellaneous Works of Joseph Addison* (London: G. Bell and Sons, 1914), II, 4.

25. Anonymous, Preface to *Constantia: or, A True Picture of Human Life*, 1751, in Barnett, p. 91.

26. Laurence Sterne, *A Sentimental Journey through France and Italy* [1768], ed. Graham Petrie (Harmondsworth: Penguin Books, 1967), p. 40. The introduction to this edition, by A. Alvarez, begins with the type of assertion I am calling into question: "Laurence Sterne is a distinctly 'modern' novelist" (7).

27. J. Paul Hunter, "Response as Reformation: *Tristram Shandy* and the Art of Interruption," *Novel* 4 (1971), 132–46.

28. Samuel Johnson, the *Rambler*, no. 4, 31 March 1750, in *The Yale Johnson*, III, 21–22.

29. Thomas Holcroft, Preface to *Alwyn: Or the Gentleman Comedian*, 1780, in Barnett, p. 150.

30. See Tompkins, pp. 367–68.

31. Quoted in Tompkins, p. 110.

32. Both quotes are from Tompkins, p. 101.

33. Quoted in Tompkins, p. 110.

Chapter 5

1. In just the first sentence, for example, differences between oral and written cultures are elided, writing becomes a problem of the "author," and the author is assumed to be a self constituted by the presence of an individual "will."

2. For an exception to this disciplinary approach to revision, see Jonathan Arac's suggestive analysis of Wordsworth as a "spectator ab intra" in "Bounding Lines: *The Prelude* and Critical Revision," *Boundary 2* 7:3 (Spring 1979), 31–48.

3. The most imposing example of a struggle to come to terms with all the "new" texts is the effort by Kenneth Johnston to find biographical patterns of crisis and

resolution in Wordsworth's many efforts to write *The Recluse*. See his *Wordsworth and The Recluse* (New Haven: Yale University Press, 1984).

4. For a relevant discussion of the concept of interrelations, see Ralph Cohen, "On the Interrelations of Eighteenth-Century Forms," in *New Approaches to Eighteenth-Century Literature: Selected Papers from the English Institute,* ed. Phillip Harth (New York: Columbia University Press, 1974), pp. 33–78.

5. Edward Young, *Conjectures on Original Composition,* ed. Edith J. Morley (London and New York: Longmans, Green and Co., 1918). This edition is reprinted in *Criticism: The Major Statements,* ed. Charles Kaplan (New York: St. Martin's Press, 1975), pp. 220–50. All further references to the *Conjectures* are hereafter cited in the text; the page numbers refer to Kaplan's collection.

6. In the first preface to the *Castle of Otranto,* for example, Horace Walpole's disavowal of authorship manifests both thematic and generic embarrassment; his use of the supernatural, and the dramatic features and structure of the tale, are excused by the pretense of discovering an ancient manuscript. Walpole is thus able to argue that the real author lived in a time in which superstition was widespread and his talents were probably best suited to the theater.

7. For a brief account of the terms of this debate, see Ricardo Quintana and Alvin Whitley, eds., *English Poetry of the Mid and Late Eighteenth Century* (New York: Alfred A. Knopf, 1963), pp. 18–23.

8. Cohen, "Innovation and Variation," p. 36.

9. Cited in Quintana and Whitley, *English Poetry,* p. 20.

10. The paragraph containing this "caution" is "substantially Richardson's" according to Louis Bredvold, Alan McKillop, and Lois Whitney, eds., *Eighteenth-Century Poetry and Prose* (1939; rpt. New York: Ronald Press, 1978), p. 464. Since my historical argument is not an attempt to assess individual authorial achievement, the issue of Richardson's contributions is relevant here only as evidence of another authorial deception to be classified under the historical rubric of embarrassment.

11. See Kaplan's editorial comments in *Conjectures,* p. 220.

12. Edmund Burke, *A Philosophical Enquiry into the Origin of Our Ideas of the Sublime and the Beautiful,* ed. James T. Boulton (1958; rpt. Notre Dame: University of Notre Dame Press, 1968).

13. In his "Introduction on Taste" Burke argues that "the senses are the great originals of all our ideas" (23). For an overview of the poetic manifestations of this epistemology, see Ralph Cohen, "The Augustan Mode in English Poetry," *Eighteenth-Century Studies* 1 (1967), 3–32.

14. See Cohen's discussion of the eighteenth-century concept of limits in "The Augustan Mode," pp. 28–29.

15. See David Simpson's discussion of "simultaneity" and the "hermeneutical" in *Irony and Authority,* pp. ix–x.

16. Wordsworth offers an instructive point of comparison not only because his revisionary activity is so obviously extensive, but also because his innovative role has often been underestimated and/or misconstrued. Recent efforts to uncover Wordsworth's roots in eighteenth-century notions of the Imagination (Engell's *Creative Imagination*) and of Sensibility (James H. Averill, *Wordsworth and the Poetry of Human Suffering* [Ithaca: Cornell University Press, 1980]), for example, have fallen victim to organic metaphor and have failed to recognize that even when Wordsworth's Romantic "opinions," in the words of P. W. K. Stone, "are most apparently in concord with the

views of the preceding age, they have in fact a different bearing." See Stone, *The Art of Poetry, 1750–1820* (New York: Barnes and Noble, 1967), p. 136. Stone recognizes the discontinuity in change but, lacking a theory to explain it in relationship to continuity, he comes to a number of very problematic conclusions about Romanticism.

17. I use the word "interpretative" to refer specifically to the *Romantic* procedure for engaging texts based on this particular part/whole relationship. Because of the persistence of that procedure in our time, its historicity has been largely ignored.

18. In this chapter, all quotes from the 1799, 1805, and 1850 *Preludes* are taken from William Wordsworth, *The Prelude, 1799, 1805, 1850,* ed. Jonathan Wordsworth, M. H. Abrams, and Stephen Gill (New York: Norton, 1979).

19. The adverb ("steadily") thus suggests the subjectivity of the action, for looking is steady in relationship to habit.

20. Ferguson, *Language as Counter-Spirit,* p. 33.

21. *The Letters of William and Dorothy Wordsworth: The Middle Years,* ed. Ernest de Selincourt, 2nd ed., revised by Mary Moorman (Oxford: Clarendon Press, 1969), I, 146. Cited hereafter as *Middle Letters,* I.

22. For the Duke of Argyle's account and the Fenwick note, see *Poems,* II, 417. The accuracy of the Duke's account of the poem's composition has been called into question by J. Bard McNulty, "Self-Awareness in the Making of 'Tintern Abbey,'" *The Wordsworth Circle* 12:2 (Spring 1981), 99. See the possibilities raised by Mark Reed in *Wordsworth: the Chronology of the Early Years, 1779–1799* (Cambridge, Mass.: Harvard University Press, 1967), p. 243.

23. *Poems,* II, 517. McNulty (p. 99) offers some interesting thoughts on "Tintern Abbey" as an ode, but his argument founders on a distinction between "true" and "conventional" momentum; he accepts uncritically and ahistorically the Romantic distinction between natural free expression and the unnatural restriction of form.

24. Joseph Trapp, *Lectures on Poetry* (London, 1742), p. 215.

25. Roland Barthes, *Image-Music-Text* (New York: Hill and Wang, 1977), pp. 147–48.

26. See *Poems,* II, 539–49.

27. *The Letters of William and Dorothy Wordsworth: The Later Years,* ed. Ernest de Selincourt (Oxford: Oxford University Press, 1939), III, 1248–49. Cited hereafter as *Later Letters.*

28. For a discussion of Wordsworth's career-long concern with classification systems, see Arthur Beatty, *William Wordsworth: His Doctrine and Art in Their Historical Relations* (Madison: University of Wisconsin Press, 1962), pp. 195–205.

29. *The Letters of William and Dorothy Wordsworth: The Middle Years,* ed. Ernest de Selincourt, 2nd ed., revised by Mary Moorman and Alan G. Hill (Oxford: Clarendon Press, 1970), II, 191.

30. Thomas McFarland pursues connections between Romantic fragmentation and organic unity in *Romanticism and the Forms of Ruin.*

31. James Heffernan, "Mutilated Autobiography: Wordsworth's *Poems* of 1815," *The Wordsworth Circle* 10:1 (Winter 1979), 109–10.

32. Gene Ruoff, "Critical Implications of Wordsworth's 1815 Categorization, with Some Animadversions on Binaristic Commentary," *The Wordsworth Circle* 9:1 (Winter 1978), 75–82. Judith Herman, "The Poet as Editor: Wordsworth's Edition of 1815," *The Wordsworth Circle* 9:1 (Winter 1978), 82–87. Donald Ross, Jr., "Poems

'Bound Each to Each' in the 1815 Edition of Wordsworth," *The Wordsworth Circle*
12:2 (Spring 1981), 133–40.

    33. *Henry Crabb Robinson on Books and Their Writers,* ed. Edith J. Morley
(London: J. M. Dent and Sons, 1938), II, 484.

    34. Cited in *Prelude,* p. 512.

    35. See 1799, II.364–66; 1805, I.625–29, II.335–36; 1850, I.597–601, II.316–17.

    36. See Beatty, *Wordsworth,* pp. 196–97.

    37. *The Correspondence of Crabb Robinson with the Wordsworth Circle,* ed.
Edith J. Morley (Oxford: Clarendon Press, 1927), I, 161. The whole passage is a fine
illustration of the same ambivalence and defensiveness toward his own extratextual
material that we earlier saw exhibited in regard to the prefaces.

    38. See the Norton edition, pp. 391, 508, 520, 522. Donald Reiman has called
attention to *The Prelude* as sonnet in a footnote to "Poetry of Familiarity: Wordsworth,
Dorothy, and Mary Hutchinson," in *The Evidence of the Imagination,* ed. Donald H.
Reiman, Michael C. Jaye, and Betty T. Bennett (New York: New York University
Press, 1978), pp. 176–77.

    39. See the suggested etymologies for "hallow" and "holy" in the *OED.*

Chapter 6

    1. *Memoirs and Letters of Sara Coleridge,* edited by her daughter (New York:
Harper and Brothers, 1874), p. 77.

    2. I am not implying, of course, that anyone can step out of any discourse at any
time. It is our *historical* relationship to Romantic discourse that makes this particular
maneuver possible at this time. Such a step, as I have been emphasizing in this generic
history, never entails an absolute break with the past, but a reclassification of features
(my re-placing of Wordsworth's turn) that involves discontinuity and continuity.

    3. Sir Walter Scott, unsigned article in *Quarterly Review* 14 (October 1815),
reprinted in *Jane Austen: The Critical Heritage,* ed. B. C. Southam (London: Routledge & Kegan Paul, 1968), p. 63 (cited hereafter as Southam). References to how
Austen "excites" the reader occur throughout the selections that make up this volume.

    4. Virginia Woolf, "Jane Austen at Sixty," *Nation* 34 (15 December 1923), 433.

    5. This is not, of course, a personal attack on Woolf's competence. I am only
pointing out how certain critical assumptions surface in her language.

    6. See Daniel Cottom, "Austen's Attachments and Supplantments," *Novel* 14:2
(Winter 1981), 152–67.

    7. Scott's review is dated October 1815 and was issued in March 1816. See
Southam, p. 63.

    8. Richard Whateley in *Quarterly Review* 24 (January 1821), reprinted in
Southam, p. 87.

    9. Watt places the geniuses, of course, in opposition to an "uncritical" and self-
indulgent "public."

    10. Much of the historical work on the novel in recent years has focused on the
texts that Watt's developmental history could not engage: the Gothic and Domestic
novels of the late eighteenth century.

    11. Watt's Austen is finally of this type: she climaxes one century and mothers the
next. As Norman Page has pointed out, F. R. Leavis was another literary historian who
had a great need for Austen but did not know what to do with her. See Page, "The

Great Tradition Revisited," in *Jane Austen's Achievement,* ed. Juliet McMaster (New York: Barnes and Noble, 1976), pp. 44–63.

12. T. B. Tomlinson, *The English Middle Class Novel* (New York: Barnes and Noble, 1976), p. 24.

13. Igor Webb points out the social significance of "choice" in Austen in *From Custom to Capital: The English Novel and the Industrial Revolution* (Ithaca: Cornell University Press, 1981), pp. 43–44.

14. All quotations from Austen's novels are taken from *The Novels of Jane Austen,* ed. R. W. Chapman, 3rd ed. (Oxford: Clarendon Press, 1932, 1933). This quotation is from *Emma,* p. 84. All further references will appear in the text.

15. The surge effectively began with *The Wordsworth Circle* 7:4 (Autumn 1976), a special issue. In addition to those studies and others cited below, see A. Walton Litz, *"Persuasion:* Forms of Estrangement," in *Jane Austen: Bicentenary Essays,* ed. John Halperin (Cambridge: Cambridge University Press, 1975), pp. 221–34.

16. Joseph Kestner, "Jane Austen: The Tradition of the English Romantic Novel, 1800–1832," *The Wordsworth Circle* 7:4 (Autumn 1976), 297–311.

17. Susan Morgan, *In the Meantime: Character and Perception in Jane Austen's Fiction* (Chicago: University of Chicago Press, 1980), pp. 3, 11.

18. Butler, *Romantics, Rebels and Reactionaries,* p. 6.

19. A. Walton Litz, "'A Development of Self': Character and Personality in Jane Austen's Fiction," in McMaster, *Jane Austen's Achievement,* p. 74.

20. This is the major difficulty in Morgan's useful study. Patricia Spacks suggests an alternative in her provocative analysis of the "poetics of growth" in "Muted Discord: Generational Conflict in Jane Austen," in *Jane Austen in a Social Context,* ed. David Monaghan (Totowa, N.J.: Barnes and Noble, 1981), pp. 159–79.

21. "The history of narrative art since the Romantic period," observes John. O. Lyons, "has been in one sense the history of the devices by which writers give the illusion of a real character. The necessity of such an illusion did not occur to earlier ages, and their use of puppets and masks and mirror images suggested an aspect of the character's artistic existence." See Lyons, *The Invention of the Self: The Hinge of Consciousness in the Eighteenth Century* (Carbondale: Southern Illinois University Press, 1978), p. 226. Also, for a suggestive analysis of how E. H. Gombrich's work on representations of the "real" relates to the concept of genre, see Adena Rosmarin, *The Power of Genre* (Minneapolis: University of Minnesota Press, 1985), pp. 10–22.

22. Henry Fielding, *Joseph Andrews* [1741] and *Shamela* [1742], ed. Martin Battestin (Boston: Houghton Mifflin, 1961), pp. 7–12.

23. We need to distinguish here between the forms discussed as "high" by the writers of a particular time and those that we, as literary historians, now understand to have been hierarchically dominant. In this case, the latter forms include the satiric and the georgic-descriptive. Thus, in accord with the principle of interrelations, the function of the "high" epic features of Fielding's text was satiric. The novelistic use of georgic-descriptive features is discussed in chapter 4. For a discussion of the eighteenth-century generic hierarchy, see Cohen's "Augustan Mode" essay.

24. For a discussion of order in variety in the eighteenth-century novel, see Eric Rothstein, *Systems of Order and Inquiry in Later Eighteenth-Century Fiction* (Berkeley: University of California Press, 1975), pp. 1–21.

25. Samuel Richardson, *Clarissa or, the History of a Young Lady* [1747–48], 4 vols., introduction by John Butt (London: Dent, Everyman's Library, 1962), I, xiv.

26. See my discussion of *Otranto* in "Wordsworth's Gothic Endeavor."

27. Henry Mackenzie, the *Lounger* no. 20 (18 June 1785), reprinted in *Novel and Romance, 1700–1800: A Documentary Record,* ed. Ioan Williams (New York: Barnes and Noble, 1970), pp. 328–29.

28. See Watt, pp. 296–97. Also Barbara Hardy, *A Reading of Jane Austen* (London: Peter Owen, 1975), pp. 11–15. This approach does produce some helpful insights; it is the use of Austen as a "solution" that I find problematic.

29. Austen is leaving it to the reader to sympathize ("concern") and to judge; as I have already shown, this is a characteristic Romantic ploy.

30. *Jane Austen's Letters: To Her Sister Cassandra and Others,* ed. R. W. Chapman, 2nd ed. (London: Oxford University Press, 1952), pp. 468–69, 452.

31. Donald Greene, "The Myth of Limitation," in *Jane Austen Today,* ed. Joel Weinsheimer (Athens: University of Georgia Press, 1975), p. 166. Drawing distinctions between Fielding and Richardson, as many of their contemporaries did, is not the problem; the difficulty lies in elaborating a literary history out of them.

32. Dorothy Marshall, *Industrial England, 1776–1851* (New York: Scribner's, 1973), p. 91.

33. See Spacks's discussion of the growth of a literature of growth in "Muted Discord."

34. Cottom discusses the impersonality of the family in "Austen's Attachments," p. 162.

35. See Nancy Armstrong, "The Rise of Feminine Authority in the Novel," *Novel* 15:2 (Winter 1982), 127–45.

36. Diana Spearman, *The Novel and Society* (London: Routledge & Kegan Paul, 1966), p. 37.

37. Frederick Engels, *The Condition of the Working-Class in England: From Personal Observation and Authentic Sources,* English ed. (1892; rpt. Moscow: Progress Publishers, 1973), pp. 329, 332.

38. See Coleridge's description of the plan for *Lyrical Ballads* in *Biographia Literaria,* II, 5.

39. These line numbers and those that follow refer to the Norton version of the 1850 *Prelude*.

40. For a discussion of the internalization of form in Austen, see Henrietta Ten Harmsel, *Jane Austen: A Study in Fictional Conventions* (The Hague: Mouton, 1964), p. 163. Karl Kroeber discusses Romantic "transformations of genre and mode" in "Jane Austen, Romantic," *The Wordsworth Circle* 7:9 (Autumn 1976), 295.

41. Gene Ruoff offers a very valuable comparison between Austen and Wordsworth in "The Sense of a Beginning: *Mansfield Park,*" *The Wordsworth Circle* 10:2 (Spring 1979), 174–86.

42. Unsigned review from *New Monthly Magazine* 95 (May 1852), 17–53, reprinted in Southam, pp. 137–38.

43. G. H. Lewes in *Blackwood's* 86 (1859), reprinted in *Literary Criticism of George Henry Lewes,* ed. Alice R. Kaminsky (Lincoln: University of Nebraska Press, 1964), p. 92.

44. Robert Langbaum, *The Poetry of Experience: The Dramatic Monologue in Modern Literary Tradition* (New York: Norton, 1957). Wayne Booth, *The Rhetoric of Fiction* (Chicago: University of Chicago Press, 1961), pp. 243–64.

45. See Southam, pp. 117, 126–28.

46. Alistair Duckworth, *The Improvement of the Estate: A Study of Jane Austen's Novels* (Baltimore: Johns Hopkins University Press, 1971).

Chapter 7

1. Neil McKendrick, John Brewer, and J. H. Plumb, *The Birth of a Consumer Society* (Bloomington: Indiana University Press, 1982), pp. 2, 5. Let me acknowledge, at the start of this section, my debt to Michel Foucault, particularly his analysis of how, since the advent of subjectivity, knowledge has assumed a disciplinary power: "power would be a fragile thing if its only function were to repress, if it worked only through the mode of censorship, exclusion, blockage and repression, in the manner of a great Superego, exercising itself only in a negative way. If, on the contrary, power is strong this is because, as we are beginning to realise, it produces effects at the level of desire—and also at the level of knowledge. Far from preventing knowledge, power produces it" (*Power/Knowledge*, 59). As literary historians clarify literature's role in the construction of subjectivity, they will find Foucault's work—particularly his later efforts such as *Discipline and Punish* and *The History of Sexuality*—a more and more valuable resource.

2. The most notable exception has been J. Bronowski, *William Blake and the Age of Revolution* (London: Routledge & Kegan Paul, 1972). The book concludes, however, with a Romantic theory of individual "dissent." Also useful for seeing Blake in a different light is Minna Doskow, "The Humanized Universe of Blake and Marx," in *William Blake and the Moderns*, ed. Robert J. Bertholf and Annette S. Levitt (Albany: State of New York Press, 1982), pp. 225–40.

3. *Blake*, p. 670. In his note to the text on p. 805, David Erdman indicates that this prospectus was "etched by Blake."

4. Although money wages did rise in the 1790s, inflation resulted in a drop in real wages. See John Rule, *The Experience of Labour in Eighteenth-Century English Industry* (New York: St. Martin's Press, 1981), p. 68. Also, E. A. Wrigley, "Malthus's Model of a Pre-industrial Economy," in *Malthus and His Time*, ed. Michael Turner (London: Macmillan, 1986), p. 11.

5. Nathaniel Forster, *Enquiry into the Causes of the Present High Price of Provisions* (1767), cited in A. W. Coats, "Changing Attitudes to Labour in the Mid-Eighteenth Century," in *Essays in Social History*, ed. M. W. Flinn and T. C. Smout (Oxford: Clarendon Press, 1974), p. 83.

6. Richard C. Wiles, "The Theory of Wages in Later English Mercantilism," *Economic History Review*, 2nd series, 21 (1968), 113–26. Also of particular value in understanding eighteenth-century attitudes toward labor are: T. A. Critchley, *The Conquest of Violence* (London: Constable, 1970); J. L. Hammond and Barbara Hammond, *The Skilled Labourer, 1760–1832* (London: Longmans, Green & Co., 1919; rpt. New York: Augustus M. Kelley, 1967); *Society and Politics in England, 1780–1960*, ed. J. F. C. Harrison (New York: Harper & Row, 1965); Dorothy Marshall, *Eighteenth Century England* (London: Longman, 1962); Ian R. Christie, *Wars and Revolutions: Britain, 1760–1815* (Cambridge, Mass.: Harvard University Press, 1982); E. P. Thompson, *The Making of the English Working Classs* (New York: Vintage Books, 1963).

7. See Coats's Postscript to "Changing Attitudes," p. 91.

8. Samuel Crumpe, *An Essay on the Best Means of Providing Employment for the People* [1795] rpt. (New York: Augustus M. Kelley, 1968), p. 9.

9. For an example of this view, see the "Editor's Introduction" in Joseph Priest-

ley, *Priestley's Writings on Philosophy, Science, and Politics*, edited with an introduction by John A. Passmore (New York: Collier Books, 1965), pp. 7–38.

10. David Hume, *Enquiries Concerning the Human Understanding and Concerning the Principles of Morals*, ed. L. A. Selby-Bigge (Oxford: Clarendon Press, 1902), p. 47.

11. On the relationship between Hume's psychology and his economics, see his editor, Eugene Rotwein, in David Hume, *Writings on Economics* (Madison: University of Wisconsin Press, 1955), pp. xxxii–liii. Also, see Coats's use of Rotwein in Coats, "Changing Attitudes," p. 82.

12. Cited in Coats, "Changing Attitudes," p. 84.

13. John Clarke, *The Price of Progress: Cobbett's England, 1780–1835* (London: Granada Publishing, 1977), p. 95.

14. Perkin, *The Origins of Modern English Society*, p. 91. In "Conspicuous Consumption by the Landed Classes, 1790–1830," David Cannadine claims that "the whole home demand argument needs fundamentally rethinking" (Turner, *Malthus*, 107), but the "recent research" he cites are articles published in 1976 and 1977. Since then, McKendrick's book has provided the most convincing evidence that home demand was an essential ingredient in economic progress.

15. G. F. Wendeborn, *A View of England* (London, 1791), I, 191, 225, cited in Clarke, *Price of Progress*, p. 96.

16. Wedgwood's contribution to commercialization is treated at length in McKendrick, *Birth*, pp. 99–144.

17. *The Sovereignty of the Law: Selections from Blackstone's Commentaries on the Laws of England, (1765–1769)*, edited with an introduction by Gareth Jones (Toronto: University of Toronto Press, 1973), pp. 123–24.

18. See my review of Aers, Cook, and Punter, *Romanticism and Ideology*, in *Comparative Literature Studies* 21:2 (Summer 1984), 228–32.

Chapter 8

1. Thomas Robert Malthus, *First Essay on Population, 1798*, with notes by James Bonar (New York: Augustus M. Kelley, 1965), pp. 217–18. This reprint contains the text of the first version of Malthus's essay, the preface to the 1803 edition, and some correspondence with Godwin.

2. Quoted in Patricia James, *Population Malthus: His Life and Times* (London: Routledge & Kegan Paul, 1979), pp. 388–96.

3. William Hazlitt, *A Reply to the 'Essay on Population' by the Rev. T. R. Malthus* [1807] (New York: Augustus M. Kelley, 1967), p. 371.

4. Gertrude Himmelfarb, *The Idea of Poverty: England in the Early Industrial Age* (New York: Vintage Books, 1983, 1985), p. 105.

5. My emphasis on the politics of developmental desire does not preclude other kinds of political analyses, such as Himmelfarb's charting of the changing conceptions of poverty and of images of the poor. See, for example, her comments in *Idea of Poverty* on the bottom of p. 118.

6. This passage appeared only in the second edition of 1803 (pp. 549–50). Severe criticism of it as an argument against marriage caused Malthus to delete it from subsequent editions. That deletion did not, however, signal a change in Malthus's attitude toward the female body. Patricia James describes the circumstances in *Population Malthus*, pp. 100–101.

7. Hazlitt mocks Malthus for this "curious chapter on old maids," pointing out that "he might have written one on suicide, and another on prostitutes. As far as the question of population is concerned, they are certainly of more service to the community, because they tempt others to follow their example, whereas an old maid is a beacon to frighten others into matrimony" (*Reply*, 373). Mary Poovey addresses assumptions about "frightening" female conduct in *The Proper Lady and the Woman Writer: Ideology as Style in the Works of Mary Wollstonecraft, Mary Shelley, and Jane Austen* (Chicago: University of Chicago Press, 1984).

8. Philippe Ariès, *Centuries of Childhood: A Social History of Family Life*, trans. Robert Baldick (New York: Vintage Books, 1962), p. 339.

9. See Nancy Armstrong, *Desire and Domestic Fiction: A Political History of the Novel* (New York: Oxford University Press, 1987), pp. 59–95.

10. *Journals of Dorothy Wordsworth*, ed. Helen Darbishire (London: Oxford University Press, 1958), p. 79.

11. Nancy Armstrong's description of the domestic supervisor is in the same chapter of *Desire and Domestic Fiction* cited above. For an analysis of Dorothy Wordsworth's domesticity, see Alan Liu, "On the Autobiographical Present: Dorothy Wordsworth's *Grasmere Journals*," *Criticism* 26:2 (Spring 1984), 115–37.

12. Mary Wollstonecraft, *A Vindication of the Rights of Woman*, ed. Carol H. Poston (New York: Norton, 1975), p. 26.

Chapter 9

1. From the first edition of the *Essay*, p. 359.

2. *Allegories of Reading*, p. ix. See my discussion of this quotation in chapter 2.

3. Samuel Crumpe, *An Inquiry into the Nature and Properties of Opium* (London, 1793).

4. Molly Lefebure, *Samuel Taylor Coleridge: A Bondage of Opium* (New York: Stein and Day, 1974), p. 14.

5. For a study of Keats's use of medical knowledge and figures, see Donald C. Goellnicht, *The Poet-Physician: Keats and Medical Science* (Pittsburgh: University of Pittsburgh Press, 1984).

6. Meyer Howard Abrams, *The Milk of Paradise: The Effect of Opium Visions on the Works of DeQuincey, Crabbe, Francis Thompson, and Coleridge* (Cambridge, Mass.: Harvard University Press, 1934), pp. 4–5, 49.

7. *The Eclectic Review*, 2nd ser., 19 (1822), 366–71. See Alvin Sullivan, ed., *British Literary Magazines: The Romantic Age, 1789–1836* (Westport, Conn.: Greenwood Press, 1983), p. 130. Also, see Elisabeth Schneider, *Coleridge, Opium and Kubla Khan* (New York: Octagon Books, 1975), p. 28.

8. Paul-Gabriel Boucé, Preface, in Boucé, ed., *Sexuality in eighteenth-century Britain* (Manchester, Eng.: Manchester University Press, 1982), p. xi.

9. Julian Drachman, *Studies in the Literature of Natural Science* (New York: Macmillan, 1930), p. 17.

10. Dr. Andrew Jacob, *An Essay on the Influence of the Imagination and Passions in the Production and Cure of Diseases* (Dublin, 1823). For a discussion of the entry of Imagination into medical literature, see G. S. Rousseau, "Nymphomania, Bienville and the Rise of Erotic Sensibility," in Boucé, *Sexuality*, pp. 94–119.

11. For a historical survey of efforts to present the imagination as a physiological

fact, see G. S. Rousseau, "Science and the Discovery of the Imagination in Enlightened England," *Eighteenth-Century Studies* 3 (1969), 108–35.

12. Alethea Hayter, *Opium and the Romantic Imagination* (Berkeley: University of California Press, 1968), p. 334.

13. Malthus also participated in this medicalization. As Ann Digby points out, "Malthus' own experience gave him a view of pauperism as a moral disease whose contagious qualities provided a built-in multiplier to an ever increasing, dependent population." See "Malthus and Reform of the English Poor Law," in Turner, *Malthus*, p. 167.

14. See M. H. Abrams, *Natural Supernaturalism*.

15. Leslie Brisman, *Romantic Origins* (Ithaca: Cornell University Press, 1978), p. 385.

16. See Raymond Williams's analysis of the formation of this myth in *Culture and Society, 1780–1850* (New York: Doubleday, 1960), p. 39.

17. Virginia Berridge and Griffith Edwards, *Opium and the People: Opiate Use in Nineteenth-Century England* (London: St. Martin's Press, 1981), p. 281.

18. Dr. John Jones, *The Mysteries of Opium Reveal'd* (London, 1701), p. 27.

19. See Berridge and Edwards, *Opium*, p. xxv.

20. Crumpe, *Inquiry*, p. 177. See Glenn Sonnedecker's discussion of eighteenth-century treatises on opium in *Emergence of the Concept of Opiate Addiction* (Madison: American Institute of the History of Pharmacy, 1962), pp. 11–16.

21. E. W. Adams, *Drug Addiction* (London: Oxford University Press, 1937), p. 22.

22. P. M. Latham, *The Collected Works of Dr. P. M. Latham*, ed. Robert Martin (London, 1876), I. 392.

23. Alfred Lindesmith, *Addiction and Opiates* (Chicago: Aldine Publishing Company, 1947, 1968), p. 8.

24. See Berridge and Edwards, *Opium*, p. 170.

25. *The Opium Habit, with Suggestions as to the Remedy* (New York, 1868), p. 7.

26. *Poems*, II, 468. This edition details the differences between the three manuscript versions of the poem; it also includes the relevant section of Milton's *History of England* in the notes.

27. Geoffrey of Monmouth, *The History of the Kings of Britain*, trans. Lewis Thorpe (Harmondsworth: Penguin Books, 1966), p. 104.

Index

211